D1242861

LOOKING FOR WORK, SEARCHING FOR WORKERS

The dynamic character of American industrialization produced imbalances between the supply of and demand for labor across cities and regions. This book describes how employers and job seekers responded to these imbalances to create networks of labor market communication and assistance capable of mobilizing the massive redistribution of population that was essential to maintain the rapid pace of the nation's economic growth between the Civil War and World War I. It combines a detailed description of the labor market institutions that emerged in this period with a careful analysis of a variety of quantitative evidence to assess the broader economic implications of these institutions for geographic wage convergence and for American economic growth more generally. Despite a remarkable expansion of the geographic scope of labor markets at this time, the evidence suggests that labor market institutions reinforced regional divisions within the United States and left a lasting impact on the evolution of many other aspects of the employment relationship.

Joshua L. Rosenbloom is Professor of Economics at the University of Kansas and Research Associate at the National Bureau of Economic Research.

LOOKING FOR WORK, SEARCHING FOR WORKERS

AMERICAN LABOR MARKETS DURING INDUSTRIALIZATION

JOSHUA L. ROSENBLOOM

University of Kansas

CAMBRIDGE
UNIVERSITY PRESS

HD5724
.R595
2002
046937740

PUBLISHED BY THE PRESS SYNDICATE OF THE UNIVERSITY OF CAMBRIDGE
The Pitt Building, Trumpington Street, Cambridge, United Kingdom

CAMBRIDGE UNIVERSITY PRESS
The Edinburgh Building, Cambridge CB2 2RU, UK
40 West 20th Street, New York, NY 10011-4211, USA
477 Williamstown Rd., Port Melbourne, VIC 3207, Australia
Ruiz de Alarcón 13, 28014 Madrid, Spain
Dock House, The Waterfront, Cape Town 8001, South Africa

http://www.cambridge.org

© Joshua L. Rosenbloom 2002

This book is in copyright. Subject to statutory exception
and to the provisions of relevant collective licensing agreements,
no reproduction of any part may take place without
the written permission of Cambridge University Press.

First published 2002

Printed in the United Kingdom at the University Press, Cambridge

Typeface Sabon 10.25/14 pt.   *System* LATEX 2$_\varepsilon$ [TB]

A catalog record for this book is available from the British Library.

Library of Congress Cataloging in Publication Data
Rosenbloom, Joshua L.
Looking for work, searching for workers : American labor markets during
industrialization / Joshua L. Rosenbloom.
p. cm.
Includes bibliographical references and index.
ISBN 0-521-80780-8 – ISBN 0-521-00287-7 (pc.)
1. Labor market – United States – History.   2. Labor demand – United States –
History.   3. United States – Economic conditions – 1865–1918.   I. Title.
HD5724 .R58   2002

331.12'0973 – dc21   2001035671

ISBN 0 521 80780 8   hardback
ISBN 0 521 00287 7   paperback

For Mary

1957–2001

CONTENTS

LIST OF FIGURES AND TABLES

Figures

Tables

PREFACE

This book grew out of my desire to understand how markets arise and how they work. Market processes of exchange are central to modern economics, and the development of efficient markets is widely regarded as an important factor in the speed of American economic growth. Yet the way in which markets develop, and the institutions through which they accomplish the task of matching supply and demand are rarely addressed by economists. In the pages that follow, I describe the development of American labor market institutions during the late-nineteenth and early-twentieth centuries, focusing in particular on the ways in which they facilitated the matching of job seekers and employers across space. During this period, the industrialization of the American economy was associated with both substantial growth in aggregate employment and marked shifts in the location of economic activity. These developments would not have been possible in the absence of market institutions capable of mobilizing labor both internationally and internally.

My primary goal has been to contribute to our understanding of the process of American economic growth by illuminating the way in which labor markets responded to the shifting locations of labor supply and demand during American industrialization. But I believe that the results of this study have broader significance. For economists, this study offers an illustration of the interplay of economic and historical forces in explaining the development of institutions. As economic theory predicts, employers and workers responded to opportunities for arbitrage created by differences in the relative scarcity of labor across locations by creating labor market institutions to communicate information about supply and demand and then to make it possible for market participants to act on this information. But the channels of communication and assistance that arose from their efforts did not develop in a uniform or a priori predictable fashion. Rather, when connections between particular sources and destinations of labor were established, the actions of both employers and workers tended to reinforce these links at the expense of other potential connections. The result was a path-dependent process of labor market integration that perpetuated patterns of regional separation from the pre–Civil War era until well into the twentieth century.

In addition to their effects on the spatial organization of economic activity within the United States, the labor market institutions that emerged during the nineteenth century to facilitate geographic mobility also had unanticipated effects on other aspects of the employment relationship. Especially important was the interaction between the development of institutions for the external recruitment of labor and the internal allocation of labor within firms. Although the geographic scope of markets for both skilled and unskilled workers expanded substantially during the nineteenth century, the labor market institutions that encouraged mobility proved more effective at increasing supplies of unskilled workers than they did at increasing supplies of skilled workers. This difference contributed to the increasing subdivision of labor by many American employers and encouraged a growing reliance on on-the-job training as a source of skilled workers. Yet high rates of labor mobility and the resultant turnover of the manufacturing workforce created an increasing tension between the goals of promoting the efficient allocation of labor and encouraging adequate investment in the training of skilled workers.

For historians, the following chapters illustrate the importance of markets in shaping the context of social and economic history. Labor and social historians have produced a wealth of studies documenting the impact of industrialization on labor relations and social conflicts in the late-nineteenth century. For the most part, however, their work has been based on the study of particular workplaces or communities. Market forces of supply and demand, however, impinged on communities and factories in ways that shaped and constrained the options and opportunities available to both workers and employers. Evidence of the scope of market integration as well as the use of strikebreakers that I present here clarifies the fact that there was in most cases only limited room for local variation in wages and working conditions. Broader market pressures constrained the kinds of labor market bargains that were possible, and the development of labor market institutions promoting geographic mobility helped to undermine workers' ability to use strikes to increase their bargaining power vis-à-vis employers. Similarly, the apparent de-skilling tendency of manufacturing technologies in the late-nineteenth century takes on a rather different appearance when set in its broader market context. It is true that the tendency of technological change in the late-nineteenth and early-twentieth centuries reduced employer demand for traditional categories of skilled labor. But evidence on employment and wages makes it clear that these changes were a response to the growing relative scarcity of skills and were only partially effective in offsetting the rising demand for skilled workers.

Writing this book has taken me much longer than I ever anticipated. My research on this topic began in my doctoral dissertation, completed in 1988, and has continued on and off in the more than 13 years since then. In this time, I have benefited greatly from the advice and assistance of many people. My earliest debts are to my dissertation advisors, Gavin Wright and Paul David, whose patient guidance helped me to formulate and develop the outlines of this project. Beginning when we were both graduate students, Bill Sundstrom and I have shared an interest in many of the issues considered in this volume. Over the years, we have collaborated on research on some of these topics, and I am indebted to Bill for all that I have learned with and from him over the years. Parts of Chapter 4 began as a paper written jointly with Bill, and some of the material in Chapter 5 also derives from our collaborative efforts. My colleague Tom Weiss has read and commented on countless drafts of many papers over the years. I am grateful to him for his patience, good judgment, and sound editorial advice. I am indebted to Gerald Friedman for providing the data that underlie the analysis in Chapter 6 and for his comments on earlier drafts of that chapter. I am indebted as well to Bill Collins, Stan Engerman, Price Fishback, Claudia Goldin, Peter Mancall, Bob Margo, Tom Weiss, and Gavin Wright, all of whom read some or all of this manuscript. Their advice and encouragement have made this a much better book.

The University of Kansas General Research Fund has provided support for this project through several summer grants. A research fellowship provided by the Hall Center for the Humanities at the University of Kansas and a sabbatical leave provided much needed time away from teaching to concentrate on this book. During my sabbatical, the Economic Growth Center and the Department of Economics at Yale University provided a very hospitable home to pursue my research.

Last, but not least, my greatest debts are personal: to my wife, Mary; and our children, Nathan, Benjamin, and Timothy; for their patience and understanding while I have worked on this project. Words cannot adequately express my sorrow that Mary is not here to celebrate with me the completion of this book. In gratitude for all that she has given me, this book is dedicated to her memory.

Joshua L. Rosenbloom
Lawrence, Kansas
June 2001

LABOR MARKETS AND AMERICAN INDUSTRIALIZATION

On August 8, 1904, John Achzener met a man on the street in Baltimore who asked him if he "wanted to go along with some other men to Chicago to work as butchers at $2.25 a day." After inquiring if there was a strike and being assured that there was not, Achzener accepted the offer and boarded a train for Chicago.[1] When William Rees, a weaver living in Philadelphia, needed work, he would walk from one employer to the next seeking a job, sometimes traversing four miles or more on his rounds. At other times he would get lucky and "stumble in just when they need[ed] a weaver" (Licht 1992, p. 1). In December 1915, the superintendent of the Robesonia Iron Company, located in Pennsylvania, wrote to Thomas Armato of the Industrial Labor Agency, an employment agency in Brooklyn, to inform him that "we expect to extend our operations soon, and will likely want more men. At our quarry we have mostly Italians, and here nearly one half foreigners, of whom about one half are Italians and one half Slavonians."[2]

These transactions between employers and job seekers, and millions of others like them, were all part of the operation of American labor markets during the late-nineteenth and early-twentieth centuries. Economists often use the term "market" to describe a group of buyers and sellers of a particular good or service or to refer to

[1] As it turned out, there was a strike, and Achzener soon left his new employment. His account of how he came to Chicago was recorded by striking union members and is reproduced in Tuttle (1966, p. 195–96).

[2] This letter and the series of correspondence from which it comes are reproduced in Bodnar (1974).

the transactions that take place between these buyers and sellers.[3] Market participants could not carry out these transactions, however, without information about specific opportunities to exchange goods and services and the means to act on this information. Markets are embedded then in specific institutions that serve to channel information, establish prices, and bring buyers and sellers together so that they can carry out transactions. Economists typically take the existence of smoothly functioning markets for granted, but the fact is that the institutions necessary to establish such markets do not simply emerge full-blown but must be created by self-interested individuals – either market participants themselves or third-party intermediaries. How these institutions operate can have important impact on the outcomes that they produce.

During the nineteenth century, industrialization and other structural changes in the American economy increased the importance of labor markets while substantially compounding the problems that labor market institutions had to resolve. As these changes transformed the United States from a primarily rural and agricultural society to an urban and industrial society over the course of the nineteenth century, wage labor assumed an increasingly prominent role in the economy. At the beginning of the nineteenth century, most Americans, with the exception of slaves, worked as independent farmers or artisans. There were, of course, wage workers, but most of these people found employment as trade workers or farm laborers and could reasonably expect that their status as employees was a step toward becoming an independent proprietor themselves. By the end of the century, the typical worker was much more likely to be employed for wages in a large factory.[4]

---

[3] See, for example, the definition of markets in Mankiw's (1998, p. 62) widely used introductory economics textbook.

[4] The career prospects of late-nineteenth century wage laborers are hard to characterize. Although it seems likely that many remained wage laborers throughout their lives, many must have harbored the expectation that such work was a temporary interlude. Piore (1979, ch. 3) argued that many of the immigrant workers – who made up an important segment of the industrial labor force – expected at first that they would return to their homelands and use their earnings to purchase farm land or secure a higher status at home. High rates of return migration suggest that many of them may have realized their expectations. But it is equally clear that not all were successful in this quest.

One manifestation of this transformation was the growing prominence of labor issues in the decades after the Civil War. During the economic depression that followed the Panic of 1873, for example, unemployment emerged as a major policy concern in the more industrialized parts of the country, where public officials confronted the problems raised by large numbers of idle workers unable to support themselves. Irregular employment was not a new problem, but as growing numbers of workers became dependent on wage labor for their livelihood, the nature of the problem was transformed, prompting officials to acknowledge for the first time that many of those without work were unemployed "through no fault of their own" (Keyssar 1986, ch. 2). In the 1880s, the nation was swept by an unprecedented wave of labor conflict and strikes. Unemployment, strikes, and other labor issues prompted a growing number of states as well as the federal government to establish bureaus of labor statistics to study the operation of labor markets and track the conditions of wage workers.[5]

The 1880s also mark the beginnings of what might be termed the modern era of organized labor. During the 1880s, the Knights of Labor successfully organized large numbers of workers. Although this organization collapsed as quickly as it had emerged, in the 1890s the American Federation of Labor rose to prominence, successfully promoting the spread of unionization. By the early twentieth century, nearly 10 percent of nonagricultural workers were union members (Freeman 1998, pp. 291–3). Organized labor's advances both benefited from and contributed to the growing importance of labor issues in the political arena. Organized labor and social reformers turned increasingly to the political arena in their efforts to limit the use of child labor, regulate safety conditions for women and children, establish maximum hours and minimum wages, create old-age pensions, unemployment and sickness insurance, and reform workers' compensation laws (Fishback 1998, p. 751).

---

[5] The first such bureau was established in Massachusetts in 1870. By the end of the 1870s, it had been joined by similar organizations in Pennsylvania (established 1873), Ohio (1877), New Jersey (1878), Indiana, Missouri, and Illinois (all 1879). By 1900, 30 states and the federal government had all established agencies to monitor and study labor conditions. See Carter, Ransom, and Sutch (1991).

Although the roots of American industrialization lie in the ante-bellum period, the pace of change quickened substantially after the Civil War. The integration of national rail and telegraph systems in the 1860s helped to create national markets for processed foods and consumer goods and encouraged manufacturers in a wide range of industries to build new capital- and scale-intensive factories to exploit economies of scale that larger markets made possible (Chandler 1977).[6] Some sense of the transformation in manufacturing is conveyed by the rapid growth in the size and capital intensity of manufacturing establishments at this time. Between 1870 and 1900, the average number of employees per establishment more than doubled in 11 of 16 manufacturing industries. More striking is the growth of truly large factories. In 1870, the McCormick plant in Chicago, with an employment of 400 to 500 workers, was considered one of the largest in the nation. By 1900 there were 1,063 establishments employing 500 to 1,000 workers, and 443 employing more than 1,000 workers (Nelson 1975, pp. 4–5). Capital accumulation was proceeding even more rapidly as indicated by the fact that the real value of capital per worker in manufacturing more than doubled between 1879 and 1899 (U.S. Bureau of the Census 1975, series P-5 and P-123). These developments could not have taken place without the development of mechanisms capable of mobilizing vast numbers of workers and facilitating their redistribution over long distances.

During the nineteenth century, the geographic scope of American labor markets expanded in response to the demands created by industrialization. In 1790, when Almy and Brown opened the first American textile mill using British spinning technology, the workforce consisted of a single adult supervisor and nine children between the ages of 4 and 10, all of whom were drawn from the

---

[6] According to Perloff et al. (1965, p. 191), "For practical purposes, the joining of the Union and Central Pacific railroads in Utah on May 10, 1869, may be said to symbolize the beginning of a truly nation-wide economy." Between 1865 and 1900, railroad mileage in operation increased more than fivefold, rising from 35,000 to 193,000. At the same time, the adoption of a standard gauge, improved coordination between lines, and a host of technological innovations – including larger engines, automatic couplers, and air brakes – increased the speed and lowered the costs of travel and transportation (Stover 1961, pp. 143–80; Taylor and Neu 1956). These developments were paralleled by the growth and improvement of telegraph and telephone networks (Field 1992; DuBoff 1982).

families of nearby farmers (Ware 1931, p. 23). Two decades later when the Boston Manufacturing Company established the first integrated spinning and weaving mill in Waltham, Massachusetts, in 1814, it was unable to find the hundreds of workers it needed in the immediate area. To staff the factory its owners dispatched recruiters throughout most of the New England states to attract young women from the region's agricultural districts. To house these women they established dormitories near the factory.

In retrospect, it seems almost inevitable that the founders of the early textile mills sought to meet their labor needs by expanding the horizons of the labor market. But there was nothing natural or inevitable about this process. Indeed, the conventional economic analysis of markets treats the supply of labor as given. In this analysis, an increased demand for labor would shift the market equilibrium outward along a fixed supply curve causing wages to rise. The increase in wages would serve both to induce the available workforce to supply more effort and to cause employers to temper their labor demands until supply and demand were brought back into balance. If the founders of the Boston Manufacturing Company had been content to accept this market equilibrium, they would likely have abandoned their efforts to establish factory production of textiles because the costs of labor were prohibitive. Instead of accepting high labor costs, however, they chose to adjust along a different margin, taking steps that would lower the supply price of labor through the development of new channels of communication that expanded the pool of workers on which they could draw.

As the century progressed, the growth of factories along with the need to build railroad lines, cities, and urban infrastructure multiplied the scale of employers' demand for labor and obliged employers everywhere to address the same problems of labor supply that had confronted the Boston Manufacturing Company. In most cases, they followed a similar route, pursuing strategies that helped to expand labor markets over broader and broader areas.[7]

---

[7] A comparable broadening of markets for finance capital was also required. Davis' (1963, 1965) work on the emergence of a national financial market stimulated a large literature tracing the development of financial markets in this era. Among the subsequent studies, see especially Carosso (1970), Sylla (1969), James (1978),

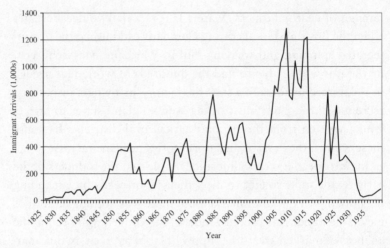

Figure 1.1   Number of Arriving Immigrants, 1825–1939. *Source*: U.S. Bureau of the Census (1975, series C-89).

By the 1840s the pool of underemployed rural workers had begun to diminish, obliging northern manufacturers to turn increasingly to foreign immigrants for labor. As Figure 1.1 illustrates, despite sharp short-run fluctuations linked to macroeconomic cycles, the number of arriving immigrants followed an increasing trend, reaching roughly 800 thousand per year in the decade after 1900. Between 1870 and 1915, nearly 30 million immigrants entered the country. Reflecting this influx, the foreign-born share of the population increased from around 13 percent in 1860 to a high of nearly 15 percent in 1890. Because of the selective nature of immigration, the foreign born were an even larger fraction of the labor force, accounting for 20 percent of gainfully employed workers in 1870 and 26 percent at the end of the century. The foreign-born presence was especially significant in the most rapidly growing sectors of the economy. The native-born people tended to concentrate in agriculture, and the foreign-born workers provided nearly a third of the nation's manufacturing and transportation labor force and made up a majority of the labor force in many of the largest and most rapidly growing cities.

and Snowden (1987a, 1987b). As a result, we know a great deal both about the development of financial institutions involved in the mobilization of capital and the extent to which these institutions gave rise to a unified national financial market.

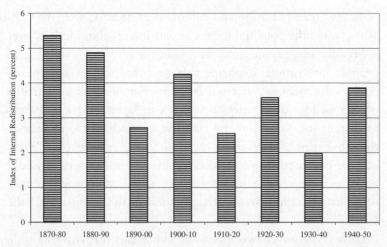

Figure 1.2   Index of Internal Redistribution of Population, 1870–1950.
Note: The index is the sum of positive (or negative) changes in the percentage of total national population residing in each state during each time period. *Source*: Eldridge and Thomas (1964, p. 28).

The beginning of World War I brought the era of mass migration to an abrupt end. With the outbreak of the war, immigration slowed to a trickle. There was a brief recovery in arrivals at the end of the war, but the passage of restrictive legislation in the early 1920s slowed the flow of immigrants substantially.

Paralleling these international population movements was an equally massive internal redistribution of population. Because of data limitations, population movements within the country are less well documented than international ones, but Figure 1.2 shows one index of population redistribution constructed by summing changes in the percentage of the nation's population in each state between successive censuses beginning in 1870.[8] The two largest changes took place in the 1870s and 1880s. Subsequent decades show a pattern of oscillations around a generally declining trend, with each peak or trough lower than the preceding one.

---

[8] Because the positive and negative changes in state shares of the population must sum to zero, the index is constructed by summing either the positive or the negative changes. Clearly, the measure here captures only net migration between states. Data available since 1940 show that there may be substantial offsetting migration flows, which will be missed by this measure. See Eldridge and Thomas (1964, ch. 1) for further discussion.

Falling transportation and communication costs after the Civil War created the potential for the expansion of labor markets over a broader geographic area, and hence a growing level of geographic integration. Realizing this potential, however, required the development of effective labor market institutions capable of channeling information between employers and job seekers in distant locations and the creation of mechanisms to finance the movement of workers in response to this information. Without the development of these labor market institutions it would have been impossible for the United States to follow the path of industrialization that it actually took in the decades after the Civil War.

This book poses two questions about this formative episode in the development of American labor markets: What labor market institutions promoted the geographic mobility of labor during American industrialization? And how did these institutions influence the course of American economic development? The answers to these questions yield a number of important insights. The first is the prominence of employer recruitment in promoting the geographic expansion of labor markets. Economists and historians interested in migration have long recognized the important place of friends and family in facilitating long-distance migration, but I show both that employers were instrumental in initiating migration flows that were later perpetuated by friends and family and that the reliance of job seekers on kin- and friendship-based information channels was effective only because employers adopted hiring and personnel policies that were complementary to the operation of these informal labor market channels. Labor market institutions, in other words, were the product of the interaction between employers and workers.

The second point that emerges from this investigation is the importance of historical forces in shaping the patterns of labor market integration that emerged in the course of the nineteenth century. The complementary actions of employers and job seekers created labor market institutions that were highly effective in mobilizing labor over long distances, resulting in a considerable degree of market integration. Yet the labor market channels of communication and assistance that they promoted evolved in a fundamentally historical, or path-dependent, manner. Patterns of labor market recruitment that emerged during the first half of the nineteenth century, when slavery separated southern from northern labor markets, were perpetuated and reinforced by the reliance on kin- and friendship-based networks of labor market information. After the abolition of slavery, well-integrated southern and northern labor markets remained largely isolated from one another until large-scale European immigration was terminated by the beginning of World War I.

The third point is that the development of late-nineteenth century labor market institutions that promoted geographic mobility involved trade-offs with other labor market outcomes. Although employers recruited both skilled and unskilled workers over long distances, late-nineteenth century labor market institutions proved more effective at integrating markets for less skilled workers than they were for more skilled ones. This difference encouraged American employers to reorganize production processes – introducing specialized machinery and increasing the division of labor – to reduce their reliance on skilled craft workers. Their efforts did not so much eliminate the need for skilled labor as alter the types of skills that were required. Factory methods of production required a new class of semiskilled operatives who could best acquire the skills they needed through on-the-job training rather than formal apprenticeships. The high rates of turnover that characterized late-nineteenth and early-twentieth century labor markets limited the ability of workers and employers to make investments in training, however, and contributed to a growing tension between the goals of efficient spatial allocation of labor and the training of adequate numbers of skilled workers.

PLAN OF THE BOOK

The next two chapters describe the development of those labor market institutions that facilitated increasing geographic integration in the late-nineteenth century. In Chapter 2, I describe the dominant methods by which labor market information was communicated and transactions were accomplished. As is true today, labor markets after the Civil War were highly decentralized.

The primary channels of communication were informal networks of friends and relatives. These same friends and family also provided assistance in financing the direct and indirect costs of long-distance migration. When these networks came into existence, they proved highly efficient mechanisms for mobilizing long-distance movements of labor and were strongly encouraged by employers. Because they linked specific sending and receiving regions, however, the development of kin- and friendship-based labor market recruitment mechanisms tended to reflect the influence of historical accidents. After a particular pattern of migration had become established, it tended to be perpetuated, while other potential sources of labor supply were neglected because comparable mechanisms of recruitment had not been established.

But finding that kin- and friendship-based networks dominated the recruitment of labor at this time provides only a partial answer to the question of how labor markets worked; it is also necessary to determine how these networks came into being in the first place. As I show, employers played an essential and purposeful role in establishing these networks through their recruitment of migrants, either directly or through the services provided by employment agencies. In principle, the activities of employers should have tended to offset the tendency of the labor market to become locked-in to particular patterns of connections. However, I find that patterns of employer recruitment were also prone to a considerable degree of path-dependence in their evolution because of the coordination problems associated with the decentralized decisions made by employers and job seekers. For employers, recruiting was most effective where there were large concentrations of mobile job seekers. For job seekers, the prospects of finding a job were clearly greatest where many employers were likely to be. The mutually reinforcing nature of these concerns then tended to push job seekers and employers to concentrate their search efforts in a few major centers of labor distribution. By the time of the Civil War, New York, Chicago, and a small number of other major cities had emerged as focal points for both groups, and this pattern persisted without significant disruption until the influx of foreign workers was interrupted by the outbreak of World War I.

Although labor market intermediaries – employment agencies and labor exchanges – did develop during the late-nineteenth century, their role in the mobilization of labor remained significantly constrained. In Chapter 3, I offer an explanation for the limited role of labor market intermediaries based on a careful examination of the operation and characteristics of the intermediaries that did emerge in this period. Drawing on a wide array of sources, I show that the operation of successful labor market intermediaries closely paralleled the workings of the informal networks of friends and relatives that were the primary source of labor market information. The close correspondence in the operation of formal intermediaries and informal channels suggests that rather than seeing intermediaries as a potential alternative to these networks, they should be viewed as a commercialized extension of them. Only where informal connections were not viable were labor market intermediaries capable of surviving for any length of time.

In Chapters 4 through 6, I turn to an examination of the impact of late-nineteenth century labor market institutions on the course of American economic development. Chapter 4 considers the interaction between the development of mechanisms to facilitate the external recruitment of labor and the ways in which employers allocated labor internally, and especially how they filled positions requiring specialized skills. External recruitment was an important source of skilled and unskilled workers in this period. But, evidence on employment trends and the evolution of skill premia indicate that at the aggregate level the supply of skilled workers was less elastic than that of unskilled workers. In part, this inelasticity may reflect the weakness of American apprenticeship, but it also reflects the greater reluctance of skilled European workers to emigrate to the United States. Responding to the high and rising costs of recruiting traditional categories of skilled labor, employers turned to technological solutions – reorganizing work processes by introducing specialized capital equipment and an increased division of labor. These changes did not so much eliminate the need for skilled workers as alter the types of skills required and increase the importance of on-the-job training in employer-specific skills. These changes created incentives to increase the duration of worker-employer attachment, a fact reflected in the emergence of a substantial minority of workers with long job tenures. But continued reliance on immigrant laborers with relatively low attachment to factory work appears to have slowed the adoption of internal promotion and long-term jobs. Not until the end of mass migration after World War I did employers begin to invest significantly in the development of so-called internal labor markets.

Chapter 5 uses data on wages and earnings to trace changes in the geographic scope of labor markets across much of the nineteenth and early-twentieth centuries. In the theoretical ideal of a market with no information or transactions costs, comparable workers would earn the same wage regardless of their location, a fact sometimes labeled the "law of one price." Because obtaining information and carrying out transactions involve real costs, however, actual markets will never attain this theoretical ideal. The more efficient the institutions that emerge, however, the smaller the degree of variation in wages across different locations.[9] Spatial variations in wages thus provide one important measure of the efficiency of market institutions.

Consistent with evidence developed in Chapter 2 that patterns of migration tended to follow well-established routes, these data show that the expansion of American labor market boundaries after the Civil War was impressive, but strikingly uneven. By the end of the nineteenth century, labor markets in the northern United States had been linked in a tightly integrated regional market, and were, in turn, closely linked to northern European labor markets. Yet this regional and international integration coincided with the persistent isolation of northern and southern labor markets in the United States from one another.

Chapter 6 considers the impact of market expansion on labor relations, through an examination of variations in employers' use of strikebreakers in late-nineteenth century labor conflicts. The

---

[9] Suppose that the range of prices is from a low of P_l to a high of P_h. Clearly buyers who paid P_h would have preferred to buy at P_l, and sellers who received P_l would rather have sold at price P_h. That these traders did not encounter each other is a consequence of their lack of complete information, and the range of prices then provides one metric for assessing the extent of the costs imposed by lack of complete information in the market.

progress of labor markets toward increasing regional and international integration tended to break down barriers isolating local markets, making it more difficult for workers in any one place to affect the terms of their employment. One visible manifestation of this was the widespread use of strikebreakers at this time to undermine the bargaining power of workers engaged in labor disputes. In the 1880s and 1890s, employers used strikebreakers in over 40 percent of strikes, and the use of strikebreakers substantially reduced striking workers' chances of success. Labor historians have suggested that worker and community solidarity may have been stronger in smaller places, thus making it easier to prevent strikebreaking. It also seems possible that workers in some industries or skilled occupations may have been more insulated from competitive pressures than were others. In this chapter, I examine and largely reject these conjectures. Rather, I find that the use of strikebreakers did not vary appreciably by region or city size and that industry and occupation effects were quite limited as well. I do, however, find that the source of strikebreakers varied systematically with location, with employers in smaller communities and in locations outside the Northeast most likely to use outside strikebreakers.

2

JOB SEEKERS, EMPLOYERS, AND THE CREATION OF LABOR MARKET INSTITUTIONS

Understanding how labor was mobilized in response to the shifting pattern of labor demand created by industrialization requires an examination of the mechanisms that labor market participants created to convey information and facilitate transactions between job seekers and employers. A complete account of these institutions would require considering all the transactions that took place in the labor market. Since the late 1920s, a number of studies have attempted to do just this through surveys of workers in particular industries or locations (De Schweinitz 1932; Myers and Maclaurin 1943; Myers and Shultz 1951; Reynolds 1951; Rees and Shultz 1970; Granovetter 1974; and Corcoran, Datcher, and Duncan 1980). The sources available for the nineteenth century will not support such an investigation; nonetheless, it is possible to piece together from a variety of alternative sources a relatively clear picture of how labor markets worked and how they responded to the challenges created by American economic growth in this period. The account that emerges from these sources lacks some of the quantitative precision of more recent surveys, but it more clearly reveals the dynamics of labor market evolution over time than is possible based on the sort of snapshot picture provided by most worker surveys.

It is apparent from the available sources that, as is true today, most labor market information was communicated through "informal" networks of friends and relatives. When in place, such networks provided a highly efficient and low-cost mechanism of conveying labor market information. Because recruiting labor through these channels was easier than using any other mechanisms, the history of previous migration decisions exerted a powerful influence on subsequent migration decisions. Chain migration patterns were in this sense historically determined: the population movements that they produced reflected not simply the current configuration of supply and demand but also the decisions of previous migrants. Migrants at any point in time were much more likely to follow their friends and relatives than to set out for locations in which they did not know anyone.

These observations, however, leave unanswered the question of how migration flows were initiated in the first place. The evidence on this point is less complete, but a variety of sources, including the voluminous reports compiled by the U.S. Immigration Commission in its 41-volume report issued in 1911, are sufficient to construct a reasonably complete picture of how new migration flows started. This evidence supports two conclusions. First, recruitment by employers – either through their own agents or through formal intermediaries – was the crucial factor in initiating new networks of communication. Second, although employer recruitment helped to broaden the scope of labor markets substantially over time, the patterns of recruitment that were produced were influenced by the prior history of labor market arrangements. Once employers and their agents began to concentrate in a select group of cities, their presence made these places more attractive to job seekers. The more job seekers tended to gravitate to these places, the more likely employers were to search in these places when they needed to recruit workers. The interaction between these choices ensured that patterns of migration tended to persist after they became established. By the Civil War, well-established patterns of employer recruitment had already come into existence within both the northern and southern parts of the country. In the postbellum period, these patterns were reinforced contributing to the persistent lack of integration between northern and southern labor markets. Only when World War I substantially interrupted the supply of immigrant labor upon which northern employers had become dependent did northern employers begin to forge connections with sources of supply in the relatively more labor-abundant South.

INFORMAL NETWORKS, CHAIN MIGRATION, AND THE DISTRIBUTION OF LABOR

Twentieth-century studies that ask labor market participants how they found their most recent job have consistently concluded that kin and friendship connections are the dominant channels of labor market communication for blue-collar workers. In most of these studies, more than half of all workers reported having learned of their present job through information provided by friends or relatives. Another 15 to 20 percent of workers typically reported having obtained their job through direct application at the factory gate, a method of job search that in many cases may have been prompted by information provided by friends and relatives about which establishments were hiring. In contrast, with the exception of white-collar clerical workers, only a small fraction of workers reported learning of jobs through formal intermediaries like employment agencies or want advertisements.[1]

As is true in industrial labor markets today, postbellum job seekers relied heavily on information and assistance provided by friends and relatives to locate and obtain work. Although no formal surveys of job seekers were undertaken until the 1920s, a 1936 study of 2,500 workers in Philadelphia conducted by Gladys Palmer and recently analyzed by Walter Licht (1992, pp. 31–40) asked for retrospective information on the respondents' entire employment histories. In a number of cases, these histories stretched back into the 1880s. In this survey, over 50 percent of those interviewed reported that they had secured their first job through friends or relatives. This proportion declined to 40 to 44 percent for subsequent jobs, but this method of job search clearly remained quite important throughout the workers' careers. These proportions are the same for the oldest group of workers in the sample, those 45 to 77 years old in 1936, which includes many individuals who would have entered the labor market during the late-nineteenth century (Licht 1992, pp. 36–8, Table 2.6).

---

[1] See De Schweinitz (1932), Myers and Maclaurin (1943), Myers and Shultz (1951), Reynolds (1951), Rees and Shultz (1970), Granovetter (1974), and Corcoran et al. (1980).

For workers in urban areas, job search through direct application was the principal alternative to reliance on friends and family. Prior to the widespread diffusion of the automobile, factories and working-class neighborhoods clustered together, making this method practical for urban job seekers. The density of potential employers is illustrated in this account offered by an unemployed Philadelphian in the early 1910s:

I got up at 5:30 and went to Baldwin's and was told no help required. From there, I went to Hale & Kilburn at 18th and Lehigh Avenue and met with the same answer. I then walked to 2nd and Erie Avenue to Potter's Oil Cloth Works, and they needed no help. Then to the Hess Bright company, at Front and Erie Avenue, and again met with the same result. Next I came back . . . for a meal. In the afternoon, I went to Edward Bromley's; no help needed; from there to a firm at American and Girard streets with the same result. I tried two other places in the neighborhood, whose names I have forgotten, and none had any work (quoted in Licht 1992, p. 52).

In Palmer's study, 40 percent of those interviewed reported obtaining their first job through application at the factory, and 46 to 50 percent reported obtaining subsequent jobs in this manner. These proportions are roughly twice as great as those reported in more recent surveys. In contrast to the importance of direct applications and word-of-mouth methods, only 9 to 10 percent of those surveyed by Palmer reported obtaining jobs by answering want advertisements or using employment agencies.

The Role of Informal Networks in Long-Distance Migration

The mobility of labor between employers within particular urban areas was obviously important for the efficient functioning of labor markets. But the shifting patterns of labor demand that accompanied American economic growth during the late-nineteenth and early-twentieth centuries also required the redistribution of labor between cities, regions, and countries. In responding to the shifting location of labor demand, labor markets had to develop institutions to link employers and job seekers across widely separated locations. Because of the obstacle of distance, job seekers could not directly canvas potential employers. Moreover, even after they were aware of job opportunities, they had to overcome the barrier of transportation costs. For long-distance migrants, it appears that the assistance of friends and family was even more important than for local job seekers.

By far the greatest quantity of information about the institutions directing the reallocation of labor across space concerns the factors influencing the movements of European immigrants. The large volume of immigration, especially from southern and eastern Europe, was one of the most visible aspects of the social transformation of the United States after the Civil War, and it is not surprising that this phenomenon attracted considerable attention at the time as well as from historians. During the late-nineteenth century, close to one-quarter of gainfully employed workers were foreign born. Because few of the immigrants that arrived at this time went into agriculture or the professions, their contribution to the blue-collar workforce was substantially larger, especially in urban areas outside the South. The contribution of immigrants to the urban labor force is clearly illustrated in Table 2.1, which reports the proportion of foreign-born workers in selected cities and occupations in 1890. At this time, close to half of all workers in New York, Boston, Chicago, St. Paul, and San Francisco were foreign born, as were between 30 and 40 percent of workers in Philadelphia, Pittsburgh, Cincinnati, and St. Louis. Among unskilled-laborers, the proportion of foreign born was substantially higher, reaching as much as 86 percent in New York and 83 percent in San Francisco. For the country as a whole, more than one in three laborers was foreign-born. Among more skilled blue-collar occupations the foreign-born contribution was not quite so large, but it was still over 50 percent for some occupations in many of the nonsouthern cities. If the children of the foreign born are considered, the impact of immigrants on labor supply was even greater. By the early-twentieth century, the foreign born constituted well over half the labor force in many important manufacturing industries, while their children contributed another 10 to 20 percent in most cases (Nelson 1975, p. 80).

The quantitative significance of immigrants in the industrial labor force, and especially among the geographically mobile part of the labor force, makes information about their movements

Table 2.1. *Percentage Foreign Born among Gainfully Occupied Workers in Selected Occupations and Cities, 1890*

	Laborers	Blacksmiths[a]	Iron & steel workers	Machinists	Brick & stone masons[b]	Carpenters[c]	Painters[d]	All occupations
Northeast								
Boston	77.4	69.5	51.4	37.6	52.8	61.0	41.6	45.2
New York	86.0	71.3	47.9	50.7	61.2	61.4	51.4	51.9
Philadelphia	55.6	50.0	37.4	35.5	38.3	29.2	23.4	33.6
Baltimore	28.0	40.5	18.1	7.3	14.3	18.7	15.4	20.5
Pittsburgh	60.0	48.5	53.3	35.9	56.4	34.9	25.2	40.1
Midwest								
Cincinnati	38.5	38.0	31.4	30.9	55.6	40.8	23.6	30.7
St. Louis	46.5	45.9	34.1	37.1	49.7	46.7	29.1	34.6
Chicago	78.2	71.8	66.0	57.9	76.7	70.5	56.2	54.8
St. Paul	84.9	68.0	65.3	55.2	86.3	76.7	60.9	54.0
West								
San Francisco	83.2	53.9	51.7	42.4	55.1	53.4	42.1	58.1
South								
Richmond	3.8	7.3	6.4	8.6	5.6	4.0	7.1	5.1
New Orleans	15.0	25.1	18.0	21.6	13.5	22.0	16.4	19.6
United States	36.1	31.3	40.2	31.8	40.4	26.0	25.3	23.0

Note: Data for New York include workers in Brooklyn; data for Pittsburgh include workers in Allegheny.
[a] Includes wheelwrights.
[b] Includes stonecutters.
[c] Includes joiners.
[d] Includes varnishers.
Source: U.S. Department of the Interior (1897, "Population," Part II, pp. 630–743).

important in its own right, but this information should also illuminate the labor market experiences of native-born workers. Because those native-born workers seeking industrial employment had to compete in the same market with the foreign-born workers, it seems reasonable to suppose that information about how immigrants found jobs also applies to native-born workers in these same markets.

Historians and sociologists studying late-nineteenth-century immigrants are in general agreement that migration was fundamentally a social process (Bodnar 1985; Morawska 1990). According to Charles Tilly (1990, p. 84): "The effective units of migration were (and are) neither individuals nor households, but sets of people linked by acquaintance, kinship, and work experience." Rarely did immigrants leave home without a clear idea of where they were going and how they would get there. Friends and relatives not only provided advice about when and where to go but often helped to finance the costs of passage. Information provided by friends and relatives led some immigrants directly to a specific job; however, in other cases, information was more general, and new arrivals joined the pool of urban workers seeking jobs through direct application at the factory gates.

Surviving letters written by immigrants to their relatives and friends at home show that, in addition to conveying advice and information about American labor market conditions, those already in the country helped those who followed to find jobs, provided them with housing until they were employed, and paid for their passage (Erickson 1972, pp. 233–55). That many arriving immigrants were responding to information about employment opportunities provided by friends and relatives was apparent to contemporary observers. According to one immigration official, when he asked immigrants how they knew that they were going to work at a particular place, their explanation "always dwindles down to the fact that they are sent for by some friend or relative who is employed by some corporation, and their fare is usually paid by this friend" (U.S. Congress, House of Representatives 1889, p. 561). Similarly, the *New York Times* (1868a, p. 4) explained the pronounced correlation between the volume of immigration and economic conditions by observing that "when the demand for help is fair and wages are good a brisk business is done at the offices of the emigrant lines of passenger ships in receiving the money of servant girls, mechanics and laborers, to prepay the cost of bringing hither other members of their family."

The proportion of immigrants arriving on prepaid fares offers one measure of the quantitative significance of the assistance provided by immigrants already in the country in directing subsequent migration. In the 1880s, an agent for one steamship line reported to Congressional investigators that 30 to 40 percent of German immigrants were traveling on fares prepaid by someone already in the United States and that the tickets of Hungarians were "largely prepaid" (U.S. Congress, House of Representatives 1889, p. 36). By the early-twentieth century, as many as 60 percent of immigrants reported that their travel had been arranged by friends or relatives already in the country (Morawska 1990, p. 194).

As part of the voluminous investigation into the impact of immigration on the U.S. economy between 1906 and 1911, investigators for the Immigration Commission visited a large number of industrial communities throughout the country. In addition to collecting statistical evidence on employment patterns and earnings, they also interviewed knowledgeable individuals in each community to ascertain the patterns of labor movements into and out of these places. In many cases, their informants remarked on the important role of earlier immigrants in conveying labor market information to potential migrants. The Commission reported, for example, that, after securing employment, many immigrant steelworkers in the Pittsburgh area "wrote letters to their friends and relatives in their native country, setting forth the opportunities existing in this country." Moreover, many of the immigrants interviewed by the investigators cited letters they had received as an important influence on their decisions to immigrate. Most of the immigrants questioned had come because they had "heard through letters from their friends and relatives, through testimony of returned countrymen, and through the press that an abundance of employment was offered in the United States at a much higher wage than they could earn in any of the European countries" (U.S. Congress, Senate 1911, part 2, vol. 1, pp. 249, 333).[2]

Contemporary observers and later scholars have also traced the impact of these informal networks on the movements of migrants between specific sending and receiving regions. A wealth of historical accounts have described the role of pioneering migrants from a particular community in encouraging and facilitating the movement of large numbers of followers to particular destinations. Writing about the origins of Italian laborers in Hammonton, New Jersey, Meade (1907, p. 477) observed that about 1870 Matteo Campanella "sent for his brother, and the two prospered, purchased more land, and married two English girls. The Campanellas soon encouraged the coming of relatives, who in turn induced others to come, until, as a result of a continuous migration from Gesso, more than one-half the inhabitants of that town are in the United States, many of them still in Hammonton." Analyzing migration to Cleveland, Barton (1975) concluded that "more than three-quarters of the Italians, Rumanians, and Slovaks proceeded along well-travelled courses to specific destinations in the city."[3]

The consequences of so-called chain migration are readily apparent in more aggregated statistical evidence as well. Ward (1971, p. 77) documented the tendency of German and Irish immigrants in the late-nineteenth century to concentrate in different cities. A number of other studies have analyzed the intended destinations of arriving European immigrants, finding that the stock of previous migrants of the same nationality already present in a state has a positive and statistically significant effect on the proportion of new arrivals destined for that state, even after controlling for the effects of state per capita income and other characteristics likely to affect new immigrants' destinations (Gallaway, Vedder, and

[2] The Commission reported similar observations for New England textile workers; operatives in Omaha's meat-packing plants; copper miners in Calumet, Michigan; and silk workers in Patterson, New Jersey (U.S. Congress, Senate 1911, part 3, p. 283; part 11, p. 345; part 17, p. 83; and part 5, pp. 17–18).

[3] In addition to these instances, see Kamphoefner's (1987) study of migration from Westfalia to Missouri, Gjerde's (1985) study of emigration from Norway, and Moch's (1989) discussion of Polish emigration. MacDonald and MacDonald (1974) included an appendix listing instances of chain migration among Italians; Bodnar (1985, ch. 2) provided a more complete review of the literature.

Shukla 1974; Dunlevy and Gemery 1977, 1978; Dunlevy 1980). Interestingly, these studies have generally found that inclusion of the migrant stock variable reduces the magnitude and statistical significance of per capita income's effect on immigrants' choice of intended destination. While this result could have been produced in a number of ways, it is consistent with other kinds of historical evidence of the influence of friends and family in directing and assisting subsequent migrants.[4] Murayama's (1991) analysis of variations in across-prefecture emigration rates from Japan provides evidence that advice and assistance from friends and family already in the United States was important in directing Japanese immigration to the United States.

Networks based on kin and friendship connections were a highly effective means of mobilizing labor. For many employers, the referrals of current employees and the stream of applicants at the factory gate, many of whom had been attracted to a particular location through word-of-mouth channels of communication, were sufficient to meet their labor requirements. There is unfortunately little statistical evidence on hiring practices before World War I that can be used to quantify these assertions. One study conducted in 1910, however, did survey 45 large firms in Chicago about their methods of obtaining help. Of the firms surveyed, 43 reported hiring applicants at the gate regularly, 1 used this method sometimes, and only 1 stated that this method was never used. Referrals from current employees were the next most common method of hiring, being used regularly by 23 of the firms and sometimes by another 16. In contrast, newspaper advertisements were used regularly by

---

[4] Two alternative interpretations of the correlation between the intended destinations of arriving immigrants and the location of earlier arrivals are consistent with the statistical evidence: (1) that the presence of an established immigrant community reduced the psychic costs of relocation by providing a familiar environment, thus making such places more attractive as destinations; and (2) that there was some sort of national heterogeneity in preferences that caused immigrants of certain nationalities to prefer one destination over another, independent of the presence or absence of others of the same nationality (Nelson 1959). At first glance, it might appear that the weakening of the effect of state per capita income caused by the inclusion of the migrant stock variable indicates that the desire to follow past immigrants was motivated by noneconomic forces, but this fact is more reasonably interpreted as evidence that previous migrants were the channel through which information about higher incomes was communicated.

only 16 of the firms, and occasionally by 13 more. Just 9 firms reported using employment agencies either regularly or occasionally (Chicago 1914, p. 12).

Employer Encouragement of Informal Networks
Although many employers found referrals from current employees and the stream of applicants at the factory gate adequate to meet their labor needs during normal periods, it would be a mistake to interpret this as evidence that employers were passive participants in late-nineteenth century labor markets. Rather, there is evidence that they actively encouraged the use of informal channels of labor recruitment when these were available and turned to active recruitment of labor when these were not.

It is important to recognize the extent to which workers' job search strategies and employers' labor recruitment policies were interdependent. Kin- and friendship-based networks were effective means of finding jobs precisely because employers chose to adapt their recruiting policies to take advantage of them. Evidence turned up by the Immigration Commission indicates that employers commonly communicated information about anticipated job openings to their current employees before looking outside the firm. In Pennsylvania coal mines, for example, the Commission's investigators reported that when the demand for labor was strong, "the mine foremen have communicated the situation to the immigrants in their employ, with the expectation that they would send for their relatives and friends" (U.S. Congress, Senate 1911, part 1, vol. 1, pp. 532–4). Similarly, in the mining districts of Oklahoma and Kansas, they noted that all that was necessary to ensure the continued flow of workers was to encourage current employees to keep bringing their friends and relatives to the community by letting "it be known among the men employed that anyone wishing to bring in relatives or friends could do so." In such instances, the company would advance expenses for travel if two or more current employees would guarantee repayment. Occasionally, immigrant employees returning from visits to Europe would be employed to bring others with them, the mine operator advancing the cost of passage and other expenses, which would then be collected out of the workers' paychecks (U.S. Congress, Senate 1911, part 1, vol. 2, pp. 9–10, 25, 61).

Employers' decision to delegate responsibility for hiring decisions to their foremen can be viewed as another way in which they sought to adapt their personnel policies to take advantage of the workings of word-of-mouth channels of recruitment. Foremen who had moved up from the ranks of operatives were often drawn from the immigrant community and could be expected to have close ties to it, thus facilitating the use of informal channels when positions needed to be filled.[5] Roughly 10 percent of the Philadelphia workers interviewed in the 1936 survey conducted by Gladys Palmer reported securing their jobs by following a supervisor to a new job with another employer or by being hired because they were acquainted with the foreman from a previous job (Licht 1992, p. 34).

Indeed, it would appear that, in some cases, employers actually discriminated against job applicants who lacked personal connections. According to one Polish immigrant in Pittsburgh, "the only way you got a job [was] through somebody who got you in. I mean this application, that's a big joke. They just throw them away ... to get a job with the railroad my brother-in-law got it for me. My job at the hospital my dad got it for me. I got the job at the meat place ... the boy I used to play ball with he got it for me" (quoted in Bodnar, Simon, and Weber 1982, p. 56). Historians tracing the emergence of formal bureaucratic personnel policies after World War I (e.g., Nelson 1975, pp. 79–81; Jacoby 1985, p. 16) have contrasted those policies with the apparently arbitrary and capricious exercise of authority over hiring and firing that was delegated to the foreman in earlier periods; however, the foregoing observations suggest that, in delegating authority over personnel matters to their foremen, employers were simply shaping their hiring practices to take the fullest advantage of the mechanisms of labor market communication and recruitment in an era of large-scale immigration.

[5] Morawska (1990, p. 204) and Tilly (1990, p. 86) both remarked upon the importance of employers' deliberate choice of ethnic-based hiring policies mediated by their foremen in facilitating the operation of informal networks in the labor market. For instances of foremen using their contacts in the immigrant community, see U.S. Congress, Senate (1911, part 2, vol. 2, p. 44; part 12, p. 149).

EMPLOYER RECRUITING

The information and assistance provided by friends and family was of considerable importance in directing the redistribution of labor in the decades after the Civil War. After word-of-mouth channels of communication had been established, they linked particular sending and receiving regions at low cost. But the establishment of word-of-mouth channels rested on the presence of a pool of earlier migrants who could provide information and assistance to those who followed. Yet, throughout the late-nineteenth and early-twentieth centuries, new streams of migration were established in response to the shifting patterns of demand and supply. Understanding how new word-of-mouth networks were initiated is thus crucial to developing a complete account of the response of labor market institutions to the shifting pattern of labor demand in this period.

Although the evidence is scattered and incomplete, it nonetheless points strongly toward employer recruitment as the primary force in initiating streams of migration, and hence in broadening the boundaries of labor markets.[6] With the exception of employers located in sparsely settled areas, especially those with highly seasonal labor demand, however, most employers engaged in active recruitment only during brief episodes of especially intense labor demand growth. After a pool of immigrant labor had become established, they quickly shifted toward reliance on chain migration as their primary source of supply.

Canals, Railroads and Other Employers of Temporary and Seasonal Labor

The problem of inelastic local labor supply was most intense for employers located in sparsely settled rural areas and those whose demand was highly seasonal. Throughout the nineteenth and early-twentieth centuries, constructing and repairing canal and rail lines, creating urban water supply and sewage systems, cutting ice, logging, and responding to the seasonal demands of agriculture required the temporary assembly of large numbers of unskilled

---

[6] Additional support for this view is provided in Chapter 6, which shows that employers in smaller communities were more likely to have recruited replacement workers from other locations than employers in large cities.

workers, often in remote and unpopulated areas. Without an established labor force that could provide them with access to word-of-mouth channels of recruitment, employers engaged in these projects had little choice but to recruit labor themselves.

Canal construction companies were among the first to face the problem of assembling large gangs of seasonal workers. Early construction projects were on a relatively small scale, and most of the labor force retained an attachment to agriculture, doing canal work only during slack seasons. As the rate of canal construction accelerated in the late 1810s, however, recruiting labor over a broader region became necessary. Advertisements were placed in newspapers, and agents were dispatched to canvas the countryside offering to provide transportation, board, and good wages. These measures proved inadequate to the task at hand, though, prompting employers to explore more distant sources of supply. In 1817, for example, the builders of the Erie Canal sent an agent to England to recruit experienced Irish laborers. A few years later, contractors working on the Chesapeake and Ohio Canal also sent recruiters to Europe, where they advertised 10,000 jobs, hoping to obtain 3,000 to 4,000 applicants. The results of this effort were not terribly encouraging, however. Only a few hundred workers responded to these notices, and a number of these workers departed for more attractive jobs after they arrived in the United States. Perhaps for this reason most canal companies did not recruit directly in Europe. Many of them did, however, maintain agents in large eastern cities to direct immigrants seeking work to their projects, and by the 1830s the majority of canal workers were foreign born (Way 1993, pp. 18–31, 55, 79–81, 94–100).

Somewhat later in the century, railroad construction companies confronted much the same situation and responded similarly. In the 1850s, contractors for the Illinois Central Railroad dispatched agents to New York to recruit workers among newly arriving immigrants (Gates 1957, p. 70). As the demand for seasonal gang labor grew with the expansion of the railroads after the Civil War, specialized employment agencies largely took over the task of rounding up newly arrived immigrant workers in major cities, making it unnecessary for railroad construction companies or other seasonal employers to dispatch their own agents to hire workers. But the basic pattern of recruitment remained otherwise unchanged.

Mining

Like employers of seasonal gang labor, mine operators faced the problem of assembling a workforce in relatively unpopulated areas. When mining operations were begun, operators had little choice but to bring the necessary labor force to the location of production. Unlike canal and railroad construction and other seasonal activities, however, mining was conducted on a continuing basis, and the communities that developed around the mines provided the basis for subsequent recruitment through kin and friendship networks. Mine-labor markets offer numerous examples of employer recruitment and illustrate the role played by employers in encouraging the transition from direct recruitment to the use of word-of-mouth channels of communication.

The evolution of recruitment practices is clearly spelled out in the reports of the Immigration Commission from numerous mining communities.[7] By the time investigators for the Immigration Commission arrived in Pennsylvania coal mining communities in the early-twentieth century, networks of friends and family were the dominant mechanism of labor recruitment. "The principal factor in the coming of aliens," they concluded, "has been the presence of fellow-countrymen." Mine operators with whom they spoke reported making little concerted effort to attract labor other than encouraging the operation of word-of-mouth channels of recruitment. Things had not always been this way, however. The investigators reported that after 1879, when bituminous coal production had begun to expand rapidly, labor demand had outstripped supply, causing operators to turn to employment agencies in New York or to dispatch their own agents to major ports to attract arriving immigrants. There were even some reports that

---

[7] The Immigration Commission reports include studies of bituminous and anthracite coal mining, iron mining, and copper mining and smelting. Although the reports on iron and bituminous coal offer considerable detail about the operation of labor markets, the discussion of copper and anthracite coal mining provide only sketchy details, suggesting that initial episodes of recruitment were followed by the development of systems of chain migration (U.S. Congress, Senate 1911, part 17, pp. 79–86; part 19, pp. 660–1).

companies had sent agents to Europe (U.S. Congress, Senate 1911, part 1, vol. 1, pp. 532, 534, 257).

A similar sequence of events was evident in other mining districts as well. Describing the coal labor market in Kentucky, West Virginia, and Virginia, Price Fishback (1992, pp. 31–5) observed that, although friends and relatives were important in recruiting labor, "when mines first opened or during peak periods of production, word-of-mouth networks at times failed to satisfy increases in companies' demand for labor," and employers were obliged either to contract with employment agents or send their own recruiters to other regions to obtain the necessary labor. In Oklahoma and Kansas, where production began to expand in the 1880s, early mining ventures had been undertaken by skilled English, Irish, Scotch, and Welsh miners who had come to the region of their own accord. But with the expansion of production, employers began to recruit actively in eastern coal fields, as well as among immigrants arriving in New York. Mine operators sent agents to these regions, and special railroad cars were chartered to carry the recruits. By the early 1890s, though, most mines had discontinued active recruitment because a sufficient number of applicants were being attracted through the referrals of current employees (U.S. Congress, Senate 1911, part 1, vol. 2, pp. 9–10, 25, 61).

Manufacturing
Employer recruiting was least common in manufacturing, but here too employers did recruit labor when their labor demands expanded rapidly. In the early-nineteenth century, most manufacturing establishments remained relatively small affairs whose labor needs could be met without much difficulty. When Samuel Slater and his partners established the first cotton-spinning mill in the United States in 1799, for example, they staffed it with a handful of children, and a few adult supervisors, all drawn from the surrounding agricultural population. With the introduction of factory methods of production requiring a labor force of several hundred workers, however, the scale of employment expanded beyond the capacity of local labor supplies. Early textile manufacturers responded by broadening the scope of their recruiting and adapting their employment practices to take advantage of the relatively

abundant supply of young women available in New England as a result of the region's declining agricultural sector. Agents were sent into the countryside to encourage young women to work in the mills for a few years, and dormitories were built near the factories to house these women while they were away from home.[8]

The extent to which mill owners modified employment practices to make jobs attractive to the pool of potential workers in the region is testimony to the fact that their actions reflected a conscious decision to broaden the scope of the labor market rather than accept the existing configuration of labor supply conditions.[9] After the companies established a factory labor force, however, word-of-mouth networks largely took over, making continued recruitment unnecessary. Letters and visits home helped to spread knowledge of employment opportunities to siblings, cousins, and friends. At the same time, the assistance that these experienced workers could provide to new arrivals eased their transition to factory work.

Beginning in the late 1830s, the early textile labor force underwent a transition as Irish immigrants began to replace young women as the principal source of workers. On the one hand, the number of young single women living in the countryside was falling and more attractive alternatives – such as teaching – were becoming available, thus reducing the supply of native-born workers. On the other hand, the supply of immigrants was increasing as Irish emigration rates rose (Dublin 1979, pp. 132–41). At first, mill agents were dispatched to Boston and other ports to encourage new arrivals to come to the mills, but with the growing population of immigrant workers, more and more job seekers were attracted to the mills by the information and advice offered by those already employed.

---

[8] See Field (1978) for a discussion of the role of agriculture's decline in creating a surplus of labor. Dublin (1979) described the adaptation of employment practices to take advantage of this source of labor.

[9] Saxonhouse and Wright (1984) explored this theme in more depth. As they illustrated, through comparisons of the antebellum New England pattern of labor recruitment with those employed by mills in the postbellum South and in late-nineteenth century Japan, the age and sex composition of textile workers and methods of job assignment in textile factories were remarkably flexible, despite the use of similar technologies. They argued that this is evidence that differences in labor systems were the result of differences in the nature of the available labor supply in each instance.

Over the course of the century, employers continued to adapt to changing patterns of immigration, drawing in new groups as necessary. In each case, it appears that, even though recruitment was necessary at first, this effort was soon superseded by the operation of informal channels of recruitment. When investigators from the Immigration Commission visited New England textile communities early in the twentieth century, they found that most of the French Canadian and other immigrant groups employed in New England cotton textile mills had found jobs through direct application at the plant, having been attracted there by those already employed in the mills. They noted, however, that the mills had advertised extensively for additional recruits and had employed agents in Canada to recruit immigrants during earlier periods of labor shortage (U.S. Congress, Senate 1911, part 3, pp. 117, 283). Much the same situation seems to have prevailed among producers of woolen and worsted goods. Although current employees were reported to have been the primary channel through which labor demand was communicated to potential immigrants, investigators also noted that in 1906 and 1907, "competition for labor was so spirited...that it extended to the very wharves, where an agent was maintained," and companies even offered to pay prospective employees' railroad fare (U.S. Congress, Senate 1911, part 4, pp. 770–81).

Outside of textiles, few industries had made the transition to large-scale factory production before the 1860s (Atack and Passell 1994, pp. 458–62). In the next half century, however, improvements in transportation, rising population density, and the development of new capital- and scale-intensive manufacturing technologies all encouraged a rapid expansion of manufacturing establishments. As these establishments grew, one of the challenges employers confronted was how to attract adequate supplies of labor. How they responded to this challenge depended to some extent on their location. When production was located in rural areas, employers had little choice but to recruit workers actively from other places. But as we have seen, they were usually able to shift toward more passive encouragement of word-of-mouth channels once an initial pool of industrial workers had been established. When employers were able to locate their factories in more densely settled urban

areas, they could often rely on applications at the gate or recruitment efforts within the neighboring community. During periods of
especially rapid expansion, however, even urban employers sometimes turned to more active recruitment.

Although steelmaking was not as location-specific as mining, the
requirement of low-cost access to bulky raw materials and the large
scale of operations meant that steelmakers often faced the problem of meeting rapidly expanding labor requirements in locations
at some distance from established population centers. As a result,
they found it necessary to recruit labor directly during the early
stages of their growth. Although there was little evidence of active
recruitment when Immigration Commission investigators visited
communities in Pennsylvania, New York, and West Virginia, they
reported that the earliest representatives of most of the immigrant
groups employed in the steel mills had been attracted by agents
sent to New York or other immigrant centers to recruit them (U.S.
Congress, Senate 1911, part 2, vol. 1, pp. 333, 602, 744). In 1881,
for example, one plant southeast of Pittsburgh had dispatched an
agent to New York with the intention of hiring a number of Irish
immigrants. Finding few Irish workers, however, he returned with
300 Magyars instead. Letters written by these employees were in
turn responsible for the group's expanding share of the labor force
(U.S. Congress, Senate 1911, part 2, vol. 1, pp. 244–9). At another
plant in what had previously been a small country town, several
employers had in 1901 turned to labor agencies in New York and
other cities to supplement the workforce attracted from immigrant
communities in nearby towns. The investigators reported, however, that such efforts had not been required for very long because
"the constant influx of friends and relatives of immigrants already
in the community creates a labor supply sufficient to meet the demand of the various companies" (U.S. Congress, Senate 1911, part
2, pp. 602, 733–4, 744).

For employers in or near more densely settled urban areas, when
referrals from current employees and applications at the gate were
insufficient to meet labor demand, all that was usually needed was
to send their agents or foremen into the surrounding community.
In Baltimore, for example, the Immigration Commission observed
that when garment makers needed to add to their workforce,

"notices are placed in the papers, and the various foremen are sent out among the races to try to induce them to accept work" (U.S. Congress, Senate 1911, part 6, pp. 410–11). Similarly, it was reported that glassmakers in western Pennsylvania had little trouble attracting adequate quantities of unskilled labor. "This class [of labor] is found in the vicinity," the investigators reported, "and even in the periods of greatest demand for labor the employers state that it is never necessary to do more than send foremen as agents into this nearby market to secure what labor is needed" (U.S. Congress, Senate 1911, part 12, p. 149). Chicago's slaughterhouses also appear to have had little trouble attracting adequate supplies of labor. The Immigration Commission's report noted that applications at the gate were adequate to meet the needs of the packing plants and devoted little space to discussing problems of labor recruitment in the industry (U.S. Congress, Senate 1911, part 11, pp. 205–6).

Even though the workings of informal channels were adequate to meet urban employer's labor demand under normal circumstances, there is some evidence that, during occasional periods of especially rapid expansion, they were still obliged to turn to more active recruitment. This was the case in one manufacturing center the Immigration Commission visited in Indiana, where the growth of a large plow works in the 1870s had caused a sharp increase in labor demand. "Running short of labor," the company, according to the Commission report, "began to import large numbers of Poles directly from Europe and other sections of the United States" (U.S. Congress, Senate 1911, part 13, pp. 551, 571–2). Similarly, when Chicago meatpackers set up plants in Omaha, Nebraska, and Kansas City, Kansas, they were obliged at first to staff them with workers recruited from Chicago, although they soon found that an adequate supply of applicants could be had at the gate (U.S. Congress, Senate 1911, part 11, pp. 277–8, 333–4, 341–5).

LABOR MARKET INSTITUTIONS IN THE SOUTH

In the South, the Civil War and the resultant emancipation of the region's previously enslaved workers created a profound disruption in labor market institutions. After the Civil War, employers and job seekers in the South developed new mechanisms of labor recruitment that in many respects resembled northern labor markets. But southern and northern labor market institutions remained largely distinct from one another.

Prior to the Civil War, southern slave owners, with a substantial fraction of their assets in the form of slaves, opposed economic development efforts – such as canal and railroad construction – that would have encouraged an influx of immigrant labor (Wright 1979, pp. 676–9) and lowered the value of this asset. On the other hand, an active market for slave labor facilitated the inter-regional movement of labor from surplus regions in the Southeast to rapidly growing regions in the interior. Some slaves undoubtedly moved as a result of their masters' migration decisions, but the bulk of interregional slave movements were mediated by specialized slave traders and brokers, who assembled large groups of slaves in surplus regions of the Southeast and arranged their shipment to rapidly growing regions of the cotton belt. Traders located in the Southeast typically traveled around one or two counties seeking out slaves, whom they purchased from their masters and then sold either to brokers in Charleston, Richmond, and other urban centers or directly to clients from interior regions (Tadman 1989, pp. 5–8, 49–57). Between 1820 and 1860, these mechanisms contributed to the internal redistribution of an average of about 200,000 slaves per decade, or roughly 10 percent of the slave population in slave-exporting regions. In comparison, from 1870 to 1920, the migration rate of free blacks from the South Atlantic region fluctuated between 2.6 and 5.7 percent of the region's population per decade.[10]

Upon emancipation, traders could no longer purchase workers in areas of relative labor abundance and sell them in areas of relative labor scarcity. Instead, redistribution had to occur as a result of the self-interested actions of individual workers. Despite the confusions created in the immediate aftermath of emancipation, effective labor market institutions were created remarkably quickly.[11] Scholars have generally acknowledged that, in the

---

[10] See Table 2.3. As that table shows, migration rates among the region's free whites were generally even lower.

[11] Wright (1986, pp. 84–90) and Jaynes (1986) described the process of reconstructing labor markets in the wake of emancipation. Wright (1987a, p. 319–21)

period of labor scarcity immediately following the Civil War, the freedmen displayed considerable mobility. But some historians have argued that, after this initial episode, landlords used the institutions of sharecropping and debt-peonage to effectively reenslave their black labor force.[12] Gavin Wright (1987b) convincingly argued, however, that this was not the case. As he documented, high rates of mobility persisted even as the labor market softened. Studies of several Mississippi plantations in the 1870s showed, for example, that between one-quarter and one-half of the labor force was new each year, and data collected in the 1910 census shows similar rates of mobility. Even more striking evidence of the strength of market forces is provided by the fact that competitive pressures effectively equalized black and white wages for entry-level workers. Racism did, however, manifest itself in the marked segregation of southern employment along industrial lines, and obstacles to the advancement of blacks into higher paying industrial jobs (Wright 1987b, pp. 102–4, 122–31).

As was the case in northern labor markets, word of mouth was the dominant channel of labor market recruitment in the South. An official from one Alabama company described his company's labor recruitment practices as follows:

We put the word out if we wanted employees to our own people that we are going to be hiring. And they'd go home over the weekend, and they'd put the word out at the country church. And along about Tuesday we'd have the finest-looking specimens out there you ever saw, and that's who we hired (quoted in Wright 1986, p. 77).

But, even though the channels of labor market information in the South paralleled those in the North, they drew on different pools of labor. Because of the depressed condition of the agricultural sector, especially in the Southeast, and the small absolute size of the manufacturing sector, many southern employers were able to

provided a clear illustration of the range of choices that had to be settled before newly freed slaves and landowners could conclude labor market transactions.

[12] Jonathan Wiener (1978, p. 70), for example, wrote: "The coercive mode of labor control gave southern agriculture its distinctive character. Sharecropping was a form of 'bound' labor, with restrictions on the free market in labor that did not prevail in fully developed capitalistic societies such as that of the North." See also Mandle (1978, p. vi).

obtain adequate quantities of labor within the region. This was true, for example, of southern textile mills. Located in upland rural areas for the most part, these mills were able to attract families from the surrounding agricultural population by offering employment opportunities not only for adult males but also for women and children. Only after the turn of the century did the growth of these mills force employers to broaden their recruiting efforts beyond their immediate vicinity (McHugh 1988).

In some cases, however, southern employers were obliged to use recruiting to expand their labor supply. At first, many of them also turned to European immigrants, but this strategy generally proved unsuccessful. Because of low wages and poor working conditions, immigrants recruited by southern employers rarely remained for very long, and they did not encourage friends or family to follow them. As a result, the self-supporting chain migration that usually followed recruiting in the North did not develop in the South (Wright 1986, pp. 76–7).

Investigators for the Immigration Commission reporting on the coal and iron industries that developed around Birmingham, Alabama, found that because of the continuing attachment of the local population to agriculture, employers there turned to northern employment agencies to supply European immigrants. Employers reported, however, that few of these workers stayed in the South (U.S. Congress, Senate 1911, part 1, vol. 2, pp. 217–19; part 2, vol. 2, pp. 192–201). Planters in the Mississippi Delta were equally unsuccessful in their efforts to employ European immigrants on large cane and cotton plantations. When these efforts failed, they turned their efforts toward rural areas of the Southeast, where they were relatively successful in recruiting workers through the services of a number of labor agents.[13]

HISTORICAL INFLUENCES ON LABOR MARKET DEVELOPMENT

The institutions that employers and workers created in the late-nineteenth century to communicate labor market information and facilitate transactions developed in a fundamentally historical, or

[13] The work of these labor agents is described in more detail in Chapter 3.

"path-dependent" manner. That is, the patterns of resource allocation that they produced cannot be explained solely in terms of the contemporaneous configuration of supply and demand conditions. Rather, it is necessary to refer to the prior history of migration flows between specific sources and destinations to explain labor market outcomes. Chain migration and employer recruitment were effective in mobilizing millions of workers and making possible the rapid growth of American industrial might. But the connections they established linked particular sending and receiving regions, while excluding others. Once established, certain patterns of migration tended to persist, while others were simply never explored. The patterns of connection that did emerge can only be fully understood in historical context.

The path-dependent nature of patterns of recruitment operated at two distinct levels. First, after a particular stream of migration had been established, the advice and assistance offered by friends and relatives provided an effective and low-cost mechanism of labor recruitment. The diminishing cost of recruiting through these informal networks helped to encourage their persistence and expansion once in place. By its nature, chain migration linked specific sending and receiving regions. As the locations of labor demand and supply shifted over the course of time, however, new streams of migration had to be established.

The second element of historical path-dependence involved the methods of employer recruitment that were used to initiate new streams of migration. Beginning in the 1840s, northern employers seeking to expand their labor supply had begun to recruit European immigrants by sending agents to the cities through which the majority of newly arriving immigrants passed. Their efforts helped to establish the reputation of these places as centers of labor distribution, which in turn encouraged immigrant job seekers to select these places as destinations. The concentration of job seekers in these places served to attract more employers and encouraged the development of employment agencies and a broad range of other businesses catering to the needs of job seekers lacking access to informal networks.[14] These developments, in turn,

[14] See Chapter 3 for further discussion of the development of employment agencies and other businesses serving job seekers.

lowered job search costs at these places and reinforced the advantage of the existing channels of recruitment in comparison to potential alternatives. The decisions of employers and job seekers were thus interdependent and mutually reinforcing. Even though economies of scale tended to encourage the persistence of northern reliance on immigrant labor, the actions of southern employers may have added additional reinforcement. Beginning in the 1870s and continuing at least through World War I, southern employers manifested a pronounced hostility to labor agents seeking to recruit workers. In many cases, they were able to win passage of legislation imposing substantial licensing fees on labor agents who wished to recruit workers.[15]

The patterns of labor recruitment that had emerged in the North in the decades before the Civil War persisted largely unchanged in the postbellum period. Although the sources of European immigration were shifting dramatically in this period, new immigrant groups were easily incorporated into the broad outlines of this system. In contrast, even though the South, and especially the South Atlantic, emerged in the postbellum period as a labor-abundant, low-wage region within the United States, northern employers largely ignored this alternative source of labor until World War I, when the cessation of large-scale European immigration obliged them to explore new sources of supply. Strikingly, as we have seen, southern employers seeking to attract mobile workers at first turned to northern cities to recruit immigrants. Only when these efforts proved unsuccessful did they begin to develop channels of recruitment that would enable them to recruit labor within the South.

It is difficult to measure migration flows within the United States accurately. No measures of gross migration flows between different points are available, but it is possible to use measures of net migration to gain some insight about patterns of population redistribution. Net migration will obviously understate total population movements to the extent that gross flows in opposite directions

---

[15] Cohen (1991, ch. 9) listed antilabor agent legislation in the nineteenth century. According to Breen (1987, p. 76), concerns about the recruiting of laborers reached a peak during World War I, when "a number of southern communities, panicked by the exodus of black labor, reacted with blatant efforts to control the outflow of black population." In Macon, Georgia, license fees for labor agents were set at $25,000 at this time.

Table 2.2. *Net Migration, by Region and Race, 1870–1950*

Period	South		Northeast		North Central		West	
	White	Black	White	Black	White	Black	White	Black
Number (in 1,000s)								
1870–1880	91	−68	−374	26	26	42	257	0
1880–1890	−271	−88	−240	61	−43	28	554	0
1890–1900	−30	−185	101	136	−445	49	374	0
1900–1910	−69	−194	−196	109	−1,110	63	1,375	22
1910–1920	−663	−555	−74	242	−145	281	880	32
1920–1930	−704	−903	−177	435	−464	426	1,345	42
1930–1940	−558	−480	55	273	−747	152	1,250	55
1940–1950	−866	−1581	−659	599	−1,296	626	2,822	356
Rate (migrants/1,000 population)								
1870–1880	11	−14	−33	55	2	124	274	0
1880–1890	−26	−15	−18	107	−3	65	325	0
1890–1900	−2	−26	6	200	−23	104	141	0
1900–1910	−4	−24	−11	137	−48	122	329	542
1910–1920	−33	−66	−3	254	−5	421	143	491
1920–1930	−30	−103	−7	328	−15	415	160	421
1930–1940	−20	−52	2	157	−22	113	116	378
1940–1950	−28	−167	−20	259	−35	344	195	964

Note: Net migration is calculated as the difference between the actual increase in population over each decade and the predicted increase based on age- and sex-specific mortality rates and the demographic structure of the region's population at the beginning of the decade. If the actual increase exceeds the predicted increase, this implies a net migration into the region; if the actual increase is less than predicted, this implies net migration out of the region. The states included in the southern region are Oklahoma, Texas, Arkansas, Louisiana, Mississippi, Alabama, Tennessee, Kentucky, West Virginia, Virginia, North Carolina, South Carolina, Georgia, and Florida. *Source*: Eldridge and Thomas (1964, pp. 90, 99).

offset each other. One widely used index of net-migration flows is calculated using census survival methods. In this approach, the actual population in a state or region at each census date is compared to that which would be predicted by applying actual fertility and mortality experience over the preceding decade to the population at the previous census. The difference between actual and forecast population levels is a measure of net migration over the decade.

Although the net migration data are imperfect, they suggest the extent of the isolation of northern and southern labor markets from each other before World War I. The top panel of Table 2.2 shows the absolute level of net migration from different census regions for whites and blacks in each decade between 1870 and 1950; the lower panel reports these flows as rates per 1,000 population. Between 1870 and 1910 there was a net migration of only 535,000 blacks and 279,000 whites from the South to the North and West. In comparison, over this period, there was a net out migration of 709,000 whites from the Northeast and 1,572,000 whites from the North Central region.[16] Some of this difference reflects the larger population of these regions, but even normalizing migration relative to regional population, out-migration from the Northeast and North Central regions appears to have been larger than that from the South.

After 1910 the volume of migration from the South increased sharply. Between 1910 and 1920 alone there was a net movement of 555,000 blacks and 663,000 whites out of the South. This increase coincides with a decline in net migration from the Northeast and North Central regions, partly as a consequence of the influx of southerners that offset the departure of local residents. Both the level and rate of southern out-migration remained quite high thereafter, despite the effects of the Great Depression of the 1930s.

The lack of movement from South to North is not an indication that southerners were less mobile than residents of other regions. Indeed the lack of interregional migration contrasts sharply with the high rates of population redistribution that took place within the South before World War I. Blacks living outside their state of birth were more than two-and-one-half times as likely to be living in another southern state as in a northern or western one, and whites were nearly twice as likely (Wright 1986, p. 65). Table 2.3 summarizes data on rates of net migration from three subregions of the South. Rates of migration out of the states of the South Atlantic and East South Central regions were substantially higher than out-migration rates from the region as a whole. Although the census survival approach does not allow us to track the destinations of migrants from a particular region, the small rate of migration from the South as a whole implies that the majority of the migrants from the South Atlantic and East South Central regions must have been bound for the West South Central region.

---

[16] Both regions were net recipients of blacks migrating from the South.

Table 2.3. *Rates of Net Migration from Southern Subregions, 1870–1950 (migrants per 1,000 population)*

	Whites			Blacks		
Period	South Atlantic	East South Central	West South Central	South Atlantic	East South Central	West South Central
1870–1880	−6	−66	199	−26	−40	66
1880–1890	−34	−77	65	−35	−36	66
1890–1900	−28	−61	102	−53	−7	0
1900–1910	−21	−82	90	−37	−49	35
1910–1920	−10	−81	−15	−57	−109	−26
1920–1930	−24	−71	−3	−157	−82	−33
1930–1940	11	−37	−39	−69	−52	−25
1940–1950	25	−81	−44	−143	−209	−162

Note: The calculation of net migration is described in the note to Table 2.2. Regional definitions follow: South Atlantic – West Virginia, Virginia, North Carolina, South Carolina, Florida, and Georgia; East South Central – Kentucky, Tennessee, Mississippi, and Alabama; West South Central – Arkansas, Louisiana, Oklahoma, and Texas.
Source: Eldridge and Thomas (1964, p. 101).

Impressions based on patterns of net migration are reinforced by data on the state of birth and state of residence of the native-born population. Changes in the number of residents of each state born in other states provide a measure of net-migration streams between specific states and regions, at least for the native-born population. Prior to 1910, the main migrant streams originating in the South Atlantic and East South Central regions were directed toward the states of the West South Central. After 1880, there was a growing stream of migration from the South Atlantic to the Middle Atlantic states, but the size of this stream increased markedly after 1910 (Eldridge and Thomas 1964, pp. 118–19). The destinations of black migrants from South Carolina tabulated by Bernstein (1995, p. 20–1) provide a concrete illustration of these trends. Until 1920, most migrants were bound for the Southwest or for neighboring states like North Carolina and Georgia. In fact, in 1870 and 1880, there were no migrants to northern states. In 1890, New York joined the list of destinations, receiving 1,126 migrants (about 1.5 percent of the total). Bernstein reported that by 1900 3,733 black South Carolinians had moved to New York or Pennsylvania, but these two states together still accounted for less than 4 percent of blacks leaving South Carolina. Not until 1920 was there a significant northern exodus.

The small numbers of southerners migrating to the North before 1910 was not due to a lack of employment opportunities. Between 1870 and 1910 more than 20 million European immigrants entered the United States. Many of these immigrants came from agricultural backgrounds and had no more experience in industrial employment than rural southerners. Yet they came despite the obstacles of language, and the cost of trans-Atlantic travel. Despite this influx of labor, wages and earnings in the North not only remained above their level in the South but the interregional gap actually expanded as well (see Chapter 5).

Northern employers made some efforts to recruit southern workers in the pre-World War I period. Immediately after the Civil War, the Freedmen's Bureau office in Washington, D.C., received a number of requests for workers from northern employers. Cohen (1991, p. 83) estimated that between July 1865 and October 1867, when it ceased providing transportation for black job seekers, it probably sent about 9,000 workers to the North. In later decades, northern employers sometimes recruited black workers to serve as strikebreakers (Cohen 1991, pp. 97–8). As Whatley (1993) showed, however, employers were most likely to turn to black strikebreakers in periods when immigration rates were low. In any event, these efforts did not give rise to a sustained and cumulative movement of population of any significant magnitude.

Beginning with the work of Myrdal and Thomas, a number of studies have noted a negative correlation between decadal rates of European immigration and black movement to the North. Recently, Collins (1997) showed that there is also a strong negative correlation between the size of the foreign-born and black populations in cross-sectional data at the state and city level. Scholars focusing on black migration have attributed the apparent preference of employers for immigrants to racism (see Cohen 1991, p. 96; Collins 1997). But racism does not appear adequate to account for the pattern of internal population redistribution in the United States before World War I. In particular, the pattern of net migration of southern whites to the North closely paralleled that of blacks, rising substantially after 1910. Racism does not offer an explanation for northern employers' reluctance to hire native-born, English-speaking whites from the South.

Rather, I believe that the explanation is to be found in the patterns of labor recruitment developed by northern employers in the antebellum period. In the years before the Civil War, northern employers had already begun to adapt their recruitment and employment practices to take advantage of the available supply of immigrant labor. By delegating personnel decisions to their foremen and encouraging the use of referrals by their existing employees, they had created a system that was conducive to the continued recruitment of immigrants. At the same time, the combination of growing employer demand for labor and the rising volume of immigration had given rise to a relatively sophisticated set of intermediaries in major immigrant destinations in the North that made it easy for employers who lacked access to informal channels of recruitment to hire newly arriving immigrants. A corresponding development of information networks in Europe helped to encourage migration to the United States.

As long as immigrants continued to arrive in large numbers, employers had little incentive to look elsewhere for labor because it was cheaper to rely on the existing mechanisms of recruitment than to establish new ones that were capable of tapping supplies of labor in the South. In the immediate postbellum period, employers evidently experimented briefly with southern labor but concluded that immigrants were the more attractive option. Otherwise, only in extreme conditions, such as when rates of European immigration were low and their existing workforce was on strike, would employers consider recruiting in the South.

The key point to note, though, is that the cost advantage of relying primarily on immigrant labor was not an inherent characteristic of the labor market but rather the product of its particular historical development. Had the volume of immigration been lower and more labor been available in the South before the Civil War, a different set of labor market institutions might well have developed. Once established, however, the institutional patterns that had emerged in the antebellum period were self-reinforcing.

This is clearly true in the case of chain migration, but the increasing sophistication of intermediaries available to migrants who lacked access to well-placed friends and relatives helped to encourage further migration to the United States, which in turn encouraged continued employer reliance on this source of labor.

By emphasizing the historical and path-dependent evolution of labor market institutions in explaining patterns of migration in the late-nineteenth and early-twentieth centuries I do not mean to suggest, however, that racism played no role. Evidence that employers and their employees thought along racist and nationalistic lines is abundant. Employers expressed many opinions about the relative qualifications not just of blacks and whites, but of Hungarians, Poles, and Italians for different kinds of work.[17] But these modes of thinking were, themselves, at least partly a product of labor market institutions that operated along racial, ethnic, and nationality lines. Which came first is ultimately difficult to disentangle, but once established, racist attitudes and labor recruitment practices tended to reinforce one another.

Not until World War I interrupted the flow of European immigration at a time of sustained growth of northern labor demand did employers seriously begin to develop alternative sources of labor supply. During the war, for the first time, northern employment agents began to travel to the South, recruiting workers in much the same way they had previously recruited immigrants (Wright 1986, ch. 7, 1987a; Whatley 1990). Reflecting these efforts, migration from the South accelerated dramatically. As Whatley showed, the experience that northern employers gained with black workers at this time helped to open the doors of northern factories for southern workers in the 1920s. As soon as this initial foothold was established, it created the conditions for sustained and expanding migration in subsequent decades. Black industrial workers, like immigrants before them, became the basis for subsequent chain migration flows, as they encouraged and assisted friends and family to

[17] The reports of the Immigration Commission are full of statements attributing particular characteristics to different nationalities. Summarizing these opinions, Nelson (1975, p. 81) wrote that employers believed that "Poles and 'Hungarians' were suited to heavy physical strenuous work, while Italians, Portuguese, and Jews from all countries performed best at light repetitive jobs that demanded a sharp eye or nimble fingers."

move northward. The sustained rate of southern out-migration in the 1920s affirms the magnitude of this effect. Yet, the 1920s were, in contrast to the preceding half century, a period of relatively slow growth in overall manufacturing employment levels. Reflecting the diffusion of a wide range of new technologies, employers began to substitute skilled labor and capital for the abundant unskilled labor that had characterized the pre–World War I period.

3

EMPLOYMENT AGENCIES AND LABOR EXCHANGES

The Impact of Intermediaries in the Market for Labor

Networks of friends and relatives were the dominant channels of information and assistance in late-nineteenth and early-twentieth century labor markets. The information and assistance they provided directed the vast majority of long-distance migration and played an important role in the local allocation of labor as well. Nonetheless, the number and importance of employment agencies and labor exchanges did grow during the late-nineteenth century. The expansion of labor market intermediaries and other complementary businesses serving job seekers provided an important complement and extension to kin- and friendship-based networks that helped to encourage and expand European immigration in the decades after the Civil War. Their services were advertised in Europe by agents for steamship lines carrying passengers and were publicized through newspapers and other media. For potential immigrants who lacked well-placed friends and family to assist them in finding a job in the United States, the knowledge that there were employment agencies and other businesses to assist them upon arrival must have served to lower the expected costs of movement. At the same time, the rising volume of migration encouraged employers' continued reliance on immigrant labor. The mutually reinforcing nature of these decisions by immigrants and employers was central to the perpetuation of the geographic patterns of labor recruitment that had emerged in the decades before the Civil War.

Understanding the operation of the labor market intermediaries that emerged over the nineteenth century sheds considerable light on the broader issue of how labor market institutions worked at that time. In this chapter, I argue that these intermediaries developed as a commercial extension of the informal networks of friends and relatives that directed the majority of long-distance movement rather than as an alternative to them. Together with the other businesses that developed to cater to the needs of arriving immigrants, they provided the same package of services that more fortunate job seekers could obtain from friends or relatives. The importance of these additional forms of assistance is emphasized by the relatively poor performance of public labor exchanges, the operation of which was confined solely to the provision of labor market information. On the other hand, because the activities of labor market intermediaries paralleled those of informal networks, they remained confined to a marginal role in the allocation of labor: matching job seekers who lacked well-placed friends or relatives to assist them with employers whose labor needs could not be met through the referrals of current employees or applications at the gate. Because job seekers had little basis to assess the quality of information provided by formal intermediaries and directly bore most of the risks of inaccurate information, they preferred to rely on friends and relatives whenever possible.[1]

PRIVATE EMPLOYMENT AGENCIES BEFORE THE FIRST WORLD WAR

Before the Civil War, with the exception of slave traders, few intermediaries existed in the United States to organize the distribution of labor, so most transactions relied on direct contact between workers and employers. In the large eastern cities, "intelligence offices" organized local markets for domestic servants, laundresses, and clerks, but no comparable mechanisms facilitated

---

[1] The risks of unreliable information were especially large when they involved migration to a distant job because this greatly raised the cost of seeking compensation from the intermediary while lowering the likelihood that repeated interactions between job seekers and intermediaries would encourage the intermediaries to provide more accurate information. Ben-Porath (1980) and Stark (1984) provide theoretical rationalizations for the reliance on family relationships in situations of asymmetric information of the sort that characterize long-distance job search.

the distribution of labor in intercity and interregional markets.[2] Although the record is not entirely clear, it appears that after 1840 the rising numbers of European immigrants arriving in New York promoted the emergence of a range of businesses catering to their needs. By the late 1840s, the treatment of arriving immigrants by boardinghouse keepers and forwarding agents – who assisted in transportation arrangements beyond New York – was eliciting significant expressions of public concern, and published guides warned immigrants of various deceptive schemes practiced by these businesses (Ernst 1949, pp. 28–64; Kapp 1870, pp. 61–72; O'Hanlon 1976).

The first newspaper advertisements for employment agencies appeared in the early 1850s (Erickson 1957, p. 100), but the scale of their operations remained limited. In 1853, when the Illinois Central Railroad sought to hire between 7,000 and 12,000 men for the construction of over 700 miles of track, it made arrangements with labor agents in New York to forward workers to Illinois for a fee of $1 per man. But to obtain an adequate number of recruits, it also dispatched its own agents to New York and New Orleans to engage workers, and placed advertisements in New York newspapers (Gates 1957, pp. 70, 94–7).

The tide of immigration slowed appreciably during the Civil War, but by the mid-1860s Europeans were once again arriving in large numbers. With their arrival came further growth in the number of employment agencies. In New York, the number of businesses providing lodging, banking, and employment services grew rapidly (Erickson 1957, p. 100). In Chicago, whose rapid growth made it an important immigrant destination, there was a pronounced surge in the number and visibility of employment agencies and other businesses serving new arrivals. In the 1860s and 1870s, many of the immigrants arriving in Chicago were Scandinavian, and Erickson (1957, pp. 89–93) located advertisements for at least 11 different agencies engaged in the distribution of Scandinavian workers. Like the agencies in New York, they often combined their role as employment agencies with the provision

---

[2] Erickson (1984, p. 52) reported finding newspaper advertisements for intelligence offices in New York, Boston, and Philadelphia in the pre–Civil War period.

of lodging and financial services. As the sources of immigration to Chicago shifted in the 1880s toward southern and eastern Europe, these agencies disappeared, and others operated by Italians and Hungarians emerged in their stead.

As private employment agencies grew in size and number during the late-nineteenth century, they largely took over the business of recruiting unskilled gang labor for railroad construction and other seasonal or temporary projects. Although their growth cannot be traced with much accuracy, the increased attention that they attracted from public officials, social scientists, and reformers during the 1880s and 1890s provides one index of their expanded role in the labor market. One manifestation of this growing attention was the passage of legislation by a number of states requiring the licensing of employment agencies and the imposition of various regulations on their operations. Another was the proliferation of published studies of their activities and effects on the labor market.

By the turn of the century, employment agencies were found in every city in the country, but the majority were concentrated in a few urban centers (Bogart 1900, p. 343). By 1908, there were over 750 licensed employment agencies in New York and 289 in Chicago. In Boston, the number of agencies was estimated at 119 in the early 1890s and slightly over 100 during the first decade of the twentieth century. Officials in Baltimore estimated that in 1907 their city had about 150 agencies. Outside of these cities, the numbers fell off fairly quickly. Minneapolis and St. Paul had a combined total of 40 agencies; Indianapolis had just 14, and the rest of the state of Indiana had only 5; Colorado had 21 agencies, most by in Denver; and California had 69 (Bogart 1900, pp. 343–4; Abbot 1908, pp. 290–2; New York 1909, p. 112; Sargent 1911, pp. 43, 75, 128).

Even though many of these agencies simply relied on the pool of workers who applied to them seeking work, others actively undertook to expand the supply of labor by establishing networks of connections in other cities, or in Europe. In 1903, Antonio Cordasco, an Italian labor agent supplying laborers for the Canadian Pacific Railroad, corresponded with Italian labor agents in more than 12 cities in the United States, including Buffalo, Portland, Columbus, Baltimore, Philadelphia, Detroit, Chicago, and St. Louis (Harney 1979, pp. 68–9). During the following year, he expanded his recruiting efforts into Italy. Anticipating further expansion of his business he negotiated arrangements with one or more steamship lines, making him their "official representative." Under these agreements, their agents would provide Italian passengers to New York with cards advertising his services and providing directions for how to reach his offices in Montreal. In a letter addressed to several of his agents in Italy, Cordasco pledged that:

If you have any passengers you can send them without any fear. I am able to give them immediate work, the salary will be $1.50 a day. Besides that they will get a return ticket from me to the locality, they can board themselves or get board as they like. The work will last long and the payment is sure. Each man gets a contract in Italian containing the clear conditions under which they will have work and which specifies the length of time and salary. In one word there will be no tricks or schemes (quoted in Peck 1994, p. 49).

As a result of these efforts, Cordasco registered over 3,900 Italian immigrant job seekers in the spring of 1904, up from 1,200 during the previous year.

Leonidas Skliris, a Greek labor agent who came to Salt Lake City, Utah, in 1902, was soon supplying laborers to the coal and copper mines in the area, as well as the Denver and Rio Grande Railroad. To find workers, he traveled to Chicago and San Francisco, visiting Greek coffee houses and other establishments. As his business expanded, however, he also began to write to friends and relatives still in Greece to solicit additional business. By 1912, he had opened branch offices in New York, Chicago, and San Francisco and had broadened his recruiting efforts in Greece, using newspaper advertisements and hired agents as well as family and friends to direct potential migrants to him (Peck 1994, pp. 62–86).

After the Civil War, employment agencies and labor exchanges also began to emerge in the South. In many respects, their operation paralleled that of the northern employment agencies, but they operated mainly as intermediaries between employers in the rapidly growing states of the South Central region and job seekers in the more densely settled and relatively slow-growing South Atlantic states, where wages remained low. Until the interruption of European immigration caused by World War I, however, southern employment agencies did hardly any business with northern employers. Scattered evidence shows that southern employers turned to northern labor agencies as an alternative source of labor; however, most of these efforts ended unsuccessfully, and it appears that few of them were repeated.

Throughout the antebellum period, the highly productive agricultural conditions of the South Central region had promoted the redistribution of population into Mississippi, Louisiana, Arkansas, and Texas from the more densely settled and less productive areas of the South Atlantic. Even though some of this movement had occurred through the migration of individual planters with their slaves, the mobilization of labor in the antebellum South was clearly facilitated by the ability of planters to buy and sell slaves in a well-developed market (Tadman 1989).

In the postbellum period, the continuing expansion of cotton and sugar production in the South Central region, along with development of rail lines, construction and repair of levees, and other improvements created a substantial demand for labor at the same time that slow growth in the South Atlantic reduced labor demand and depressed wages (Cohen 1991, p. 44). Even if the newly emancipated blacks had information about the opportunities available to them in the South Central states, however, few possessed the resources to act on this information. In the absence of any alternative sources of supply, employers in the South Central region dispatched their own agents to the South Atlantic in search of additional hands (Cohen 1991, pp. 109–10).

Recruiting labor directly was a difficult, time-consuming, and costly process, but there was no other viable alternative. Edward J. Gay, a substantial Louisiana planter, was among those who sought to tap the more abundant labor of the Southeast in the years immediately after the War. In 1867, he sent N. G. Pierson to North Carolina and southern Virginia in search of hands. Pierson traveled first to Columbia, South Carolina, and then to Charlotte, North Carolina. From the latter location, he reported finding "The [w]hole country is Fluded With Men from all parts of the South [,] hunting Freedmen and offering Fabulies prises to get them" (quoted in Cohen 1991, p. 11). In Charlotte, Pierson was joined by his employer's son, Andrew Gay, and the two continued on together to Virginia. Pierson eventually obtained a total of 27 laborers for his employer. For his efforts, Gay paid him $125, and reimbursed expenses of $846 for hotels, food, railroad travel, and incidentals. In other words, Gay paid $36 per worker, the equivalent of about two months' wages, and if the Freedman's Bureau had not provided free transportation for the workers, Gay's costs would have been closer to $60 per worker (Cohen 1991, p. 114).

Despite the difficulty and costs that recruiting laborers entailed, Gay and others returned to the South Atlantic in the following years seeking more hands (Cohen 1991, p. 115). In December 1869, Edward Gay's brother William sent the overseer of his plantation in West Baton Rouge Parish to Liberty, Virginia, in search of 25 to 35 hands. The choice of destination was not random. The Gay family had come from Liberty and still had relatives in the area, and Gay's overseer was also familiar with the area, having been raised in Virginia. In early 1870, the overseer was joined by two other plantation managers in Gay's employ, Thomas Garret and Roman Daigre, and Gay's brother-in-law. Competition was stiff, however, and the inducements of other recruiters made it difficult to "hold one lot until another could be secured" (quoted in Cohen 1991, pp. 115–16). After several months of travels Gay's four recruiters returned with about 70 laborers at a cost of close to $1,800, or about $26 per recruit.

In view of the cost and effort involved in rounding up workers, it is not surprising that specialized intermediaries began to emerge in the South Atlantic to take over the task of finding job seekers. At the end of their 1870 recruiting trip, Garrett and Daigre turned to a newly established Richmond employment agency, Justis and McDonald, for help securing the workers they needed, and the next year, they turned first to this agency. McDonald had been hired just after the war by a group of Louisiana planters, each of whom contributed $30 toward his expenses, to recruit workers in Virginia. Building on the initial success of his efforts, McDonald made repeated visits to Virginia before joining forces with John P. Justis in early 1870.

Southern planters experimented with other sources of labor beyond the South Atlantic as well, but they apparently found the alternatives even more costly or problematic. In the fall of 1870, for example, Edward Gay arranged with sources in San Francisco to supply 52 Chinese laborers. Gay paid over $4,600 in gold to obtain these men but found it difficult to retain them once they arrived. At least 10 of them attempted to run away within the first few months. At about the same time, he also contracted with a Chicago employment agency to supply 19 German laborers. But 14 of them ran away before they had traveled as far as Memphis, presumably attracted by a better offer. Gay reported that 3 men on their steamship had offered to employ all laborers on board to work on the levees at $35 a month, or nearly twice the $20 per month that Gay had contracted to pay them (Cohen 1991, pp. 115–16). A mining company in Virginia encountered similar problems in its efforts to recruit immigrants from New York, as this account by a company official makes clear:

Tony arrived with 21 men last night. One got away in Jersey, two in Washington, D.C., 4 in Charlottesville. Some of the men are very good looking, but taken as a whole they are the worst lot I have ever seen.... Our New York transportations to this place have never been a success (quoted in Wright 1986, p. 77).

The fundamental problem was that the wages southern employers could pay were not high enough to compete with opportunities available to immigrant workers in the North.

There is little systematic or quantitative evidence about the activities of labor agents in the South Atlantic in subsequent years. A few scattered pieces of evidence suggest, however, that their operations continued to expand and played an important part in mobilizing labor within the South. One indication of their impact is the adoption of "emigrant agent laws" throughout the South Atlantic region. These laws, which were promoted mainly by local planters seeking to prevent the out-migration of their labor force, established prohibitive licensing fees for agents who transported laborers across state lines. In 1876, Georgia became the first state to introduce such legislation. It was followed by Alabama (1879), North Carolina (1891), Florida (1903), and Mississippi (1912).

Clearly these laws played some role in impeding labor mobility in the South, but the need to pass them suggests that the activities of labor agents were indeed having a noticeable effect on the distribution of labor (see Cohen 1991, ch. 9). It is also clear that few of the laws were entirely effective. In several states, fines were repeatedly raised, suggesting that the costs initially imposed were not a sufficient deterrent. In other cases, agents ignored the laws or attempted to challenge them in court.

One agent who attracted considerable notoriety in the 1880s and 1890s was Robert A. "Peg Leg" Williams. A Confederate veteran who had lost a leg during the War, Williams claimed to have been responsible for the movement of over 80,000 laborers to the Southwest between 1883 and 1890. In the early 1890s, he began to recruit blacks as part of a scheme to establish settlements in Mexico. This plan eventually collapsed, but Williams resurfaced in Georgia in the fall of 1899, where a severe drought had reduced the cotton crop and left many black laborers and tenants without work. By mid-January of 1900, it was reported that over 2,500 blacks had already departed the area. As emigration mounted, however, planters became increasingly concerned and pushed officials to arrest Williams for operating in violation of the state's emigrant agent law. They also pressured local railroads to stop providing passage to the emigrants he had recruited. Williams eventually bowed to these pressures and ceased his operations (Cohen 1991, ch. 9; Holmes 1980).

In contrast to the role that they played in encouraging and facilitating labor mobility within the South, southern labor agents apparently played a small role in intermediating between northern employers and southern job seekers in the pre–World War I period. The idea was certainly considered. In 1890, "Peg Leg" Williams, for example, advertised a scheme to export black labor to the North, but nothing much came of it, and he soon returned to his work within the South. There is also evidence that northern employers sometimes used southern employment agencies to supply blacks as strikebreakers, but this practice did not give rise to a large or continuing movement of labor. Indeed, Whatley (1993) found that the use of black strikebreakers varied inversely with the volume of immigration, suggesting that blacks were used mainly as a substitute for immigrants, when the latter were in short supply.

GAUGING THE IMPACT OF PRIVATE EMPLOYMENT AGENCIES

Private employment agencies were an important factor in the mobilization of labor in the postbellum period. But their overall impact on the labor market was limited by their concentration in a narrow market niche. Instead of offering an alternative to the advice and assistance provided by friends and relatives, private employment agencies developed as a commercialized extension of them. They were successful only in circumstances where employers and job seekers lacked access to informal channels of recruitment, and their success in these instances was dependent upon their ability to provide the full range of assistance that job seekers relied upon from friends and relatives. Ties of nationality or race were important in establishing a relationship between agencies and job seekers. In the North, where most of their clientele was foreign born, employment agencies were often operated by immigrants who dealt primarily with their fellow countrymen. Some of the larger agencies did a wider business but continued to rely on immigrant labor bosses to round up their fellow countrymen. In the South, white-run employment agencies often employed black runners to work directly with job seekers. In addition to providing labor market information, employment agencies also needed to provide assistance in financing migration and obtaining housing. In many cases, they also had to act as an intermediary between workers and their employers on the job. Because of the close parallels that developed between formal and informal channels of labor recruitment, it is hardly surprising that these formal channels tended to reinforce existing patterns of recruitment rather than promote a more general broadening of labor market boundaries.

Markets Served by Private Employment Agencies
The scope of private employment agencies' activities is clearly delineated by a number of studies undertaken during the late-nineteenth and early-twentieth centuries. Two distinct categories

of employment agencies are apparent: the first offered unskilled and semiskilled jobs primarily for immigrants, while the second helped to organize markets for skilled professionals such as teachers, nurses, and clerical and mercantile help. The agencies for the unskilled may be further subdivided into two types. The first of these specialized in supplying unskilled gang labor for temporary and seasonal work on railroad construction projects, timber and ice cutting, crop harvesting, mining, and similar activities. The second offered jobs in domestic service in homes, hotels, and restaurants. Both markets were characterized by the relative isolation of employers and job seekers from informal channels of labor market communication. Railroad construction companies and other seasonal employers who required large crews of laborers in remote locations could not possibly hope to attract adequate numbers of workers through informal channels. Although hotels, restaurants, and families employing domestics were located in urban areas, their scattered locations and the small size of their workforce made it difficult for most of them to rely on their present employees to recruit new workers. One can only speculate about the job seekers who turned to these agencies, but given the unattractive nature of the jobs that were offered and the fees involved, it seems likely that few job seekers who had alternative means of locating employment would have used their services.

Table 3.1 reproduces the results of studies of private employment agencies in Baltimore, New York, and Chicago undertaken in 1907, 1910, and 1912, respectively. For New York and Chicago, the data are for all licensed agencies, but for Baltimore the 43 agencies listed were estimated by officials to represent about one-third of the total number in the city. In all three cities, the greatest number of agencies was engaged in the distribution of domestic help and hotel and restaurant workers. Many agencies placing common or general laborers were also found in all three cities. Finally, agencies organizing markets for workers with specialized skills, such as actors, clerical and technical workers, and other professions were concentrated in New York and Chicago.

The number of agencies of each type is not, of course, a good guide to the volume of placements or labor market impacts that they had. It seems likely, however, that the largest volume of

Table 3.1. *Number of Private Employment Agencies in New York, Chicago, and Baltimore, by Occupational Specialization, 1907–1912*

Occupations served	New York (1910)	Chicago (1912)	Baltimore (1907)
Total	838	250	43
Domestic servants and hotel & restaurant workers	431	87	34
Theatrical performers	191	41	0
Common laborers	58	59	0
General laborers, farm & garden laborers, and seamen[a]	62	17	9
Technical and clerical workers	49	18	0
Nurses	24	13	0
Barbers	23	3	0
Teachers, printers, architects, and choir singers	0	12	0

[a] Includes European passage workers.
Source: New York and Chicago from Harrison (1924, p. 49); Baltimore from Sargent (1911, p. 128).

business was done by agencies dealing with unskilled labor. One study conducted in the 1920s that attempted to estimate the number of placements by different types of agencies found that 230,000 of the 470,000 placements made by private employment agencies were accounted for by general and railroad labor agencies. Agencies supplying clerical and technical work placed another 180,000 workers. Only about 25,000 jobs as domestic or hotel workers were provided at this time by private employment agencies. The remaining 37,000 job placements were accounted for by agencies supplying a range of skilled professional jobs. See Cowgill (1928, p. 14).

The makeup of private employment agencies in other cities appears to be similar to that of the cities represented in Table 3.1. For example, the Massachusetts Bureau of Statistics of Labor investigated the operations of all licensed agencies operating in Boston in 1894. Of the 98 agencies that responded to its survey, it reported that "two deal exclusively with male help, 40 with females only, and 56 with both sexes. Males find places principally as bell boys, coachmen, general farm and hotel work[ers], gardeners, domestic service [workers], laborers, stablemen and teamsters; while females are placed principally in domestic and personal service in families, hotels and restaurants" (Massachusetts Bureau of Statistics of Labor 1894, p. 11). In Indianapolis, where only six private agencies were in operation after the passage in 1910 of strict regulations governing their activities, three were involved in the placement of general laborers, and one each was engaged in the placement of nurses, domestic help, and hotel workers (Sargent 1911, pp. 43–4, 75–6).

An extensive study of Chicago employment agencies specializing in placing foreign job seekers conducted by Grace Abbot in 1908 provides additional details about the operations of private employment agencies at that time. Of 289 licensed agencies in the city, 178 (61 percent) were located in largely immigrant neighborhoods, and of these 110 specialized in placing immigrants. In this latter group, 56 furnished work exclusively for men, 33 for women, and 21 for both. The agencies for women furnished mainly domestic and hotel work; women seeking jobs in the stockyards, the clothing trades, or other industrial work were obliged to use other means. They were also typically small and informal operations. "In most cases," Abbott reported, "the agent who places women is herself a woman; her office is also her kitchen or her parlor; the place is usually dirty and almost without exception unbusinesslike" (Abbott 1908, pp. 290–1). Agencies placing immigrant men were typically located in or near saloons and cheap lodging houses and offered mainly gang labor jobs in "foundries, at the stockyards, in mines, on railroad, car-line and building construction, in the harvest fields, in ice and lumber camps, and other similar kinds of work" (Abbott 1908, p. 292).

In New York City, data collected in the early-twentieth century allow us to examine more closely the operation of private employment agencies placing workers outside the city. In May 1904, the state legislature approved a new law requiring employment agencies sending persons outside the city in which they operated to report the details of each such transaction. From the enactment of the law through July 1906, 61 of the approximately 750 licensed employment agencies in New York City reported placing a total of 40,737 persons outside the city. Because of incomplete reporting and evasion of the law, it is likely that these figures understate to some extent the volume of business done by private employment agencies. Enforcement was substantially improved in early 1906, however, and one contemporary analyst extrapolating from statistics after this date estimated that the actual number placed was probably in the range of 50,000 to 60,000 persons per year (Sheridan 1907, pp. 415–23).[3] In comparison, the 1900 census reported that there were about 99,000 laborers in New York City and a combined total of about 750,000 nonfarm laborers in the various states to which the New York agencies sent more than one thousand workers. If the typical job that these agencies filled lasted one year, then these figures would suggest that the New York agencies played an important role in allocating unskilled labor. On the other hand, if the typical job was of shorter duration – say a month or two – as seems more likely, then these agencies' role in the market for unskilled labor would have been much smaller.

The vast majority of the workers placed by the New York agencies were foreign born, many of them from among the most recent immigrant nationalities. Italians made up over 40 percent of the total, Slavs and Hungarians contributed another 13 percent, and the remainder were divided between 11 other unspecified nationalities. Unskilled gang labor was the dominant job in which the workers were placed. Table 3.2 provides a detailed listing of jobs filled by the New York agencies. Over half of all the jobs reported were for railroad construction, and another quarter were for laborers of other types. The principal alternative was mine work.[4] Few of the jobs were in urban areas; only 8 percent were in cities with populations in excess of 50,000. Many of these jobs were at a substantial distance from New York. As Table 3.3 shows, nearly half were in southern states and more than 5,000 were in Florida alone. The

---

[3] From June 1, 1909, to May 31, 1910, when the reporting was presumably more complete, the total number of placements outside the city was only 38,868 (Sargent 1911, p. 104).

[4] The expansion of coal mining before World War I resulted in extremely rapid growth in labor demand. Much of this demand was met by word-of-mouth channels, but during times of peak production or when a mine was first opened, employers were often obliged to turn to employment agencies for assistance recruiting workers (Fishback 1992, pp. 32–5).

Table 3.2. *Workers Placed Outside of New York City by New York Employment Agencies, 1904–1906*

Occupation	Number placed	Percentage of total
Laborers		
Railroad construction & repair	23,202	57.0
General, not specified	2,303	5.7
Street grading	1,680	4.1
Ditching	959	2.4
Ice cutting & storing	789	1.9
Dam & waterworks construction	390	1.0
Grading	390	1.0
Excavating	377	0.9
Concrete & cement	359	0.9
Sewer construction	216	0.5
Public road	149	0.4
Other work		
Coal mine worker	3,460	8.5
Copper & iron mine worker	848	2.1
Lumber & saw mill hand	835	2.0
Quarrymen	631	1.5
Coke oven workers	443	1.1
Miscellaneous[a]	3,706	9.1
Total	40,737	100.0

[a] Includes cotton pickers, cotton mill hands, turpentine workers, phosphate mine workers, and other occupations.
Source: Sheridan (1907, p. 421).

relatively large number of workers sent to southern states appears to be something of an anomaly reflecting the extensive railroad construction activity in the South Atlantic at this time. Southern contractors reported that they generally preferred to hire blacks but that an unusually high level of construction activity beginning in 1902 had obliged them to turn to New York employment agencies to supply additional workers (U.S. Congress, Senate 1911, part 22, p. 453). Outside the South, most of the jobs filled were located in New York or the nearby states of Pennsylvania, New Jersey, and Connecticut. The small fraction of jobs filled in the Midwest probably reflects the fact that employers in this region turned first to agencies in Chicago, St. Louis, or other cities within the region.

The reports of inspectors for the Missouri Bureau of Labor Statistics (1891, pp. 31–56) offer an especially informative picture

Table 3.3. *Destinations of Workers Sent Outside New York City by New York Employment Agencies, 1904–1906*

Northeastern states		Midwestern states		Southern states	
State	Number	State	Number	State	Number
New York	10,596	Ohio	212	Florida	5,385
Pennsylvania	3,892	Wisconsin	19	Virginia	3,818
New Jersey	2,017	Indiana	12	North Carolina	3,479
Connecticut	1,242	Nebraska	6	West Virginia	2,722
Vermont	641			Alabama	2,401
Maryland	581			Tennessee	1,008
Massachusetts	532			Georgia	903
Maine	213			South Carolina	415
New Hampshire	60			Mississippi	207
Rhode Island	29			Kentucky	173
				District of Columbia	95
				Louisiana	79
Total	19,803	Total	249	Total	20,685

Source: Sheridan (1907, p. 417).

of the operations of private employment agencies around the turn of the century. In St. Louis, there were five agencies for men, providing employment mainly as laborers on railroad construction and other similar projects; nine agencies for women, all of which provided employment as domestics; and one agency that served both men and women, placing the men in laborers, jobs and the women in factory employment. In addition, four agencies provided clerical employment for typists and stenographers. Of these, three were operated by establishments whose main business was selling typewriters, and the fourth was operated by the National Stenographers' Association, which did extensive business throughout the eastern United States. Nine more agencies were found in Kansas City: six providing employment for men in railroad construction work and three providing jobs for both men and women as laborers and domestic or hotel workers.

Table 3.4 summarizes a variety of information from the inspectors' reports for the agencies in St. Louis. At all the agencies for men, applicants for work greatly outnumbered those placed, although it is possible that some men applied to more than one of the agencies, resulting in double counting. Consistent with the

Table 3.4. *Statistics of Private Employment Agencies in St. Louis, 1891*

Agency	Applications (number/week)		Number placed (per week)	Fee charged		Years in business
	Workers	Employers		Workers	Employers	
For men						
George Lewis	500		50	$1–$2	0	11
H. P. Thiele	600		100	$1–$1.50	0	6
William Mara	500		100	$1–$2	0	16
Jerry Dignan	300–400		100	$1–$2	0	NA
Price Murray[a]	<25					NA
Conley's[a]						NA
For women[b]						
George Lewis	10–25			$0.50	$1	NA[c]
Gibbon's	100	67		$0.25	$1	<1[d]
Mrs. Krenshaw	10–12	20		$0.00	$1	NA
Mrs. Hardy	20	50		$0.50–$2	$2–$5	A few
Mrs. E. Krause	25	300		$1	$2	One of oldest
Mrs. Wendermuth		30–40		$0	$2	16
Mrs. Jacob Crist	20	300		$0	$2	16
Mrs. Gross[e]				$1	$2–$5	For some time

[a] Described as doing "a very limited business."

[b] Two other agencies for women were listed in the report, but they refused to provide the inspectors with any information.

[c] This is the same George Lewis listed in the upper half of the table. His business for women was, however, newly opened.

[d] In business for 1.5 months.

[e] Mrs. Gross reportedly was unable to supply figures on the number of applications she received but said that her business was so small that she could "no longer make her living in this business."

Source: Missouri Bureau of Labor Statistics (1891).

apparent excess of supply over demand, the costs of job search were borne entirely by the applicants, who were required to pay a fee of $1 to $2 when they were provided with work. The volume of business done by most of the agencies was fairly modest. The agencies for men reported placing from 50 to 100 men per week, but given the seasonal nature of railroad construction work it seems likely that these estimates reflect the volume of business during the most active season. Bogart (1900, pp. 344–5) estimated that private employment agencies for common laborers in Chicago and Boston placed in the neighborhood of 1,000 to 2,000 men a year, or about 20 to 40 persons a week on average. Based on his investigation of Chicago agencies in 1927–8, Cowgill (1928, p. 14) estimated that placements of general and railroad labor averaged around 800 to 1,000 workers per agency per year. In some cases, however, employment agencies might place several thousand workers per year. Antonio Cordasco, for example, supplied nearly 3,000 Italian laborers to the Canadian Pacific Railroad during 1903. It is also interesting to note that many of the agencies had been in business for a number of years at the time of the survey, suggesting that they were relatively long-lived operations.[5]

Turning to the agencies for women, it seems that the supply of domestics was generally less than the demand, since the number of applicants for work was smaller than the number of employers registering with the agencies, and employers were charged a substantial fee, while job seekers were charged little or nothing in most cases. With the exception of George Lewis, who employed a female superintendent for the branch of his business catering to women, all of the agencies for women were operated by women, and most were much smaller operations than those for men. According to the Bureau of Labor Statistics inspectors, the supply of domestics in St. Louis was quite small, because of the availability of factory jobs for young women and children, and most of the agencies reported recruiting applicants through advertisements in country newspapers. Additional applicants for work were directed to these

---

[5] This is consistent with Cowgill's (1928, p. 27) findings from the 1920s. Of 10 randomly selected agencies serving the market for general laborers in Chicago in 1928, he reported that the newest had been in operation 8 years, the oldest for 31 years, and that 6 had been in operation more than 20 years.

agencies by earlier clients, and one agency reported corresponding with postmasters in little country towns (Missouri Bureau of Labor Statistics 1891, pp. 47–8).

The Provision of Additional Services
Newly arrived immigrant job seekers, many of whom did not speak English, required more than information about the location of jobs. They needed board and lodging on arrival, they required someone to act as intermediary and translator on the job, and they might need financial assistance to defray their expenses and transportation costs until they started working. For many new arrivals, this assistance was provided by friends and relatives already in the country. But for those who were not fortunate enough to have such contacts, most of these services were available either from private employment agencies or from others who collaborated closely with them.

Many of the agencies that emerged in northern cities after the Civil War were operated by immigrants who did business mainly with their fellow compatriots. In the south, white-owned agencies often employed black runners and subagents to work directly with black job seekers. Erickson (1957, pp. 89–93) found that, with the rise of Scandinavian immigration to Chicago in the 1860s, there emerged a group of agencies operated by Scandinavians and serving primarily other Scandinavians. As Scandinavian immigration tapered off, however, these agencies disappeared and were replaced by other agencies operated by members of newly arriving nationality groups. In Montreal, two Italian labor agents – Antonio Cordasco and Frank Dini – competed for the business of Italian immigrants. In 1902, Cordasco was successful in winning appointment by the Canadian Pacific Railroad to act as its "sole *Italian* labor agent" (quoted in Peck 1994, pp. 45–6, emphasis added). The Greek labor agent Leonidas Skliris supplied Greek laborers for mining and railroad jobs in Utah. Similarly, in the Southwest, many of the agents placing Mexican workers were Mexican immigrants themselves. Investigators in Massachusetts did not comment on the nationality of the operators of different employment agencies in Boston in 1894; however, they did note a substantial degree of sorting in the clientele of the different agencies. Most of the 98 licensed agencies in the city at this time dealt primarily with immigrants, and of these "in 52 establishments... Irish applicants predominate; in four, persons born in Nova Scotia are in excess; in six others, Scandinavians lead; in six others colored applicants are in excess. Three establishments only, report that persons of American birth predominate among the applicants" (Massachusetts Bureau of Statistics of Labor 1894, p. 112).

Some agencies did expand beyond the limits of one nationality group. But when they did so, it was often by employing the services of immigrant labor bosses who acted as their representatives. For example, Achilles Oishei, a labor agent in Buffalo, New York, testified that he supplied men of various nationalities for railroad work. Asked how he obtained them, he answered, "Well, the foreman would come to me and tell me there were so many in such a place, and says 'I can fetch you so many men.'" (New York Bureau of Labor Statistics 1886, p. 496). Similarly, in the South, William Cohen (1991, p. 124) argues that black subagents were "indispensable middlemen" for the primarily white employment agents.

By building on ties of nationality or race, employment agents helped to extend informal networks of labor market information into parts of the labor market where such networks would not otherwise have been effective. But the role that friends and family played in mobilizing labor extended beyond the provision of information. The importance of the additional assistance they provided is underscored by the close connections that emerged between employment agencies and businesses providing other services for job seekers who could not rely on friends and family for assistance.

In New York City, employment agencies sprang up after the Civil War along Greenwich and Mulberry Streets near the Castle Garden depot, where immigrants could also find boardinghouses and banks to assist them (Erickson 1957, p. 100). In Chicago, Abbott's (1908, p. 295) study found that most agencies specializing in immigrant labor were located in or near saloons, boardinghouses, immigrant banks, or steamship offices. Indeed, despite a state law prohibiting agencies from conducting business in saloons, 45 percent of the agencies were found above, below, or next door to one. One study of Italian immigration in the 1890s remarked explicitly on the breadth of different services available to immigrant job seekers. Should the immigrant be "penniless," John Koren (1897, pp. 116–17) wrote:

the banker ... stands ready to provide him with food and shelter without immediate compensation until work is found. The next stop is for the new arrival to look for employment.... Employers of his own nationality are scarce and unfamiliarity with the language prevents him from applying to others for work, so he turns to one of that numerous fraternity who make it their vocation to supply contractors with cheap labor – the boss.

Another observer at the time described an immigrant bank in Boston that had an advertisement offering jobs for 200 railway workers. In addition, the business offered a notarial service, a travel agency, and an employment agency, and sold Italian patent medicines as well as imported foods and newspapers (Harney 1974, p. 109).

Even for immigrants who had been in the country for some time, or native-born workers, employment agencies were often more than just places to find employment. According to reform advocate Frances Kellor (1915, p. 158), in hard times, those men who had nowhere else to go flocked to the employment agencies by the hundreds, where they would " 'hang around' the waiting-rooms all day, and if they are permitted sleep on the floor at night."

Labor bosses played an important role in the employment of gangs of immigrant workers unable to speak English. Most bosses worked closely with employment agents, helping to round up gangs of workers, traveling with them to the location of their work, and often supervising them on the job. In a letter offering the services of the Industrial Labor Agency in securing labor to the Robesonia Iron Company, the proprietor, T. Armato, wrote: "we will take care to deliver these men on your words and our agent will start them on the job if so desired" (quoted in Bodnar 1974, p. 198). In this case, the superintendent accepted Armato's offer to supply help, responding that the company could use 10 more Italians to work at its quarrying operation, but declined the additional services he offered, explaining that: "I think the best way to do is for us to send an Italian who has worked for us for a number of years to N.Y. to bring the men out. He can tell them all about the place and the work as he speaks English and Italian. He will also be able to bring them out to the job so that there will be no danger of the men getting lost. Lastly he will be provided with transportation" (quoted in Bodnar 1974, p. 199).

In some cases, bosses might contract directly with employers to provide a number of men to perform a certain task, thus becoming employment agents as well. But the distinctive feature of the boss was that he provided the services that immigrant workers unfamiliar with the language and customs of their new country required to be profitably employed. In exchange for these services, the employer typically granted the boss the right of providing lodging, food, and other necessities to the workers (U.S. Congress, Senate 1911, part 22, pp. 334–43; Koren 1897, pp. 117–18; Nelli 1970, p. 56; Abbot 1908, p. 292).

The importance of the labor bosses in easing communication between employers and foreign-born workers is illustrated by the situation found at an upstate New York canning company employing about 600 workers, mostly Italian, during the summer harvest season. The men were provided by six bosses, who were described as men of influence within their respective communities, operating either a small store or a saloon. Early in the spring, the company would communicate its needs to the bosses, who would "go from house to house . . . telling their countrymen of the opportunity to secure work in the country." Once a sufficient number had been secured, they would be directed to the train station where the boss would arrange their transportation and accompany them to the farm. In addition to operating a small store for the workers, the boss received a salary of $12.50 a week for serving as row boss. Although the farm manager believed that they were "really useless as bosses, and must be told what to do," he explained that it was necessary to hire the bosses to "settle all disputes among his people, see that they are orderly and well behaved, act as boss in the field and as interpreter at any time he may be needed" (U.S. Congress, Senate 1911, part 24, pp. 513–14).

The Value of Services Provided by Private Employment Agencies
The same characteristics that made private employment agencies
effective extensions of the informal networks of friends and family
that directed the majority of job seekers – their roots in the immigrant community and the multidimensional nature of the services
they provided – were a source of considerable concern to public
officials and social reformers. Noting that many of the employment agencies were run by immigrants and possessed little or no
capital, these critics were highly suspicious of the quality of the information they dispensed. The report of a committee of the New
York state legislature observed, for example, that "there is also
a noticeable lack of intelligence on the part of not a few agents
as to the industrial conditions surrounding the conduct of their
business. Many cannot speak English" (New York 1909, pp. 114,
116). In another instance, several agencies in Ohio were found to
have taken their listings directly from help wanted advertisements
in the newspapers (Ohio, Bureau of the Statistics of Labor 1889,
p. 263). Others accused private agencies of purposefully misleading clients in the pursuit of profit. Many agencies collected fees
from job seekers in advance, and some may have then done little
to find them employment, or else have sent them off to distant locations where jobs did not exist or where there were fewer openings
than advertised (Sargent 1911, pp. 36–7; Abbott 1908, pp. 295,
299; Missouri Bureau of Labor Statistics 1891, pp. 41–4).

A recurrent concern expressed in this period was that labor
agents were exploiting contract labor schemes to enslave and exploit immigrant workers. Observers critical of the operation of
private labor agents often referred to them as "padrones," suggesting at least implicitly a lack of freedom on the part of their
clients. Immigrant job seekers were undoubtedly dependent on
the assistance of these agents in many ways, and agents used this
fact to profit from their roles as intermediaries between employers
and the workers they required. Yet both job seekers and employers
benefited from the agents' actions and, for the most part, appear
to have entered voluntarily into relationships with these agents.

To a considerable extent, it would appear that reformers' concerns about the operation of private employment agencies were
a manifestation of nativist sentiments rather than an accurate

assessment of the activities of these agencies. It would not be surprising to find that there were some dishonest labor agents who took advantage of their clients' inexperience with American labor markets to make a quick profit. It is also clear that sometimes agents substantially miscalculated the level of demand, as Antonio Cordasco did in 1904. Anticipating that the Canadian Pacific would require 3,000 to 4,000 trackworkers in the summer of 1905, Cordasco recruited heavily in Italy and, by the spring, registered in excess of 3,000 newly arrived immigrants. But poor weather delayed the start of construction and reduced harvest labor demand in the Canadian plains, thus releasing more resident labor, with the result that Cordasco could obtain jobs for only about 700 men (Peck 1994, pp. 54–5).

Yet it would appear that most agencies were honestly and competently run. Correspondence of the Robesonia Iron Company in Pennsylvania uncovered by Bodnar (1974) contains a number of letters from employment agencies offering their services to the company and describing information about the fees they charged. In each of these instances, the company's superintendent responded with details about their operations, the types of labor that they needed, and the wages that they were offering. These exchanges suggest that the operators of employment agencies were indeed in possession of precisely the sorts of information that would be required to serve as effective intermediaries in the labor market.

Generalizing from a few letters is, of course, unwarranted, but George Brown, the Deputy Chief of New York's Bureau of Licenses, the agency responsible for ensuring the compliance of employment agencies with state regulations, estimated around the turn of the century that his office received complaints about only 10 to 15 of the 426 licensed agencies in New York City (U.S. Congress, House of Representatives 1901, p. 232). The most telling evidence though is in the actions of employers and job seekers. The extensive business that some employers did clearly indicates that they believed the private agencies performed a valuable service for them. It is harder to assess the views of job seekers, but it seems unlikely that many dishonest agencies would have continued in operation for a long period of time. This is especially true in the years after 1890, when they began to face growing competition from publicly sponsored labor exchanges. Because the services of such agencies were available free of charge, and without risk of exploitation, their failure to displace private agencies substantially is strong evidence of the value job seekers placed on the services of the private agencies.

PUBLIC LABOR EXCHANGES

As noted earlier, the proliferation of private employment agencies during the second half of the nineteenth century provoked growing concern among public officials and social reformers. Warning of the possible exploitation of immigrants or other workers ignorant of local conditions, reformers sought to regulate the activities of private agencies and to offer workers an alternative source of labor market information through the formation of publicly supported employment bureaus. By providing a mechanism through which employers and workers could be brought together free of charge, officials hoped that these exchanges would eliminate the need for private agencies. Public efforts to organize the labor market proved largely unsuccessful, however.[6] Providing information by itself, without the other forms of assistance available through private agencies, was not enough to mobilize significant movements of labor.

The Castle Garden Labor Exchange

One of the first public efforts to organize the labor market was undertaken by New York state in the 1850s. With the rising volume of immigration into New York City during the 1840s came increased reports of frauds and deceptions practiced upon the newly arrived. Prompted both by humanitarian concerns for the welfare of these immigrants and the more pragmatic worry that immigrants cheated of their savings and unable to find employment would be more likely to require public relief, the state legislature in 1847 established the Board of Commissioners of Emigration to

---

[6] A great number of philanthropic organizations also became involved in matching job seekers and employers at this time. Most of these efforts were relatively modest in their impact, however, and were handicapped by the perception of both employers and job seekers that they were largely a form of charity work rather than an effective labor market institution.

reform and supervise the reception of immigrants arriving in New York City.[7] One of the first steps the Commissioners took was the establishment of a labor exchange, which opened in 1850. Little is known of the early history of the exchange, but by the Civil War it had become little more than an "intelligence office" supplying domestic servants to the New York market (Kapp 1870, p. 115). After the Civil War, however, the Commissioners reorganized the exchange in a more effective manner, and it emerged as a significant institution in the distribution of immigrant labor arriving in New York. Although the Commissioners were forced by a lack of funds to end their support of the exchange in 1876, the Irish and German immigrant societies of New York assumed financial responsibility for its continued operation. Under this arrangement, the exchange survived the demise of the Commissioners in 1889, when the federal government took over the reception of immigrants, and was still in operation in the early-twentieth century.

According to the Commissioners' description, following the post–Civil War reorganization of the exchange, the business of the labor exchange was conducted in a large room capable of accommodating 300 persons. Those seeking work recorded their names, nationalities, occupational skills, and whether they possessed recommendations from previous employers. Employers were required to present suitable references before they could record their needs. Clerks at the exchange helped to bring employers and workers together but did not take part in the negotiations between the two parties. After the job seeker and employer reached an agreement, exchange officials recorded the contract and could be called on to resolve subsequent disputes regarding the transaction (Erickson 1957, pp. 95–7). In its reorganized form, the exchange attracted a good deal of attention. In 1868, the *New York Times* (1868b, p. 8) reported that:

the Labor Exchange has already shown itself a great success. Its value, at first only known to the employers and unemployed of the City is now becoming generally recognized, and employers and their agents from all

---

[7] The background of these reforms is recounted in Ernst (1949, pp. 26–30), Kapp (1870, pp. 85–95), and Jones (1980, p. 1082). Not surprisingly, city officials, many of whom benefited from corruption under the city-administered system that the reforms replaced, were opposed to any change in the status quo.

Table 3.5. *Number of Persons Placed by the Castle Garden Labor Exchange and Total Alien Arrivals in New York, 1869–1887*

Year	Number of aliens arriving	Immigrants placed by labor exchange	
		Number	Percentage of arrivals
1869	258,989	34,955	13.5
1870	212,170	27,912	13.2
1871	229,639	31,384	13.7
1872	294,581	32,592	12.1
1873	266,818	25,325	9.5
1874	140,041	16,910	12.1
1875	84,264	12,440	14.8
1876	68,264	10,215	15.0
1877	54,536	10,314	18.9
1878	75,347	10,568	14.0
1879	135,070	16,533	12.2
1880	327,371	39,311	12.0
1881	455,681	49,745	10.9
1882	476,086	37,516	7.9
1883	405,909	27,903	6.9
1884	330,030	23,687	7.2
1885	291,066	15,539	5.3
1886	321,814	14,257	4.4

Source: New York, Commissioners of Emigration (1869–1874, 1880–1886); Erickson (1957, p. 193).

parts of the country avail themselves of its facilities. It is daily crowded with the unemployed, for a fair proportion of whom work is obtained.

A more precise picture of the impact of the exchange can be obtained from the statistics of its operation that the Commissioners began to collect and report following its reorganization. As Table 3.5 indicates, it was not unusual for the exchange to find employment for as many as 20,000 or 30,000 persons in a year, and this figure reached almost 50,000 in 1881. Although these figures represented only about 10 to 15 percent of arriving immigrants in any year, they compare favorably with the roughly 1,000 to 2,000 transactions that the average private employment agency studied in the 1890s and early-1900s facilitated. After 1881, however, the importance of the exchange began to decline, as both the total number of job seekers it placed and their proportion of the total stream of arriving immigrants fell. By 1886,

Table 3.6. *Location of Jobs in Which Male Immigrants Were Placed by the Castle Garden Labor Exchange*

Year	New York	New Jersey	Connecticut	Pennsylvania	Percentage of total placed in 4 states
1869	14,175	5,630	1,412	1,234	98.3
1870	11,172	4,341	927	207	93.2
1871	12,939	5,412	1,026	434	96.6
1872	13,263	5,984	1,172	1,469	93.8
1873	9,080	6,459	993	480	95.5
1874	5,133	3,855	824	82	97.5
1880	12,833	6,240	3,534	3,866	91.9
1881	13,409	5,411	3,711	8,938	81.5
1882	11,860	4,690	3,501	5,684	87.5
1883	8,102	3,711	2,210	3,590	90.2
1884	7,382	3,202	1,922	1,609	92.2
1885	5,323	1,410	872	516	94.0
1886	5,345	1,328	780	540	95.8

Source: New York, Commissioners of Emigration (1869–1874, 1880–1886).

the Commissioners stopped reporting on the activities of the exchange. Erickson (1957, pp. 95–7) suggested that the declining significance of the exchange reflects the dominant role played in its operation by the German and Irish immigrant groups that had been instrumental in the formation of the Commissioners of Emigration. Clerks of other nationalities were not employed by the exchange, and few members of the newer immigrant groups that began to arrive in large numbers for the first time during the 1880s knew of or patronized the exchange.

Even at its most successful the exchange confronted significant obstacles to the mobilization of labor over long distances. Table 3.6 details the location of jobs found for male immigrants. Throughout the period for which data are available, the vast majority of jobs were located in New York state, and, in all but two years, more than 90 percent of the positions filled by the exchange were located either in New York or the nearby states of New Jersey, Connecticut, and Pennsylvania. The jobs available for women were even more geographically confined, being almost entirely located within New York City. The obstacle does not appear to have been a lack of knowledge of or interest in the services provided by the exchange on the part of employers outside New York City, for the exchange received a large number of requests for workers from employers in distant states.[8] Rather, the difficulty arose in arranging the transportation of job seekers to distant jobs. The newly arrived immigrant without friends or relatives to assist him or her was, in the words of Commissioners, "often unable and always reluctant to pay his traveling expenses." Meanwhile employers were reluctant to remit funds for the purchase of tickets, fearing that the job seekers would take the transportation but find other jobs instead (New York, Commissioners of Emigration 1869, pp. 108–9; 1870, p. 98; *New York Times* 1868c, p. 1).

State Labor Bureaus
The efforts of the Commissioners of Emigration to match employers and workers foreshadowed a growing public involvement in the labor market. In the 1890s, state and municipal governments began to establish free public labor exchanges or employment bureaus.[9] The motivation for these efforts derived from much the same mix of humanitarian and pragmatic concerns that had prompted New York state to establish the Board of Commissioners of Emigration in 1847. To these motivations, however, was added a newfound awareness of the problem of industrial unemployment. Identifying the "disorganization" of the labor market as a factor exacerbating the effects of seasonal and cyclical fluctuations in economic activities, proponents of public employment bureaus argued that such institutions would help to reduce the severity of the resulting unemployment problem and contribute to the more efficient working of the labor market.[10]

---

[8] Erickson (1957, p. 96) advanced the argument that employers outside New York were ignorant of the exchange. But both the *New York Times* (1868a, p. 4; 1868c, p. 1) and the Commissioners in their annual report (New York, Commissioners of Emigration 1869, pp. 108–9; 1870, pp. 98–9) remarked upon the volume of requests for assistance received from employers outside the region.

[9] At about the same time, states and municipalities also began to adopt legislation regulating the activities and fees of private employment agencies. By 1900, 16 states and several municipalities had enacted such laws, accompanied in most cases by licensing and/or bonding requirements for all private employment agencies (Bogart 1900, p. 341).

[10] Sautter (1983, 1991) examined the movement to establish public labor exchanges in more detail. For a sampling of contemporary proponents' views, see Devine (1909) and Leiserson (1914). The changing perception of unemployment and the

The movement to establish public employment agencies, however, progressed gradually. In 1890, Ohio became the first state to establish such an institution, opening branches in five of its major cities. By the end of the decade, the cities of Los Angeles and Seattle and the states of New York, Illinois, Nebraska, and Montana had all established public employment agencies. In the latter two states, efforts focused primarily on organizing harvest labor markets, and in Montana a largely unsuccessful attempt was made to match workers and employers through the mail. The movement accelerated after the turn of the century, with nine more states and cities establishing agencies between 1900 and 1907 (Conner 1907, p. 3).

The volume of business done by the free public employment agencies established after 1890 varied considerably. Table 3.7 summarizes their activities, showing the number of persons placed by agencies in different cities and states during the period 1890–1910. Figures ranged from an average of more than 50,000 per year during 1906–11 for the six offices operated by the state of Illinois, to just 393 for the agency operated in Baltimore during 1903–4. In most other cities, performance fell somewhere between these extremes. The public employment office in New York City, for example, placed 4,384 persons – mostly women – during 1904–5. Most contemporary analysts explained the large differences in the volume of business done by different public employment agencies as the consequence of the differences in the financial resources committed to their operation and the varied qualifications and commitment of their superintendents, who were often political appointees rather than civil servants (Leiserson 1914; Kellor 1915, pp. 315–49).[11]

Despite the large variation in the number of positions filled by public employment agencies, the nature of these positions was surprisingly uniform across states. In every state for which there is data, unskilled workers constituted the vast majority of those served. Typically, more than half of the men obtained jobs as laborers; the jobs available for women were mainly as domestic

responses of economists, public officials, and social reformers are described in Keyssar (1986, pp. 250–9, 264–9), Garraty (1978, pp. 129–45), and Yellowitz (1968, pp. 338–60).
[11] See also Sautter's (1991, pp. 90–4) assessment of the work of the public exchanges.

Table 3.7. *Total and Annual Average Number of Persons Placed by Selected Public Employment Offices, 1890–1911*

Location	Period	Number			Annual average		
		Men	Women	Total	Men	Women	Total
Cleveland, OH	1890–1905	17,842	33,134	50,976	1,231	2,285	3,516
Columbus, OH	1890–1905	15,143	26,738	41,881	1,044	1,844	2,888
Cincinnati, OH	1890–1905	20,160	23,022	43,182	1,390	1,588	2,978
Helena, MT	1896	305	302	607	305	302	607
Seattle, WA	1895–1904	142,353	34,078	176,432	14,235	3,408	17,743
Connecticut[a]	1901–1905	12,469	23,100	35,569	2,823	5,230	8,053
Baltimore, MD	1903–1904	563	222	785	282	111	393
New York, NY	1904–1905	858	3,526	4,384	858	3,526	4,384
St. Louis, MO	1905	2,697	409	3,106	2,697	409	3,106
Kansas City, MO	1905	3,348	464	3,812	3,348	464	3,812
Milwaukee, WI	1905	5,909	1,315	7,224	5,909	1,315	7,224
Illinois[b]	1900–1905	128,123	76,591	204,714	21,354	12,764	34,119
Illinois[c]	1906–1911	219,436	88,274	307,710	36,573	14,712	51,285
Minneapolis, MN	1906–1910	17,001	10,780	27,781	4,250	2,695	6,945
Detroit, MI	1908–1911	92,460	19,938	112,398	23,115	4,985	28,100
Grand Rapids, MI	1908–1911	22,948	12,084	35,032	5,737	3,021	8,758
Boston, MA	1910–1911	9,303	6,503	15,506	9,303	6,503	15,506

Notes: The periods covered do not always correspond to calendar years, but annual averages have been adjusted to reflect partial years of coverage.
[a] Five offices.
[b] Four offices: three in Chicago and one in Peoria.
[c] Six offices: three in Chicago and one each in Peoria, Springfield, and East St. Louis.
Source: Conner (1907, pp. 12, 32, 43, 44, 50, 55, 62–4, 68, 79) and Sargent (1911, pp. 41, 46, 73, 80, 92).

servants, chambermaids, waitresses, and day workers (Conner 1907, pp. 13, 43–6, 52–6, 63–9; Sargent 1911, pp. 52, 83, 94–5). Only in the mix between men's and women's occupations was there any significant variation. In those states where overall numbers were lowest, women typically outnumbered men, suggesting that problems of funding and administration were more significant in placing unskilled men than women.

In effect, the public labor exchanges provided a mechanism for organizing local spot markets for unskilled labor. Describing the operation of one public employment office, Conner (1907, p. 78) wrote:

it is the custom when the office is opened in the morning for a crowd of applicants to be on hand ready to hear the news. When the office was visited by the writer a call came for four men to serve as masons' helpers at 35 cents an hour. After some solicitation, the superintendent succeeded in inducing three out of a crowd of over twenty idle men to accept this work.

Despite the fact that they did not charge a fee for their services and could be trusted not to offer misleading or incorrect information, the public labor exchanges had little impact on the business done by private employment agencies, especially those providing gang labor to railroad construction and other projects at a distance from the cities. This ineffectiveness is obvious in the case of New York, where the public employment agency was closed in 1906 because its function had been reduced to that of providing domestic servants. Even in Chicago, where the public agency was more active, it was reported that contractors for railroad construction work "rely upon private agencies for their men and will not hire them elsewhere." A similar situation characterized St. Louis (Sargent 1911, p. 56; Conner 1907, p. 46).

Although free public employment agencies were successful in some cities in providing a channel through which local employers of unskilled labor could locate workers, their activities in this area paralleled those of private agencies rather than replacing them. Beyond the local market, public employment agencies played essentially no role at all. The inability of the public employment bureaus to displace private employment agencies can be traced to the reluctance of both employers and job seekers to use these institutions. Because of the limited resources and poor management of most public employment bureaus, employers had good reason to be suspicious of their ability to screen skilled workers adequately, and hence were unwilling to use them except to fill the least skilled jobs. This perception was only heightened by the perception that the pool of applicants at the public labor exchanges was drawn from the least desirable segment of the labor force. According to Conner (1907, p. 78), the clientele of one public exchange he visited could best be described as "the class known locally as 'hoboes.'" This concern was self-reinforcing once it arose; the more qualified workers were aware of employers' opinions and feared being grouped with these undesirable classes of workers. Even without this obstacle, however, public labor exchanges faced the problem that they did not provide the additional support services that were likely to be required by those most likely to turn to them for assistance. Because private agencies worked closely with labor bosses, immigrant bankers, boardinghouse keepers, and other members of the immigrant community serving the newly arrived, both employers and job seekers found it advantageous to turn to these agencies despite the higher cost of their services. For job seekers, the private agencies offered access to credit, while labor bosses served as essential intermediaries between employers and gangs of non-English speaking workers, accompanying them on the way to the job site and serving as translators once they were at work.

ASSESSING THE CONTRIBUTIONS OF LABOR MARKET INTERMEDIARIES

Measured in terms of the number of transactions that they facilitated, formal labor market intermediaries occupied a small, but important niche in late-nineteenth and early-twentieth century labor markets. They served to bring together employers and job seekers who lacked access to informal channels of recruitment created by networks of friends and relatives. Although the majority of long-distance labor movements were mediated by these informal channels, the emergence of institutions serving job seekers without friends or relatives to assist them was crucial in opening new streams of chain migration.

The success of employment agencies in achieving these ends rested in large measure on their ability to mimic the operation of the informal networks for which they were a substitute. Private employment agencies were rooted for the most part in specific racial or immigrant communities. In addition to providing information, the nexus of businesses serving job seekers offered financial assistance, housing, meals, and a sense of community for the newly arrived. The importance of these additional services is underscored by the inability of publicly sponsored labor exchanges to displace private agencies. Despite the fact that they did not charge fees, and clients did not face the risk of being misled, the public agencies played only a minor role in the labor market. The additional services provided to both employers and job seekers by the private agencies thus evidently outweighed these apparent advantages.

Labor market intermediaries were an important source of flexibility in the labor market, but because the connections forged by private employment agencies followed lines already established by kin- and friendship-based networks, they did little to break down barriers between regional labor markets that had emerged in the antebellum period. In the South, employment agents recruited labor in the South Atlantic for employers primarily in the South Central region of the country. In the North, employment agents acted as intermediaries between newly arriving European immigrants and employers of gang labor. The knowledge that employment agencies stood ready to help them find work after they arrived in the United States must have been a factor in opening up new sources of labor supply across Europe and encouraging pioneering emigrants to set off in search of work in an unfamiliar destination. For employers in the northern part of the country, the continued influx of job seekers and the ease with which they could be recruited through the proliferating private employment agencies located in major cities eased the problem of labor recruitment. So long as immigration provided an adequate supply of labor, northern employers had little need or incentive to look elsewhere, and southern job seekers found it easier to look west than north, if they hoped to improve their fortunes through geographic mobility.

4

MARKETS FOR SKILLED LABOR

External Recruitment and the Development of Internal Labor Markets

The discussion in the last two chapters concentrated on the development of mechanisms of external recruitment. Recruitment from outside the firm was, by definition, the only source of unskilled labor available to employers. Employers seeking to hire skilled labor could also hire workers on the external market, selecting them from job seekers at the factory or actively recruiting workers either through their own agents or by using employment agencies and public labor exchanges. But employers seeking to fill skilled positions possessed several additional alternatives not available to employers of unskilled labor.[1] They could choose to train workers within the firm and fill skilled vacancies through internal promotions, or they could modify the production process to reduce or alter skill requirements. During the late-nineteenth and early-twentieth centuries, employers pursued all these options to varying degrees.[2] This chapter explores the interactions between

[1] Skilled labor is, of course, not homogeneous. Skilled workers possess a wide array of different kinds of training, education, and experience that serve to raise their productivity, and hence value, to employers. Because acquiring particular skills usually entails an initial investment on the part of the worker, economists often equate the acquisition of skill with the formation of "human capital." The value of investments in human capital is not fixed permanently but will depend on the prevailing level of demand and supply for the particular skills that individual workers possess. Shifts in the supply of workers with particular skills due to changes in training methods or union restrictions as well as shifts in demand induced by technological changes or shifts in taste for final products will all affect the relative value of skills.

[2] Sundstrom (1988, Tables 1 and 2) summarized responses by employers in Iowa and New York to questions about recruiting practices in a number of industries in the early-twentieth century. These data suggest that in most industries a mix of internal promotion and external recruiting was common. The building trades

these different choices, arguing that employers' responses to the relative scarcity of skilled workers in external markets were an important factor encouraging the reorganization of labor allocation and training within firms at this time.

External recruitment of skilled labor was possible only in occupations characterized by a well-defined and reasonably stable cluster of skills, the possession of which could be easily documented or verified by potential employers. In these instances, a variety of different mechanisms emerged to organize external markets. Because of the strategic value of labor market information in influencing employment conditions, however, control over these mechanisms emerged as an important point of contention between workers and employers. Even when external recruitment was possible, the relatively high cost of skilled labor – in comparison both to unskilled labor and to the supply of skilled labor in other countries – may have discouraged employers from relying on external labor markets. Instead, many employers looked for technological and organizational solutions, reorganizing the production process by introducing specialized capital equipment and subdividing tasks in ways that reduced their dependence on workers possessing traditional craft skills. These changes in the production process helped moderate the demand for skilled craft workers but often worsened the problem of scarcity for other types of labor. Workers might more easily and quickly acquire the skills necessary to fill newly created positions, but existing mechanisms of training were only further strained by the growing demand for appropriately qualified workers.

EXTERNAL RECRUITMENT OF SKILLED LABOR

External recruitment of skilled labor was most frequently found in industries that continued to rely to some degree on traditional craft skills – such as iron and steel, glass, the building trades, printing, machine tools – or in industries such as textiles, which were characterized by relatively stable technologies and well established

stand out as the primary exception, relying almost entirely on external hiring, and making almost no use of internal recruitment.

factory jobs – such as spinning and weaving. In cities, skilled workers seeking employment commonly made the rounds of local employers, and, under normal conditions, employers could count on these applicants to fill their needs. This method of job search is illustrated by the experience of William Rees, a weaver living in Philadelphia. When he needed work, Rees would simply make the rounds of the various mills with which he was familiar. On one occasion, as he described it, he was walking past a mill when: "[I] saw a man through a window whom [I] knew. [He] asked me what [I] was doing and [I] said that [I] wanted a job. [My] friend told [me] to come in.... [He] found the boss weaver and [I] was given a job" (quoted in Licht 1992, p. 1).[3]

When demand was greater, foremen might seek out acquaintances, or ask other workers to help in recruiting new hires. Employers might also attempt to lure workers from other establishments. According to Erickson (1957, pp. 34–5), in 1870, when New England cotton mills faced a shortage of skilled weavers, many of them dispatched their overseers to persuade skilled workmen to leave their current jobs by offering special inducements. When the imbalance between supply and demand was sufficiently great, employers would extend their recruitment efforts, employing agents in other centers of the trade or sending their own foremen to search out suitably skilled workers.

Long-distance recruiting was especially common when firms needed to fill specific highly skilled positions. When Richard T. Crane decided in 1855 to expand the production of his Chicago brass foundry to include finishing work, for example, he "sent for two first class workmen [he] had known in Brooklyn" (quoted in David 1987, p. 64). A decade later, when Crane needed someone to direct production of malleable-iron pipe fittings in a newly erected factory, he recruited a man with the appropriate skills from Newark, New Jersey, then the center of the malleable-iron casting trade.

In some instances, the need for specific skills might even prompt employers to recruit workers internationally. This was the case,

---

[3] Gladys Palmer's 1936 investigation of the Philadelphia labor market provides numerous examples of this sort of job search by skilled workers (personal communication).

for example, in the early textile mills, which relied heavily on English mechanics to construct their machinery and, at first, recruited skilled mule spinners and weavers from England as well (Ware 1931, pp. 203–7). Later in the century, the introduction of new lines of production sometimes necessitated recruiting foreign workers with the appropriate skills. When the managers of the Amoskeag mills, in Manchester, New Hampshire, decided to begin production of fancy ginghams – a product not previously produced in the United States – they used a British agent to locate and forward to them about 90 women skilled in weaving this kind of cloth (Creamer 1941, pp. 48–9). The same pattern is evident in other industries as well. In 1870, after installing new and extensive machinery, the Chicago Vise and Tool Company hired "a number of thoroughly experienced workmen from the celebrated establishment of Peter Wright, England" to operate its new plant (quoted in David 1987, p. 64). Likewise, until the mechanization of production in the early-twentieth century reduced their need for skilled labor, window glass producers commonly recruited glassmakers from European centers of the industry in France, Belgium, Germany, and Great Britain to fill positions in the expanding industry. During 1879 and 1880, groups of 20 to 60 blowers, gatherers, cutters, and flatteners were brought from Europe to staff newly established factories (Erickson 1957, pp. 139–41). A similar reliance on European sources of skilled labor is apparent in iron and steel, woolens, cutlery, glass blowing, and mining in this period (Erickson 1957, pp. 40–2, 110).

A distinctive feature of some skilled labor markets was the role played by labor unions in organizing local and long-distance labor markets. Where effective craft unions emerged, the local union's business agent often became – either formally or informally – a valuable source of labor market information for members of the trade. Because these agents' duties included surveying employers to ensure that they were complying with union rules, they were in close contact with potential employers and were often aware of job openings as soon as they became available. As the unions quickly discovered, control over labor market information in turn enhanced their power by encouraging workers' loyalty to the union. For job seekers, union contacts could be a source of additional information about matters such as the personality of the foreman and working conditions at different establishments (Jackson 1984, pp. 191–7; Smelser 1919, pp. 60–2; Harrison et al. 1924, p. 72). At the same time that union business agents were helping job seekers, they also provided employers with a valuable service by helping to screen workers. As one agent observed, "I tell the men what jobs there are and they can take their pick. Of course, if I'm pretty sure a man can't handle a particular job I tell him so and can generally convince him" (Harrison et al. 1924, p. 72). This observation is corroborated by John R. Commons' investigation of pattern makers in Chicago. According to Commons, "most employers employ through the union as a matter of choice; it is much easier to telephone to a union headquarters for a man than to get one in any other way, and the opinion prevailed as a rule that the union did try to send an employer a man who was best suited to his need" (U.S. Department of Labor 1904, p. 189).

Union organization of skilled labor markets was most fully developed in the building trades, where the small size of many employers and the highly variable nature of demand made employment relationships especially unstable (Smelser 1919, p. 59). But the union's role in organizing the labor market also reflected the value of this service for employers. Employers at first resisted unions, but by the 1890s builders in most major cities had come to accept a significant degree of cooperation with the building trades unions. This acceptance reflected both the informational advantages that they provided in the labor market and the recognition that the unions could help to reduce competitive pressures on prices by making it difficult for new entrants to cut costs by hiring lower cost labor (Jackson 1984, pp. 240–1).[4]

In many cities, unions and their business agents also played an important part in organizing markets for skilled metal workers. Like the employers in the building trades, small-job foundries and machine shops faced unpredictable and highly variable demands for small batches of customized products. These conditions

[4] As Friedman (1992) pointed out, the strength of urban building trades had much to do with their ability to form political alliances as well.

resulted in high rates of turnover. By maintaining close contact with employers and unemployed members, the unions emerged as an important organizing force in the distribution of labor. Most of the skilled workers that employers required were union members, and reliance on the union provided a way of organizing the labor market, facilitating worker mobility across firms, and preventing price competition between employers (Klug 1989, p. 47).

In contrast to the building trades, however, metal trades employers associations in a number of cities set up competing employment bureaus in an effort to counterbalance union power. In 1903, the Employers' Association of Detroit established an employment bureau, which kept files on workers that allowed it to screen workers and blacklist union activists (Klug 1989, pp. 47–54). Not all such efforts were explicitly motivated by antiunion sentiments, however. In Philadelphia, for example, the Metal Manufacturers Association was composed of both union and nonunion shops, so its labor bureau did not maintain a blacklist. Instead, it attempted to steer union members to union shops. Based on his examination of the association's records, Howell Harris concluded that the success of the Philadelphia bureau reflected its ability to capture or create the externalities of greater stability in labor demand and supply by facilitating the movement of workers from one firm to another (Harris 1991, p. 126).

In addition to their role in organizing local labor markets, a number of unions attempted with limited success to organize the allocation of labor across larger distances. Lloyd Ulman attributed the rise of national trade unions in the years after the Civil War to the threat that "travelling members" posed to local unions' control over labor supply in their communities (Ulman 1955, pp. 68–87). National unions provided a means of establishing uniform criteria for membership and developing methods of transferring membership from one local to another. Although the initial impetus for the formation of national trade unions arose from a desire to regulate or reduce mobility, many national unions eventually became involved in the dissemination of labor market information. D. P. Smelser (1919, pp. 75–84) reported that 14 national unions had attempted to establish some form of employment bureau for their members by 1919. Of these, he believed that half had achieved "some success."[5]

Short of establishing formal employment bureaus, many national unions provided labor market information through their publications (Smelser 1919, p. 86). Soon after its formation in 1881, for example, the Brotherhood of Carpenters and Joiners of America began to publish a monthly newspaper entitled *The Carpenter*. Among the regular features of this paper were reports on local labor market conditions from affiliated local unions. Ulman (1955, pp. 72–5) argued that locals often played down favorable conditions in an effort to discourage migration, but inspection of these notices reveals that many in fact described local conditions in quite positive terms.

EMPLOYMENT AND WAGES IN MARKETS FOR SKILLED LABOR

Despite the development of both informal and formal mechanisms of communication designed to facilitate the external recruitment of skilled labor, late-nineteenth and early-twentieth century American employers found that skilled labor was in relatively scarce supply. The problem was not so much that market institutions were poorly suited to the problem of allocating the existing stock of skilled labor, but rather that they were unable to increase the nation's stock of appropriately skilled workers at a rate comparable to the increase in demand at this time. In other words, even though the ability to recruit skilled labor externally meant that the supply of skilled workers to individual employers was relatively elastic, the economy-wide supply of skilled workers was relatively inelastic compared to that of unskilled labor. As a result,

---

[5] Smelser's (1919, pp. 76–81) list of successful unions included the granite cutters, glass bottle blowers, flint glass workers, lithographers, photoengravers, potters, and pattern makers. Among the unsuccessful attempts, he listed the locomotive firemen, railway conductors, bookbinders, typographers, and leather workers on horse goods. Smelser also noted that a number of unions experimented with advancing travel funds to members, but that none of these unions had been successful in this effort because of the difficulties involved in getting local unions at the destination to collect repayments and forward them to the local that had advanced the money.

rising demand for skilled workers caused their relative wages to rise during the late-nineteenth and early-twentieth centuries. By the late-nineteenth century, wage premia for skilled workers in the United States had risen to historically high levels and were generally well above those in major European economies.

The argument that skilled labor was relatively scarce appears to conflict with the widely held view among labor historians that the late-nineteenth century was a period of "de-skilling" technological change in which employers used the techniques of scientific management to wrest control of the work process from their skilled employees through an increasingly fine division of labor and the introduction of new capital-intensive production techniques (see Gordon, Edwards, and Reich 1982). For the most part, this view rests on relatively disaggregated data from particular plants or industries. Such evidence captures an important facet of the history of this period, but it cannot be used to draw inferences about the direction of aggregate trends in the economy. Manufacturing production was indeed becoming more concentrated in large establishments that employed vast numbers of relatively unskilled factory operatives. But data on the occupational composition of the labor force and the behavior of wages suggest that, contrary to the deskilling hypothesis, the relative demand for skilled labor was actually rising, rather than falling, at this time. In light of this evidence, it seems most appropriate to interpret the direction of technological change in this period as an endogenous response to the continued scarcity of skilled labor rather than an exogenous shock to the economy.

Occupational data derived from the IPUMS (integrated public use microdata) samples of the federal censuses between 1870 and 1920 indicate that the share of skilled craft workers in the male labor force was stable or increasing after 1870.[6] Table 4.1 traces

[6] This finding is consistent with Alan Dawson's (1979) analysis of published census returns. According to Dawson, from 1870 to 1910 the number of workers in a range of skilled occupations that he termed the "labor aristocracy" grew at approximately the same rate as the labor force as a whole and more than kept pace with the growth of workers in what he termed "working class" occupations. The occupations Dawson included in the labor aristocracy are enginemen, firemen and conductors, carpenters and joiners, brick and stone masons, painters

Table 4.1. *Shares of Male Workers by Occupation, 1870–1920*

Occupation	1870	1880	1900	1910	1920
Professionals and technical workers	2.8	3.1	3.6	3.4	4.1
Farmers	25.7	26.2	15.9	15.6	15.9
Managers, officials, and proprietors	5.5	5.2	5.4	7.4	7.3
Clerical and kindred workers	1.4	2.1	4.2	4.5	5.4
Sales workers	3.2	3.4	4.1	4.7	4.8
Service workers	2.6	3.4	4.5	4.8	4.6
Skilled craft workers	13.9	12.3	15.2	15.2	19.3
Apprentices	0.6	0.3	0.2	0.3	0.2
Operatives	13.0	13.7	14.0	15.1	15.1
Laborers	31.3	30.1	32.9	29.2	23.4

Note: The occupational classifications used here follow the 1950 census occupational categories, into which the IPUMS has recoded the original occupational data. Labor force shares were calculated for all males aged 16 to 65 who reported an occupation. Excluded from the calculation are those men who gave a response coded by the IPUMS as "nonoccupational" responses. Shares may not sum to 100 in each year because of rounding.
Source: IPUMS samples for 1870, 1880, 1900, 1910, and 1920.

changes in the distribution of males aged 16 to 65 across broad categories of occupations.[7] Because microdata for 1890 are not available there is no information for this year. As these data make clear, this 50-year period was characterized by substantial shifts in the occupational composition of the labor force. But these shifts do not point to any decline in the employment of skilled craft workers. Reflecting the relative decline of the agricultural sector,

and glaziers and varnishers, paper hangers, plasterers, plumbers and gas and steam fitters, mechanics, glassworkers, blacksmiths, machinists, steam boilermakers, wheelwrights, cabinetmakers, coopers, gold and silver workers, bookbinders, engravers, printers, lithographers and pressmen, and model and pattern makers. The working class included blue-collar manufacturing workers, agricultural laborers, a variety of domestic service workers, and some trade and transportation workers.

7 A variety of different approaches to occupational classification have been used in the census. Here I employ a consistent set of occupational classifications based on 1950 census occupational codes that were generated by IPUMS investigators. The underlying occupational data come from the unedited responses of individuals to questions about their primary occupation, which IPUMS investigators used to assign individuals to particular occupational categories. Clearly the specific skills and technical content associated with job titles are likely to change over time, and no occupational classification scheme is perfect, but the socioeconomic approach of the 1950 scheme does a good job of capturing the sort of broad shifts in labor force composition with which I am concerned here. See Sobek and Dillon (1995) and Sobek (1995) for further discussion of IPUMS methods.

the share of farmers (including farm owners and tenants) dropped sharply after 1880. Consistent with the rise of large factories and bureaucratic organizations, the shares of operatives and clerical and kindred workers were both rising in this period. The proportion of clerical and kindred workers increased especially dramatically, rising nearly threefold over this period. Turning to skilled craft workers, after a small drop between 1870 and 1880, their share of the labor force rose slightly between 1880 and 1900, and then increased by nearly one-third from 1910 to 1920. Excluding farmers from the data, the share of skilled craft workers among all nonagricultural workers held roughly steady from 1870 to 1910 – dropping from 18.7 percent to 18.0 percent – and then shot up from 1910 to 1920 – reaching 23 percent.[8] Thus, in aggregate there is no evidence of a tendency toward de-skilling.[9]

While the relative employment of skilled craft workers was holding steady, their wages were rising relative to those of less-skilled workers. Figure 4.1 graphs two series of data on skill margins compiled by Williamson and Lindert (1980). Both series suggest an increase in skill margins after 1850, and the series for urban skilled workers shows that this increase intensified after 1890. By 1914, wages of urban skilled workers had risen nearly 20 percent relative to those of the unskilled. Figure 4.2 graphs another set of comparisons for the post-1890 period drawn from Dawson (1979). Between 1890 and 1914, these data indicate that nominal wages of skilled blue-collar workers, what Dawson calls the "labor aristocracy," increased by 73 percent, that those for all manufacturing workers grew by 54 percent, and that those of the unskilled grew by just 31 percent.[10]

---

[8] These calculations exclude farmers, but they still include agricultural laborers on the grounds that many of these workers may have worked part of the year in industry and, in any event, could easily move back and forth between the agricultural and nonagricultural sectors.

[9] In the absence of technological changes in the production process, the demand for and employment of skilled workers might have risen even more rapidly than they actually did. In this sense, comparing what actually happened to a counterfactual alternative, one can still portray the technological innovations of this period as de-skilling.

[10] In contrast to the rising trend in returns to skill over the late-nineteenth century, there is considerable evidence that skill premia declined sharply between 1900 and 1940. The data make it difficult to date the turning point precisely; however, the most careful analysis suggests that much of the narrowing in skill

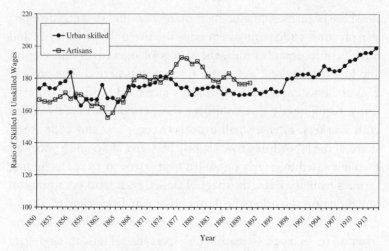

Figure 4.1   Wages of Urban Skilled Workers and Artisans Relative to Wages of Unskilled Labor, 1850–1914. *Note*: The urban skilled series is the ratio of wages of urban skilled workers to those of unskilled workers in manufacturing and building trades. The artisans series is the ratio of wages of artisans to common laborers. *Source*: Williamson and Lindert (1980, pp. 306–8).

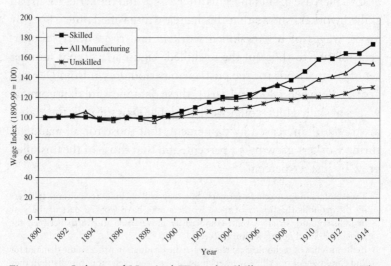

Figure 4.2   Indexes of Nominal Wages by Skill, 1890–1914. *Note*: The index of skilled occupations is constructed as an employment-weighted average of wages of enginemen, firemen, bricklayers, carpenters, machinists, blacksmiths, compositors, and pressmen. *Source*: Dawson (1979, p. 333).

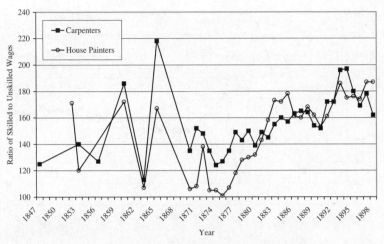

Figure 4.3   Ratio of Skilled to Unskilled Wages in the Building Trades, Chicago, 1847–1898. *Source*: David (1987, p. 88).

Paul David's (1987) examination of labor market dynamics in Chicago provides further support for the view that the relative cost of skilled labor was rising in the post–Civil War era. Figures 4.3 and 4.4 graph the relative wages of specific categories of skilled workers in construction and metal working, respectively, in Chicago from mid-century through 1898. During the early years covered by the data, when Chicago was still a relatively small city in a rapidly growing region, cyclical fluctuations in demand caused wide swings in skill margins, but as the city grew, relative wage levels tended to become more stable, and after 1870 skill premia followed a gradually rising trend.

The gradually rising trend in skill premia within the United States indicates that, in comparison to unskilled labor, skilled labor was becoming relatively less abundant during the late-nineteenth century. At the same time, international comparisons of skill premia indicate that the problem of skilled labor supply was more pressing for American employers than it was for Europeans. Table 4.2 reports data on nominal wages for a variety of different occupations in Birmingham, England, and Pittsburgh, Pennsylvania, in 1905 originally assembled by Peter Shergold, along with the

premia took place between World War I and the early 1920s. See Goldin and Katz (1999, p. 6).

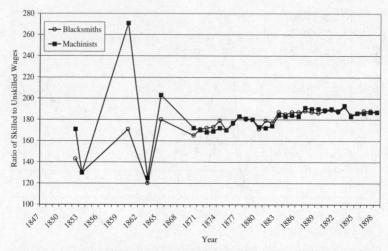

Figure 4.4   Ratio of Skilled to Unskilled Wages in the Metal-Working Trades, Chicago, 1850–1898. *Source*: David (1987, p. 88).

ratio of wages in each occupation to those of unskilled laborers. In every instance, this ratio was larger in Pittsburgh than in Birmingham. Moreover, using the level of wages in Pittsburgh as a rough guide to the level of skill embodied in different occupations, the gap in skill premia between the two cities was largest for the most skilled occupations and smallest for those requiring the least skill.

One might be suspicious of comparisons based on just two cities at a single point in time. But the picture that emerges from other data sources is consistent with Shergold's findings. Between 1905 and 1910, the British Board of Trade collected wage data from a large number of American and European cities and towns to make comparisons with comparable occupations in Britain. Although the range of occupations included in this study is narrower than that represented in the data gathered by Shergold, the results again clearly show that skilled workers in the United States earned considerably more in comparison to unskilled workers than was true of their European counterparts. Table 4.3 reports skill premia for the United States, Britain, Belgium, Germany, and France calculated from the data gathered by the British Board of Trade. Because the Board of Trade did not report a wage for unskilled laborers in the building trades, I have compared wages of skilled

Table 4.2. *Occupational Wage Ratios in Birmingham, England, and Pittsburgh, Pennsylvania, 1905*

	Pittsburgh		Birmingham		
Occupation	Hourly wage (cents/hour)	Skill premium	Hourly wage (cents/hour)	Skill premium	Ratio of skill premia (U.S./Britain)
Steel mill laborer	15.5	1.00	9.9	1.00	1.00
Baker, third hand	18.5	1.19	10.3	1.04	1.15
Baker, second hand	21.5	1.39	11.5	1.16	1.19
Baker, first hand	27.7	1.79	13.7	1.38	1.29
Building laborer	29.9	1.93	13.7	1.38	1.39
Foundry blacksmith	29.0	1.87	11.7	1.18	1.58
Bookbinder	30.6	1.97	15.0	1.52	1.30
Machinist	31.6	2.04	16.5	1.67	1.22
Boilermaker	33.4	2.15	17.5	1.77	1.22
Pattern maker	36.3	2.34	17.5	1.77	1.32
Machine woodworker	39.2	2.53	17.3	1.75	1.45
Painter	42.6	2.75	17.3	1.75	1.57
Carpenter	43.8	2.83	19.3	1.95	1.45
Plumber	50.0	3.23	19.3	1.95	1.65
Stone mason	55.0	3.55	20.3	2.05	1.73
Plasterer	56.3	3.63	20.3	2.05	1.77
Compositor, newspaper	58.6	3.78	22.8	2.30	1.64
Bricklayer	63.1	4.07	19.3	1.95	2.09

Note: The skill premium shows the ratio of wages in each occupation to those of steel mill laborers in the same city.
Source: Shergold (1983, p. 82).

workers in this industry to those of hod carriers – a semiskilled occupation.

In three of the four building trades occupations represented, skill premia in the United States were substantially higher than in all the European countries represented. Only carpenters and joiners appear to have enjoyed no advantage in the United States. Among the skilled trades in engineering, skill premia for both blacksmiths and pattern makers were higher in the United States

Table 4.3. *Ratios of Skilled to Semiskilled and Unskilled Wages in the United States and Selected European Countries, 1905–1910*

Occupational comparison	United States	Britain	Belgium	Germany	France
Skilled building trades (relative to hod carriers or bricklayer laborers)					
Bricklayers	1.98	1.52	1.36	1.34	1.41
Stonemasons	1.74	1.49	1.51		1.62
Carpenters and joiners	1.34	1.47	1.38[a]	1.34	1.52[a]
Plasterers	1.85	1.52	1.37		1.48
Skilled engineering trades (relative to engineering laborers)					
Fitters	1.71	1.70	1.46	1.45	1.52
Turners	1.71	1.70	1.54	1.50	1.57
Blacksmiths	1.90	1.70	1.53	1.54	1.64
Pattern makers	2.06	1.80	1.49	1.39	1.59

Note: When occupational wages were reported as a range of values, I used the midpoints in calculating pay ratios. Although data for different countries refer to different years, the Board of Trade believed that changes in wage levels between these years would not affect comparisons.
[a] This ratio is for carpenters only.
Source: Great Britain, Board of Trade (1911), U.S. Department of Labor (1908, p. 349; 1909, p. 81; 1910, p. 621).

than in Britain, and the gap was even larger compared to the other countries included in the data. Wage premia for the two categories of machinists – fitters and turners – represented in the data were above those in Belgium, Germany, and France, but equal to those in Britain. The relatively low skill premia for American machinists may be explained, however, by the much more extensive division of labor in work performed by this class of artisans in the United States than in Europe. The authors of the Board of Trade study noted that because of the subdivision of engineering labor in the United States they had difficulty finding workers in the United States whose skills were comparable to those of British workers in these occupations.

It is also possible to make some more limited comparisons for 1890 using data gathered by the U.S. Department of Labor through correspondence with officials in several European countries. These are reported in Table 4.4. Again, these data indicate that skill premia in the United States were generally greater than in Europe. The ratios of skilled to unskilled wages in the building trades were

Table 4.4. *Ratios of Skilled to Unskilled Wages in the United States, Britain, France, and Belgium, 1890*

Skilled occupation	U.S. Northeast	U.S. North Central	France (Paris)	Belgium (Liege)	Britain (Manchester)
Building trades					
Bricklayers	2.83	2.75	1.70		1.54
Carpenters	1.81	1.64	1.61	1.50	
Foundries and machine shops					
Blacksmiths	1.33	1.41	1.62	1.50	
Iron molders	1.76	1.75	1.35	1.33	

Source: France and Belgium from U.S. Department of Labor (1898); Manchester, bricklayers' wages from U.S. Department of Labor (1898), unskilled wages from Allen (1994). U.S. wage data from calculations in Coelho and Shepherd (1979) based on wage data from the Aldrich Report; and Sundstrom and Rosenbloom (1993) based on U.S. Department of Commerce and Labor (1905).

considerably higher in the United States than in any of the European countries represented. Similarly, the ratio of iron molders, wages to those of unskilled workers was higher in the United States, though the relative wage of blacksmiths appears to have been lower in the United States than in Europe.

APPRENTICESHIP, TRAINING, AND THE SUPPLY OF SKILLED LABOR

With relative wages rising and the labor force share of skilled workers essentially constant, it appears that the aggregate supply of skilled workers was relatively less elastic than that of unskilled workers. What explains this difference? Apparently – given the international differences in skill premia noted earlier – international migration was more effective at mobilizing unskilled than skilled labor. Compounding this problem, the institutions that might have facilitated the training of skilled craft workers domestically were weak or nonexistent in nineteenth-century America. The lack of effective apprenticeship institutions in the United States contrasts sharply with the situation in Britain, where well-developed union apprenticeship programs provided a much more abundant supply of skilled workers.[11] Traditional apprenticeship involving a period of indenture had never strongly taken root in the United States (Elbaum 1989). Even in those industries where craft skills continued to be important, apprenticeship was in decline by the late-nineteenth century. By the 1890s, according to Jackson (1984, p. 225), "most of the men who became journeymen carpenters had not served a regular apprenticeship." Although trade-union ideology advocated formal apprenticeship as a means of controlling the supply of skilled craftsmen, by 1890 only a minority (16.5 percent) of trade unions regulated apprenticeship at the national or international level. In most of the trades where unions did restrict the number of apprentices per journeyman, so few apprentices were employed that very few of the restrictions were binding (Bemis 1891).

Quantitative evidence about apprenticeship is scarce, and international comparisons are problematic, but the magnitude of the differences is so large that it is hard to dismiss.[12] For the United States, data collected as part of the population census indicate that after 1880 just over 1 percent of manufacturing and mechanical workers were employed as apprentices. In comparison, data for Germany suggest that in the late-nineteenth and early-twentieth centuries roughly 8 percent of manufacturing workers were apprentices. For Britain at this time, data are available only for engineering trades. As of 1914, slightly more than 15 percent of employees in these trades were apprentices. Even if apprenticeship levels for the economy as a whole were only half this amount, apprenticeship would still have been vastly more important in Britain than in the United States.[13]

Table 4.5 provides more disaggregated data drawn from a survey conducted by the New York State Bureau of Labor Statistics (1909) for a report on industrial training.[14] In all but one industry

[11] See Gospel (1992, p. 8) and Hanagan (1997) for additional evidence suggesting that the British apprenticeship system tended to create a much more abundant supply of traditionally skilled workers than was true elsewhere.

[12] Broadberry (1997, pp. 110–17) reported and discussed the comparative data for the United States, Britain, and Germany that form the basis for this paragraph.

[13] For the post–World War II period, the percentage of apprentices in all manufacturing was about two-thirds that for the engineering trades.

[14] The New York survey is probably biased in a number of ways, but two of the most important biases in the reports on apprenticeship might offset each other. First, the survey is for the state of New York, which being an older industrial center

Table 4-5. *Apprenticeship and Training in New York Industries, 1907–1908*

| | Employment characteristics | | | | Survey responses[a] | |
Industry	Number of establishments	Total employment	Percentage female	Percentage employing apprentices	Percentage for whom apprentices met skilled labor needs[b]	Percentage for whom a majority of skilled employees trained in establishment
Glass products	22	4,179	5.3	31.8	36.4	59.1
Metals, machines, conveyances	285	110,762	5.6	37.5	27.1	49.8
Wood manufactures	103	17,902	2.0	27.2	35.7	52.4
Leather and leather goods	47	14,182	32.7	0.0[c]	NA	55.4
Printing and paper goods	135	26,222	37.5	50.4	41.4	47.8
Textiles	114	52,554	57.1	0.0[c]	NA	71.1
Clothing, millinery, etc.	242	53,317	65.4	7.4	34.6	44.9
Cigars and confectionery	31	12,625	65.0	0.0[c]	NA	58.3
Building industry	197	26,189	0.0	43.1	34.0	5.6

[a] Percentage of establishments.
[b] Of those establishments responding that they employ apprentices.
[c] No response to question reported by these industries
Source: New York State Bureau of Labor Statistics (1909, pp. 2–29).

represented in the survey, apprentices were employed by a minority of establishments. Moreover, even among the minority of employers answering the questions about apprenticeship, fewer than half felt that apprenticeship met their needs for skilled workers. Even in a traditional craft-oriented industry like construction, only 43 percent of establishments employed apprentices. Apprenticeship was especially rare in industries employing large numbers of women.

Still, it cannot be concluded from the New York survey that apprenticeship was irrelevant by 1908. In the production of blown glass, machinery, pianos, lithography, and some of the building trades, apprentices were still used in fairly large numbers (see also Stephens 1911). Moreover, the views of individual employers that apprenticeship failed to meet their needs for skilled workers is not a complete assessment of the system given that many trained apprentices probably left their original employers for jobs with other firms. A reasonable summary of these findings would be that apprenticeship continued to be a significant source of supply of trained workers in a select group of craft occupations that was of declining proportional significance in the American labor force.

Various theories have been advanced to explain the weakness of apprenticeship in the United States. Elbaum (1989) argued that apprenticeship never gained the customary acceptance among employers in the United States that it did in Britain because the high degree of geographic mobility in America made indentured apprenticeship contracts almost impossible to enforce.[15] According to this line of reasoning, differences in external conditions led to

and more heavily unionized than average, may have had a stronger apprenticeship system than elsewhere in the United States. Second, the survey tended to select the larger establishments in the state, which may have been less traditional in their organization and more reliant on semiskilled or specialized production workers.

[15] See also Douglas (1921). Erickson (1984) also stressed the difficulty of enforcing indentures in the American setting as an explanation of the failure of contract labor arrangements in the nineteenth century. Hamilton's (2000) study of apprenticeship contracts in Montreal provides additional evidence that the difficulty of enforcing contracts was an important factor in the decline of apprenticeship. In particular, she finds that the decline in contract numbers coincided with shifts in the length of contracts and the structure of pay for apprentices that indicate that masters were becoming increasingly concerned about the risk that apprentices would break their contracts before their completion.

divergent patterns of recruitment and training that might be described as alternative equilibria. In Britain, the preference of firms for workers whose skills were certified by documentation that they had completed their apprenticeship indenture raised the value of this credential and thus made it extremely costly for apprentices to leave before they had completed their training. This disincentive to mobility in turn allowed employers to invest substantial resources in training with the knowledge that they would be able to recoup this investment before the trainee left. In the United States, however, high rates of geographic mobility led employers to discount formal credentials and rely more heavily on other criteria to assess a worker's abilities. As a result, the value of completing one's indenture declined, reducing the incentives that kept trainees in place. With little assurance that apprentices would serve out their indentures, employers had little to guarantee that their investments in training would be recovered. As Stanley Lebergott (1984, p. 372) observed, "workers' incessant mobility made it thoroughly unwise for any employer to invest much in training his employees. Why train workers who could, and did, quit at any time, thus walking off with their employers' investment in training?"

Recently Jacoby (1991a) suggested that even though American courts were willing to enforce apprenticeship agreements by forcing apprentices to finish their terms, employers were reluctant to enter legal apprenticeship contracts because they could interfere with their ability to dismiss at will. This argument emphasizes employers' desire for flexibility in responding to temporary declines in demand. But such a strategy could only make sense if employers were confident that they could once again hire workers with the requisite skills when demand conditions improved. Implicitly, then, Jacoby's interpretation reflects another channel through which the relatively high mobility of workers in the United States may have discouraged investment in formal training programs.

After 1900, the view that traditional apprenticeship was not meeting the country's need for trained workers spurred a growing interest in vocational education and the "new apprenticeship" (Nelson 1975; Douglas 1921; Jacoby 1991b). According to Douglas's (1921) survey of the range of programs and institutions involved in vocational education – manual training in high schools, specialized trade schools, and so-called corporation schools set up within business firms – none had achieved much quantitative significance prior to World War I. Indeed, Douglas notes that such programs as the corporation schools encountered problems similar to those associated with traditional apprenticeship in the United States: the difficulty of the firm reaping a return on its investment in general training given the interfirm mobility of employees. Douglas does not explain why firms were unable or unwilling to impose this cost on their trainees, as the model of human capital accumulation would predict, but informational asymmetries or capital-market imperfections seem likely to have made it difficult or risky for trainees to foot the bill.[16]

If the weakness of apprenticeship and training programs restricted expansion of the supply of skilled workers in the United States, one alternative was to import workers with the desired skills from Europe. As we have already seen, there is evidence that American employers did sometimes recruit skilled labor overseas. But the same conditions that discouraged employers from investing in training workers would also have discouraged investment in locating and transporting workers across the Atlantic. Once skilled workers entered the United States, they might be recruited away by other employers who could afford to offer them higher wages because they did not have to recoup the additional costs of recruitment and transportation. In the early 1880s, for example, the Pepperell Company attempted to recruit weavers from Glasgow, Scotland, for its plant in Biddeford, Maine. Although an initial group of 19 women worked out well, the next group proved to be less skilled than the first, and 20 men soon departed for jobs at other mills (Erickson 1957, p. 38).

An additional factor discouraging efforts to import skilled labor was the divergence of American and European manufacturing techniques. As the next section describes, many American employers responded to skilled labor scarcity by increasing the subdivision of labor and introducing more capital-intensive production processes. While these measures made it easier for employers to use

---

[16] Elbaum (1989, p. 343) offered some evidence of the size of the investments in training that British apprenticeship programs required and argued that these costs would have been difficult for trainees to finance.

semiskilled workers, they reduced the relevance of skills acquired in Europe and hence the value of workers possessing these skills for American employers.

TECHNOLOGICAL CHANGE, ON-THE-JOB TRAINING, AND INTERNAL LABOR MARKETS

Faced with rising costs for traditional types of skilled labor, many American employers opted to redesign their production processes, either through the purchase of capital equipment that substituted for certain types of skilled workers or by adopting a finer division of labor that allowed them to make use of less-skilled workers. In the first half of the nineteenth century, American makers of small arms pioneered these techniques in developing a distinctive American system of manufacturing. In the second half of the century, their methods were diffused much more widely as a consequence of the technological convergence of production techniques across a broad array of precision manufacturing activities (Hounshell 1984; Rosenberg 1976, ch. 1).

Among the manufacturers adopting these solutions in the late-nineteenth century was the Baldwin locomotive works, located in Philadelphia. To meet growing demand, Baldwin's production managers redesigned production processes to reduce dependence on craft skills, by increasing reliance on standardized parts and subdividing labor. As John K. Brown (1995, p. 129) noted in his recent study of the company, "although many jobs still required skilled hand and machine work, locomotive building had been so carved up into specialized tasks that most workers were essentially industrial operatives rather than craftsmen." Labor market concerns were a central factor motivating changes in the production process. "With work tasks narrowed and divided under piecework," Brown (1995, pp. 143–4) wrote, "Baldwin found it easier to take on men quickly during market rebounds, since many new workers needed only a specialized competence."

There can be little question that many of the production technologies introduced in this period did have the effect of reducing the relative employment of workers possessing traditional craft skills. But the effect of these reductions was offset partially or completely by capacity expansion. For example, at the Baldwin locomotive works, employment increased from around 1,000 men in 1866 to 3,500 in 1896, and then to over 18,000 by 1907. Rather than reducing Baldwin's reliance on skilled labor, the changes in the organization of production made the company more dependent on a core of skilled workers, who were kept on even in lean times, while less-skilled workers bore the brunt of fluctuations in the firm's labor demand (Brown 1995, pp. 130, 144–5). Moreover, the aggregate evidence on employment and wages reviewed earlier makes clear that at the economy-wide, level the demand for skilled labor was stable or rising relatively, not declining.[17] That overall demand for skilled workers was rising does not refute the argument that many employers were motivated to introduce new technologies because of their desire to gain a greater degree of control over the production process, but it does suggest that this desire is best seen as an endogenous response to the high and rising costs of reliance on skilled labor, rather than as an exogenous cause of technological innovation.[18]

Technological changes that reduced the relative skill intensity of production moderated increases in the demand for some skilled craft workers, but these very changes in skill requirements and job definitions only worsened the problem of labor scarcity among newer categories of skilled or semiskilled labor.[19] Employers in

[17] More narrowly focused studies provide additional support for this conclusion. In coal mining, for example, between 1890 and 1900, machine-cut coal increased from 6 percent to 25 percent of output. However, because of the extensive growth of the industry the amount of hand-cut coal actually increased by close to 50 percent, and the number of skilled pick miners in West Virginia – the center of bituminous coal mining – continued to increase until 1909. Not until 1919, when fully 72 percent of coal was mined by machine, did the number of pick miners fall to its 1900 level (Fishback, personal communication).

[18] That some skilled workers bore significant costs of adjustment as a result of being displaced by new technologies is beyond doubt, but it is apparent that in aggregate the demand for skilled workers was increasing. Such a situation is entirely consistent with the considerable labor conflict evident in this period, since employers' efforts to reduce their dependence on inelastically supplied skilled labor threatened to reduce scarcity rents that were reflected in the relative high wages of skilled workers, and no doubt also helped to increase uncertainty among skilled workers about their future employment prospects and control over the shop floor.

[19] The lack of formal training programs for factory operatives should not lead us to conclude that these positions did not require substantial investments in human capital. On-the-job training of factory workers is most clearly evident in rising

large-scale manufacturing industries found that technological innovations and the subdivision of labor required constant adjust-
ments of task assignments and qualifications. The rapidity of the
changes did not allow sufficient time for standardized occupational
markets to emerge. This lack of standardization may well have exacerbated problems encountered in trying to fill skilled positions
through external recruitment.

The nature of the problem was well described by Weyl and
Sakolski (1906, p. 694) in a survey of the conditions of entrance
into skilled jobs in a variety of industries:

Occupations have multiplied so rapidly and the gradations of skill and
workmanship have become so numerous and imperceptible that it is
frequently exceedingly difficult, if not impossible, to specify the distin-
guishing marks and characteristics which separate one group of workers
from another.

Such ambiguities had serious repercussions for trade unions, lead-
ing to jurisdictional disputes and difficulties in defining qualifications for membership. But of greater importance here is how
employers designed institutions to increase the supply of workers
to these new positions.

The logical solution was on-the-job training within the firm,
usually coupled with some form of internal promotion.[20] As
Doeringer and Piore (1985) point out, the provision of on-the-
job training is an important function of modern internal labor
markets, so it is hardly surprising that the need for training motivated the early development of such institutions in American

levels of output per worker with increasing job tenure. The length of such training
periods was relatively short compared to traditional apprenticeship programs,
but the value of this investment gauged by the foregone output during training
could be quite large. Because much of this investment was specific to a particular
plant and production process, it was financed largely by employers rather than
workers, with the result that employers rather than workers retained much of
the revenue resulting from the increase in productivity. See James Bessen (2000)
for a discussion of the nature of factory skills and calculations of the value of
investments in human capital in the New England textile industry at mid-century.
Although I am unaware of any comparable calculations for other industries or
time periods, much of what he finds seems likely to apply more generally.

[20] Informal, on-the-job training continues to be the most important mode of skill
acquisition for blue-collar workers in the modern U.S. economy (U.S. Department
of Labor 1985).

industries.[21] On-the-job training took advantage of the stock of skills acquired by existing workers and supervisors, who helped with the training, and it could be tailored to firm-specific technologies and task assignments. Even when the skills acquired were general, the establishment of internal labor markets may have been necessary for firms to finance workers' training in the absence of apprenticeship institutions. Promoting workers from within also gave the firm the chance to screen diligent and trustworthy candidates for its more important positions, including supervisory positions.

Railroads were among the first businesses to confront the problem of rapidly expanding demand for nontraditional categories of skilled labor during the nineteenth century, and among the first to adopt internal promotion systems to train skilled workers. In the early phases of railroad growth, engineers and mechanics were recruited from among skilled workers in related industries – especially machine building. In the earliest railroading days in New England, for example, most locomotive engineers were recruited from among the most skilled and reliable shop mechanics (Minnesota Bureau of Labor 1895, p. 326). Locomotive manufacturers frequently provided engineers to drive and repair the engines they sold (Licht 1983, p. 41). Over the ensuing decades, however, as operations became regularized and the work involved more routine, a more detailed division of labor emerged, with locomotive engineers specializing in engine driving and being held responsible for fewer and fewer repair tasks on their trains. Under these technological and organizational conditions, "what was essential for an engineer to know could be learned 'on the footboard' itself" (Stromquist 1987, p. 105). Spurred by the desire to increase the supply of engineers and reduce wage pressures, the railroads adopted a system whereby engineers were promoted from the ranks of the firemen (Stromquist 1983,

---

[21] According to Doeringer and Piore (1985, ch. 3), modern internal labor markets are characterized by three distinct but interrelated elements: (1) labor allocation takes place within the firm in the form of promotion, often along predetermined job ladders, and ports of entry into the firm may be limited to certain entry-level positions; (2) workers enjoy considerable job security, and employment relationships are often long term; and (3) the employment relationship is governed by impersonal, bureaucratic rules and procedures.

pp. 494–6).[22] Describing the response of the Galena and Chicago Union Railroad to demand pressures in the 1850s, one contemporary wrote:

Master mechanics everywhere found it necessary to promote firemen to be engineers as fast as they could possibly be trusted to serve as runners; they did not call them engineers; about all they needed to know was to tell the difference between the sound of steam and of water as they opened the gauge cocks to find out how much water there was in the boiler. (glass water gauges were then unknown.) (Quoted in David 1987, p. 66.)

By 1873, the job ladder on the locomotive led from fireman to engineer in "90 percent" of the cases, although there remained holdouts for the old system of promoting mechanics (Richardson 1963, p. 154).[23] In the "train service," a parallel job ladder emerged, along which conductors typically were recruited from the ranks of the brakemen.

In manufacturing industries, on-the-job training usually took the form of assigning new recruits to be assistants or "helpers" of more skilled workers, or by starting learners on simple operations and moving them through a sequence of more demanding positions as they gained experience. The latter system evolved into fairly standardized job ladders in a number of industries. Outside of transportation and manufacturing, little is known about internal labor markets, but it is possible that promotion along internal job ladders developed early, especially in large financial, trading, and utilities firms. Carter and Carter (1985), for example, described the development of internal labor markets in New York retailing before World War I.

The helper system increasingly took the place of formal apprenticeship in many industries. For example, in machinery and engine construction, traditionally bastions of skilled machinists who trained apprentices, advances in metal-working machinery and the

---

[22] A partial exception to this pattern occurred in the South, where black workers were frequently employed as firemen and brakemen but were prohibited from advancing to engineer or conductor.

[23] In practice, the promotion path was somewhat more complex, as engineers typically started on freight trains and were promoted to passenger service only after acquiring additional experience.

factory division of labor reduced skill requirements and encouraged the growth of the helper system. Even in the job and repair shops, where the highest skills were still required, the helper system supplanted the old apprenticeship system. Although "all highly skilled workers were supposed to have passed through an apprenticeship," the New York Bureau of Labor Statistics (1909, p. 56) found that in many shops, "as a matter of fact the class is largely recruited from the ablest and brightest of the machine hands or helpers."[24]

A similar pattern was apparent in the building trades. For example, in carpentry, the widespread use of prefabricated components produced in woodworking factories helped to reduce the need for all-round skills. Meanwhile, the growing size of construction companies meant that employers were less likely to work alongside their employees and, thus, were reluctant to take on the traditional responsibilities of training new workers. The decline of apprenticeship is apparent in census statistics, which show that by 1890 the number of apprentice carpenters was far below that needed to replace those who would leave the profession within the next five years. Most journeymen carpenters instead had received their training informally, beginning as helpers in small, nonunion firms engaged in residential construction (Jackson 1984, pp. 225–7).

Another alternative to the traditional apprenticeship involved an initial period of training on simpler or less-demanding machines, followed by promotion to journeyman status. This situation was common, for example, in the printing industry around the turn of the century. Weyl and Sakolski (1906, p. 769) reported that:

Under modern methods of running press rooms, . . . a number of years of practical work on small presses is essential for one desiring to take

---

[24] Because of their small size, the specialized nature of their products, and substantial fluctuations in demand, however, many machine shops were unable to fill skilled positions entirely through internal promotion and continued to rely to a large degree on external recruitment. The emergence of either union or employer association organized employment bureaus for machinery workers was one mechanism that helped to internalize some of the externalities associated with general training. By facilitating the movement of workers between shops within a locality, the bureau helped to retain an adequate pool of skilled labor, while also promoting the acquisition of a wider set of skills by exposing workers to a broader range of production problems. See Harris (1991).

charge of a rotary press and to perform the higher grades of work. Accordingly the young men who should be rated as apprentices in a press room are feeders and job pressmen, who attend the small presses or assist in the operation of large cylinder presses. When they have had sufficient experience and have proven themselves capable of taking charge of the operation of a large press, they can be promoted to this higher position.

In industries where there was a considerable division of labor and most jobs involved operating machines, workers could be expected to advance to more complex or difficult steps in the production process as they demonstrated their abilities. "Beginners are generally put first at the simpler operations," stated the New York Bureau of Labor Statistics (1909, p. 27), "and as they show ability and application are advanced to somewhat more difficult processes or the manipulation of less simple machines. This advancement may continue up to that particular point in the organization beyond which the capacities or ambition of the worker are not sufficient to carry him." According to the report, this "system of developing skilled workers" was quite common, especially in female-dominated trades such as clothing, millinery, and laundries and in boot, shoe, and textile manufacturing.[25]

In several industries where mass production technologies were quite advanced, the helper system had already evolved into formalized job ladders by the early-twentieth century. Production in the large Chicago packing houses, for example, was arranged in long, continuous-flow "disassembly lines." Tasks were specialized, and jobs were arranged in standard ladders. Novice "splitters" were low-skilled workers in the plant who had worked their way up and received their training by working alongside experienced main splitters; learners typically were given the smaller and hence easier animals to work on. Training for other jobs in the packing industry was often picked up by "go-betweens," lower-skilled workers who divided their time between their regular tasks and higher-paying jobs (Thompson 1907, pp. 90–1). For a brief period in 1902–3, the meat cutters' union succeeded in enforcing a strict promotion

---

[25] Dublin (1979, pp. 186–7) provided further detail on the early emergence of job ladders for female workers in textile mills.

ladder with an associated pay scale and seniority promotion, but the job ladder appears to have antedated these years (Commons 1904; Thompson 1907, p. 103). A similar association between the introduction of continuous-flow production and the introduction of job ladders is evident in the steel industry (Stone 1974; Elbaum 1984).

One of the best cases for the importance of machine-based, mass production technologies in the evolution of job ladders is made in Brown and Philips's (1985, 1986a, 1986b) studies of the canning industry. Their work also underscores the prominent part played by rising product demand and inelastic supplies of traditional skilled labor in initiating the introduction of machine-based production methods. In the face of rapidly growing demand for canned goods after the Civil War and a limited supply of skilled processing labor, skilled workers were able to capture scarcity rents, a fact reflected in the decline of the ratio of value added to wages from 4.97 in 1860 to 2.07 in 1880 (Brown and Philips 1986b, p. 748). These circumstances in turn precipitated the adoption of newly developed automated canning machinery. The new technology created several semiskilled positions for which workers "gradually accumulated skills and knowledge through incremental, on-the-job training" (Brown and Philips 1986a, p. 134). Although in principle the skills thus learned were applicable throughout the industry, Brown and Philips argue that an employer could only gauge the level of a worker's skill through direct observation – hence the skills were not readily transferred between firms.

Some general quantitative evidence on the importance of internal training during the decade preceding World War I is provided in reports on industrial training prepared by the New York and Iowa State Bureaus of Labor Statistics analyzed by William Sundstrom (1988). More than half the establishments responding to the New York bureau's survey in 1907–8 said that internal training and recruitment supplied at least half of their skilled workers. Only in the building industry was internal training of negligible importance. A similar survey conducted in Iowa in 1913–14 found that only about a third of firms recruited their highly skilled workers from within the firm, but that over 60 percent recruited supervisory employees from within (Sundstrom 1988). Of course, training for many tasks was not necessarily a long-term project. In many industries, attaining a low-grade operative's skills required only 6 months to 3 years, but attaining high-grade skills more typically required 3 to 6 years (New York Bureau of Labor Statistics 1909, pp. 8–11).

As with more traditional skills, on-the-job training required institutions or contracts that would provide both employers and workers with reasonable assurance that they would receive a return on their investment. To the extent that training was general, employers needed to keep the trainees around long enough to recover any training costs incurred. To the extent that training was firm specific, both parties could benefit from a long-term employment relationship in which they would share firm-specific rents. As the example of the canning industry suggests, the firm specificity of a semiskilled worker's skills may have had more to do with information about the worker's effort and reliability than with his or her actual ability to perform certain tasks.

Formal regulation of internal labor markets by personnel departments and union contracts was uncommon before World War I (Jacoby 1985; Baron, Dobbin, and Jennings 1986). But the worker's anticipation of promotion and the employer's desire to retain trained workers may have provided enough glue to keep the two parties together for an extended period. This situation was certainly true at the Baldwin locomotive works, where a core group of the most skilled workers was kept on regardless of short-term fluctuations in the firm's production (Brown 1995, pp. 144–5). Evidence on job duration in this era is far from complete. Nonetheless, it seems likely that although employment relationships were shorter in the late-nineteenth century than they are today, a significant minority of workers did have relatively long job tenures with a single employer. Table 4.6 reports one set of comparisons assembled by Jacoby and Sharma (1992) for selected industries in 1913–14 and 1973. Illustrating the lengthening of job tenures, the number of workers in their present job less than 1 year dropped substantially, and the number in their jobs five years or more increased between

Table 4.6. *Length of Censored Job Spells, 1913–1914 and 1973*

Year	Manufacturing	Machinery	Metals	Chemicals	Textiles and apparel
Percent of (censored) job spells over 5 years					
1913–1914	31	32	32	10	51
1973	49	48	24	55	44
Percent of (censored) job spells under 1 Year					
1913–1914	38	37	24	64	15
1973	22	22	18	16	25

Note: The title of the lower half of the table is corrected following Fishback (1998, p. 727). For 1913–14, the data come from a sample of 45,791 workers in 40 manufacturing establishments.
Source: Jacoby and Sharma (1992, pp. 173–4).

these dates. On the other hand, even in 1913–14, 31 percent of manufacturing workers were in jobs that had lasted at least five years.[26]

That 31 percent of manufacturing workers in 1913–14 were in jobs that had lasted at least five years is striking evidence of the importance of long-term jobs even at this date. Yet the figure might have been even higher had the industrial labor force been less transient. High rates of European immigration were important in facilitating external recruitment but they also created a labor force composed of workers with limited interest in long-term jobs (Piore 1979, pp. 149–54). In its 1911 report, the Immigration Commission concluded that many immigrant workers:

have no intention of permanently changing their residence, their only purpose in coming to America being to temporarily take advantage of the greater wages paid for industrial labor in this country. This, of course, is not true of all the new immigrants, but the practice is sufficiently common to warrant referring to it as a characteristic of them as a class. From all data that are available, it appears that nearly 40 per cent of the new immigration movement returns to Europe and that about two-thirds of those who go remain there (U.S. Congress, Senate 1911, vol. 1, p. 24).

[26] For additional evidence and discussion, see Sundstrom (1986, ch. 3), Carter and Savoca (1990), and James (1994).

Quantitative evidence on return migration is incomplete, but for 1908–10, the Commission found that, for every 100 European immigrants, there were 32 European emigrants returning to their homeland. The close correlation of arrivals and departures of Europeans with each other and with the business cycle further confirms the transience of the immigrant labor force, since the increase in departures during good times indicates that departures were not the result of difficulty finding work but rather reflected the fact that immigrants had not intended to stay in the first place.[27]

Given the up-front costs of on-the-job training, it seems likely that the low attachment of immigrant workers was an important factor inhibiting employers' efforts to introduce production methods that relied more heavily on such training. By cutting off both the influx of new workers and eliminating the possibility of return migration, World War I initiated a significant shift in the composition of the labor force that altered employers' calculations about the costs and benefits of investments in training. By the 1920s, American workers were, in Gavin Wright's (1987a, p. 335) words, "more mature, more experienced, more American, more educated, more stable geographically, and above all more committed to industrial work as a career than ever before."[28] With a more stable and committed labor force, investments that previously appeared uneconomic would have become profitable. It is thus hardly surprising that employers for the first time began to centralize personnel decisions, formalize labor relations policies,

[27] More direct, but necessarily less comprehensive, evidence is available from surviving letters written by immigrants. Summarizing information from letters of immigrant steelworkers, historian David Brody (1960, pp. 97–8) wrote: "From the peasant viewpoint the longer move to America differed from seasonal migration only in degree.... A Polish immigrant expected to 'remain for some years and return with something to our country so that later we might not be obliged to earn [as hired laborers].'... The immigrant hoped to earn a stake and return to his village." Similarly, Charlotte Erickson (1972, p. 236) observed: "The new, more economically oriented immigrants did not go to the United States with the fixed intention of staying there. Even among those who did remain, the possibility of returning to Britain constituted an active alternative choice for a long time."

[28] One quantitative indication of this shift is the drop in worker turnover between the 1910s and 1920s, which was driven largely by a fall in quit rates. Between 1910 and 1914, turnover rates per 100 manufacturing workers ranged from about 90 to over 130. Throughout the 1920s, they were below their minimum prewar level, and by 1928, they had fallen to just 37.1. See Brissenden and Frankel (1920) and Berridge (1929).

and introduce incentives to reward long-term employees (Slichter 1929).

The internal labor markets of turn-of-the-century American firms were largely nonbureaucratic, leaving most personnel decisions in the hands of foremen and shop supervisors (Nelson 1975).[29] Jacoby (1985) argued that dissatisfaction with this "foreman's empire" on the part of workers and reformers eventually led employers to adopt centralized personnel management rules and departments, but only under pressure from unions and government. Such a view is, however, difficult to square with evidence of relatively slack labor markets during the 1920s. More plausibly, the formalization of employment practices at this time seems to have codified preexisting informal practices, while the greater emphasis on training and retaining workers was made possible by the greater commitment of the labor force to industrial work. Indeed, it may have been precisely because workers had come to expect a reasonably long-term job with prospects of advancement that they increasingly resented the insecurity and arbitrariness associated with the foreman's empire.

SUPPLY, DEMAND, AND THE INSTITUTIONAL STRUCTURE OF SKILLED LABOR MARKETS

As the American economy expanded in the half century after the Civil War, employers repeatedly confronted the problem of labor recruitment. Even though many employers were able to meet their needs for skilled labor by hiring it on external markets, the relative inelasticity of skilled labor in the aggregate prompted many of them to pursue alternative approaches to meeting their labor requirements. In particular, employers looked to an increased division of labor and new manufacturing technologies that substituted capital for traditional skills. Although this course moderated demand, the wage data suggest that it was insufficient to eliminate

---

[29] A notable exception to this generalization is provided by the railroads, which by the turn of the century operated with highly bureaucratic internal labor markets, often regulated by union contracts, where official seniority rules and formal examinations played important roles in promotions and dismissals. See Licht (1983), Richardson (1963), and Mater (1940).

the problem. In addition, new production technologies did not so much eliminate the demand for skills as shift it to new categories of semiskilled operatives. Because the skills required by these operatives were specific to particular production processes and plants, technological innovation was accompanied by a rise in the importance of on-the-job training and internal promotion schemes. Investments in training were, of course, practical only if trained workers could be retained long enough for their increased productivity to repay the initial outlay involved in their training. Despite high rates of turnover, some workers do appear to have forged the sort of longer term attachments that would justify investment in training. Although these developments were rarely accompanied by the introduction of formal, bureaucratic employment management, the foundations were nonetheless being laid for the post–World War I development of full-fledged internal labor markets.

5

ONE MARKET OR MANY? INTERCITY AND INTERREGIONAL LABOR MARKET INTEGRATION

Between the Civil War and World War I, the effects of emancipation in the South, ongoing transportation improvements, the continuing process of western settlement, increasing urbanization, and industrialization combined to produce a spatially unbalanced pattern of economic growth in the United States. The previous chapters have examined how labor market institutions developed in response to the resulting imbalances between the supply of and the demand for labor. This chapter examines wage and earnings data to provide an assessment of how well these institutions worked in promoting geographic mobility and creating a broad, geographically integrated labor market.

Based on a broad range of evidence, it appears that the market institutions that emerged in response to American industrialization produced a remarkable but uneven expansion of labor market boundaries. By the 1880s, cities throughout the Northeast and Midwest were part of a single, effectively unified market. This market was, in turn, closely linked to labor markets in northern Europe. A parallel process of integration is also apparent between the eastern and western regions of the American South. Yet, interregional and international market integration coincided with the persistent isolation of northern and southern labor markets from one another.

The message of this chapter is twofold. First, markets worked well. As economic theory suggests, competitive forces created strong pressures toward wage equalization. Presented with opportunities for spatial arbitrage between regions with relatively abundant labor and regions with relatively scarce labor, market participants developed effective institutions to mobilize labor. But, second, the geographic scope within which these institutional responses took place was not determined solely by economic forces. Rather it reflected the continuing imprint of temporally remote events of the eighteenth century that had divided the country between slave and free states. Not until the interruption of European mass migration caused by the onset of World War I were the barriers separating northern and southern labor markets effectively bridged.

THE MEANING AND MEASUREMENT OF MARKET INTEGRATION

The function of a market is to bring together sources of supply and demand. The efficiency that economists attribute to market processes of allocation thus depends critically on the formation of channels of communication linking employers and job seekers as well as mechanisms to facilitate the movement of job seekers in response to employment opportunities. Because it is difficult to measure directly the information and transactions costs associated with the institutions through which the market operates, research on market integration must proceed indirectly. Most tests of market integration are derived from the "law of one price," which states that within an integrated market, the free flow of information and labor will ensure that wages (for the same type of labor, employed under the same conditions) at different locations will "tend to equality easily and quickly."[1]

The relationship between wage equalization and market performance is most easily illustrated by reference to a relatively stylized model. Suppose that there are just two locations – for concreteness call them Philadelphia and Chicago. The upper panel of Figure 5.1 depicts the determination of wages and employment in both places as a result of the intersection of local labor supply

---

[1] Cournot, quoted in Marshall (1961, pp. 324–35). We need to hold constant the conditions under which the work is performed because workers seek to maximize their well-being, not their monetary earnings. Presumably, locations that offer more attractive conditions – better climate, lower risk of unemployment, and so on – would be preferred if wages were equal.

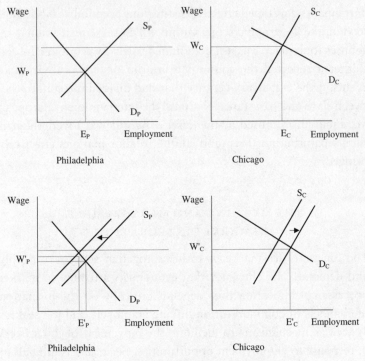

Figure 5.1   Wage determination in Two Cities.

and demand curves.[2] If each location were isolated from the other, then the labor market equilibrium in each place would be determined solely by local supply and demand conditions, and wages in the two cities would bear no necessary relationship to each other. If, on the other hand, workers can move between locations, then the level of wages in one city would influence those in the other. Denote the cost of moving between cities by C. This cost includes not only the direct expense of travel between places (e.g., railroad fares) but also a variety of indirect costs such as the expense of obtaining information about employment conditions, conducting a job search, and any transactions costs associated with financing the costs of movement.[3]

[2] I am assuming implicitly that there is just one, homogeneous, category of labor.
[3] If workers have an attachment to a particular location, either because of certain
     locational amenities or because they face psychic costs associated with moving
     to a new residence, then these would also be included in the movement cost
     variable, C.

If wages in Chicago exceed those in Philadelphia by an amount greater than C, then workers will move from low-wage Philadelphia to high-wage Chicago. As the lower panel of Figure 5.1 shows, this movement causes the supply curve to shift outward in Chicago and inward in Philadelphia. As a result, wages fall in Chicago and rise in Philadelphia. The movement of labor between the two locations will continue until the wage differential is equal to C. At this point, the geographic distribution of labor may be said to have reached an equilibrium. Migration thus constrains equilibrium wage differentials to be less than or equal to the costs of movement, C, between locations.

Having established what a spatial equilibrium looks like in our two-city example, we need to consider the observable consequences of two kinds of shocks that might occur: localized supply or demand disturbances and changes in the cost of movement between the two cities. First, consider the effects of a demand shock in Chicago. Beginning in equilibrium, with the differential between wages in Chicago and Philadelphia less than the cost of movement, C, suppose that the productivity of labor in Chicago rises for some reason. As a result, the demand for labor in Chicago would shift outward-causing the city's wage to rise. If the shock is small, the wage differential would still be less than C, and there would be no effect on the Philadelphia labor market. If, however, the wage gap between the cities increased sufficiently, the differential would be large enough to induce a movement of labor from Philadelphia. The resulting inward movement of the supply curve in Philadelphia and the corresponding outward shift of the supply curve in Chicago would cause wages to rise in Philadelphia and fall in Chicago. Migration and the resulting wage convergence would continue until the wage gap is reduced to the same size as the cost of movement, C. At this point, the markets have returned to spatial equilibrium, and there would be no more migration. Following the entire sequence, we would observe that wage movements in the two cities were positively correlated with one another. If, however, our initial observation is made after the demand shock, the movement of wages will be negatively correlated, as the reallocation of labor produces a convergence in wages.

Now consider the implications of an improvement in transportation or an institutional change in the labor market that reduced the transactions cost of movement between cities. If the cost of movement fell sufficiently, the existing wage differential would induce migration from Philadelphia to Chicago. As a result, wages would converge, and long-run variations in wages between the two cities would be constrained to fall within a narrower range than had been true before. In addition to reducing the absolute size of intercity wage differentials, a reduction in movement costs would, other things being equal, increase the correlation of wage movements across cities, since smaller local labor market shocks would induce migration between locations. Thus, as costs of movement fall and market integration rises, this fact should be reflected in both an increasing similarity of wage movements across locations and greater wage equalization. This observation suggests two alternative quantitative measures of integration. The first focuses on the correlation of wage movements across locations; the second concentrates on the magnitude of differences in wage levels between geographically distinct markets.[4]

Neither the convergence of wage levels across locations nor the strength of correlation of wage movements is an unambiguous measure of integration, however. Using the correlation of wage movements across locations requires relatively frequent observations on wages at different locations, data that are not always available. Moreover, it is possible to find spuriously high levels of correlation when imperfectly integrated markets are subjected to common disturbances, such as macroeconomic fluctuations or

[4] Historical studies have generally relied upon the criterion of price equalization. On labor market integration, see, for example, Lebergott (1964), Coelho and Shepherd (1976), Rothenberg (1988), Rosenbloom (1990, 1996), and Margo (2000); on financial markets see Davis (1965), Smiley (1975), and James (1978). Although Boyer and Hatton (1994) focused on the correlation of wage movements, most work using this criterion has been done in the context of contemporary studies of industrial organization. See, for example, Stigler and Sherwin (1985). Spiller and Huang (1986) used a switching regression model to estimate transaction costs between markets as a model parameter. Odell's (1989) study of the integration of financial markets in the late-nineteenth century suggested a method for combining data on the magnitude of wage differentials and the correlation of wage movements, but her approach would become unwieldy if applied to more than a small number of locations.

movements in the aggregate price level.[5] Another potential problem with using the correlation of wage movements arises because the observed level of correlation is likely to depend on the magnitude of the disturbances to which local markets are subjected. If local shocks produce only small wage movements, they are unlikely to result in wage differentials large enough to encourage migration and, hence, affect wages in other locations. Larger wage movements, on the other hand, are more likely to result in wage differentials large enough to encourage the movement of workers and, hence, influence wages in other places.

The use of wage differentials as a measure of integration is intuitively appealing because the equilibrium wage gap between locations can be interpreted as an upper-bound measure of movement costs at a point in time, and the convergence of wages over time would imply a reduction in these costs. The connection between wage convergence and increasing integration is not perfect, however, because, as we have seen, wages will also appear to converge as the market returns to equilibrium after a disequilibrating shock. Another potential complication that should be noted is the possibility that the balance of supply and demand conditions in two entirely isolated labor markets could produce the appearance of wage equalization despite the absence of any real linkage. Because of these ambiguities, there is no single conclusive measure of market integration. Instead, it is necessary to combine data on wages with the available evidence on labor force movements and other information to construct plausible inferences about the scope of labor market boundaries.

WAGE AND EARNINGS DIFFERENTIALS WITHIN THE UNITED STATES

During the late-nineteenth and early-twentieth centuries, a variety of government studies collected geographically disaggregated data

---

[5] In Rosenbloom (1988, pp. 83–96), I found that between 1870 and 1898 much of the correlation in year-to-year movements of wages across locations in the United States was the result of the common effects of macroeconomic fluctuations in output and prices.

on wages. Among the most important of these are the *Nineteenth Annual Report of the Commissioner of Labor* (U.S. Department of Commerce and Labor 1905) and the Weeks and Aldrich Reports (U.S. Congress, House of Representatives 1886; U.S. Congress, Senate 1892).[6] The data contained in these studies permit comparisons of wage rates across locations for specific occupations, thus controlling for potential heterogeneity in human capital and working conditions that could otherwise produce spurious variations. On the other hand, these data are limited in both their chronological and geographic coverage, as well as in the small size and possibly unrepresentative composition of the samples on which they rest. Wage data are available only for occupations sufficiently ubiquitous to be found in a large number of locations. Consequently, most of the wage quotations refer to skilled craft workers engaged in production for local markets. Even so, the available figures often rest on small samples of employers and workers and cover a restricted, and in some cases changing, sample of locations and years.[7]

The principal alternative to using occupational wage data is to use average factory earnings calculated from the censuses of manufacturers. Average factory earnings cover a much larger segment of the labor force and are available for 100 or more cities at each census date beginning in 1880. But because they are an average over possibly heterogeneous groups of workers, it is more difficult to control for the effects of labor force composition on wages.

Neither the wage nor earnings data are perfectly suited to evaluating the extent of market integration, but their imperfections are different, and both types of data point to substantially similar conclusions. Reflecting the more rapid pace of economic growth

---

[6] Another wage study reported in *Bulletin* 18 of the Department of Labor (U.S. Department of Labor 1898) provided annual observations on wages for a variety of occupations in 12 cities from 1870 through 1898, but the small size of the samples on which the results are based and the peculiar sampling framework, in which only firms that had been in existence for the entire period of the study were included in the data makes this source problematic. Although I used these data to analyze interregional real wage differentials in Rosenbloom (1990), subsequent comparison of the *Bulletin* 18 data with the other available data sources suggests that they may not accurately reflect trends in geographic wage differentials. See Rosenbloom (1996).

[7] See Long (1960, pp. 7–12) for further discussion of these sources.

in the North Central region, wages there remained higher than in the Northeast throughout the pre–World War I era. Although the East-West differential was relatively large as late as 1870, within the northern part of the country there was a very rapid convergence after this date. Viewed in conjunction with Robert Margo's (2000) recent work on wage differentials before the Civil War, this convergence suggests that a substantially unified labor market across the Northeast and North Central regions existed well before the end of the century. Wages in the Mountain and Pacific regions remained higher than those in the Northeast and North Central regions. Substantial population flows into this area suggest that these differentials did induce the expected supply response but that the existing institutional arrangements were inadequate to eliminate the wage gap in the face of the rapid growth of demand in the western regions of the country.

In the South, wage levels were generally below those in the North and were falling farther away from prevailing northern levels over time. As was true in the North, southern wages exhibited an East-West gap, with wages in the South Central well above those in the South Atlantic in the 1870s and 1880s. As a result, North-South wage differentials were largest for the South Atlantic region and smaller for the South Central region. Over time, however, there was a pronounced convergence between the two southern regions. Wages throughout the South declined relative to the North after 1870, resulting in a widening North-South wage gap at the same time that wages across the South were becoming more equal. Despite declining southern wages, rates of migration from the region remained extremely low until the 1910s (see Chapter 2). Thus, it appears that regional integration within the North and South coincided with the persistent isolation of the two regions.

Geographic Variation in Wages

Geographically disaggregated wage data from a variety of studies can be combined to trace the scope of market integration from the Civil War until the early-twentieth century. The Weeks Report, conducted as a special supplement to the 1880 census, gathered data on wages and prices extending back to 1850 or earlier from 627 manufacturing, mechanical, and mining firms in

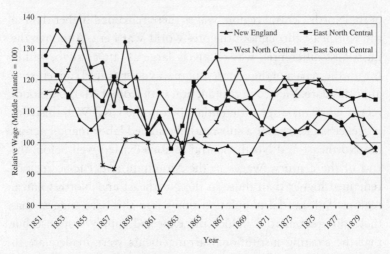

Figure 5.2   Relative Real Wages of Common Laborers, 1851–1880. *Notes*: Real wages in the Middle Atlantic equal 100 in each year. *Source*: Coelho and Shepherd (1976, p. 218).

38 states, 2 territories, and the District of Columbia. Although data were collected from all parts of the country, 83 percent of the employers surveyed were concentrated in the Northeast and North Central regions. In addition, because the data were collected retrospectively, the number of observations fell sharply for the earlier years. Coelho and Shepherd (1976) used these data to examine regional differences in real wages from 1851 to 1880 for common laborers and engineers – the two most numerous occupations in the data – as well as to construct a combined regional index based on wages for six occupations.[8]

Based on Coelho and Shepherd's analysis of the Weeks Report data, Figure 5.2 plots real wages of common laborers in New England, the East North Central, the West North Central, and the East South Central regions relative to those in the Middle

[8] The six occupations are engineers, blacksmiths, machinists, painters, carpenters, and common laborers. Because each observation in their data represented the average wage for a particular occupation paid by a particular employer and the mix of occupations differed across regions, average wages in each region could differ because of differences in occupational mix as well as differences in earnings within occupations. To control for differences in occupational composition across regions, Coelho and Shepherd regressed each wage observation on region and occupation dummy variables and used the coefficient on the region dummy to measure interregional earnings differences.

Atlantic region over the entire 1851–80 period.[9] Because of the small number of observations available, Coelho and Shepherd did not report real wages for the South Atlantic or other regions. Within the North, a clear tendency toward wage convergence is apparent. In the early 1850s, real wages in the North Central regions were 20 to 30 percent higher than in the Middle Atlantic, and wages in New England were from 10 to 20 percent above the Middle Atlantic. By the early 1860s, wages in New England had fallen to near equality with the Middle Atlantic, and wages in the West North Central region appear to have converged shortly after the end of the Civil War. Although wages in the East North Central region remained above eastern levels, the wage gap was clearly smaller in the 1870s than it had been in the 1850s. In the one southern region, wage behavior was more erratic, fluctuating widely around the level of wages in the Middle Atlantic, with no clear trend.

Two sources of wage data – the Aldrich Report and the *Nineteenth Annual Report of the Commissioner of Labor* – are available for 1890.[10] Although differences in geographic and occupational coverage between these sources and the Weeks Report mean that wage differentials for 1890 cannot be directly compared to those based on the Weeks Report, both sources suggest that within the North convergence continued over the course of the 1880s. Table 5.1 shows real wages for a number of occupations in each region as a percentage of the wage level of the corresponding occupation in the Middle Atlantic based on Coelho and Shepherd's (1979) analysis of regional wage and price data from the Aldrich Report. Although relative wages varied across occupations, wages in New England and the East and West North Central regions were generally within 5 to 10 percent of those in the Middle Atlantic by 1890. In contrast, wages further west – in the Mountain and Pacific regions – remained 15 to 25 percent above eastern levels.

---

[9] Coelho and Shepherd adjusted for regional differences in the cost of living using price indices constructed from data on the retail prices of 58 commodities contained in the Weeks Report. See Coelho and Shepherd (1974) for a complete description of the data and the construction of their cost-of-living index.

[10] The Aldrich Report also included retrospective wage data for New England and the Middle Atlantic regions, but not for other parts of the country.

Table 5.1. *Relative Regional Real Wages of Selected Occupations in 1890 from the Aldrich Report (Middle Atlantic = 100 for each occupation)*

Occupation	NE	ENC	WNC	SA	ESC	WSC	MTN	PAC
Blacksmith	94	94	104	89.5	105	113	115	113
Machinist	92	103	106	103	114	143	113	115
Iron molder	87	105	103	104	107	119	117	123
Tinsmith	82	96	100	96	102	111	121	112
Carpenter	93	94	96	81.6	101	122	117	94
Mason	91	109	104	84	111	114	122	130
Painter	80	92	94	70	94	103	110	103
Bricklayer	82	102	103	79	109	97	119	123
Plumber	103	105	122	91	121	112	125	121
Baker	104	114	114	90	114	105	95	134
Cabinetmaker	92	85	98	82	100	109	116	94
Stonecutter	86	108	111	80	102	114	119	114
Common laborer	101	108	110	67	79	100	148	121
Farm laborer	126	114	123	67	78	90	124	129
Median regional wage ratio	92	103	104	83	104	112	118	118

Note: Regional abbreviations: NE – New England; ENC – East North Central; WNC – West North Central; SA – South Atlantic; ESC – East South Central; WSC – West South Central; MTN – Mountain; PAC – Pacific Coast.
Source: Coelho and Shepherd (1979, p. 77).

The data for the South present a more complicated picture. The South Atlantic was clearly a low-wage region for all types of labor. The median occupational wage ratio was just 83 percent of the corresponding northern wage, and in just two occupational categories – machinists and iron molders – were wages in the South Atlantic equal to or above those in the Middle Atlantic. Generally, the interregional differentials were largest for laborers and other unskilled workers and smallest among skilled workers, especially those in the metal trades. The same pattern of variation in relative regional wages is apparent in the East South Central and West South Central regions. Wages of unskilled laborers lagged behind northern levels, but wages of skilled occupations were equal to or above those in the North. In the East South Central region, laborers' wages were 20 percent below northern levels by 1890. In the West South Central region, laborers' wages were comparable to those in the Mid Atlantic region, but

Table 5.2. *Relative Regional Real Wages of Selected Occupations in 1890 from the Nineteenth Annual Report of the Commissioner of Labor (Northeast = 100 for each occupation)*

Occupation	North Central	South East	South Central	West
Bricklayer	110	63	117	138
Carpenter	99	71	102	116
Hod carrier	104	62	91	128
Machinist	103	100	125	115
Iron molder	105	92	117	118
Pattern maker	104	88	110	110
Common laborer, building	107	53	92	116
Common laborer, foundry and machine shop	106	74	99	120
Median regional relative wage ratio	105	73	106	117

Source: Sundstrom and Rosenbloom (1993, p. 386).

the wages of agricultural laborers were 10 percent lower than those of comparable workers in the Mid Atlantic region. The small size of North-South wage differentials for skilled workers in the South Central regions could be evidence of greater integration in the markets for these workers. In light of the limited volume of migration from the South at this time, it seems more likely, however, that it was produced fortuitously by the relatively greater scarcity of skilled than unskilled labor in these regions of the country.[11] In the absence of occupation-specific evidence on migration patterns, though, it is impossible to offer a conclusive test of these competing hypotheses.

Table 5.2 shows relative regional real wages for eight occupations in 1890 based on Sundstrom and Rosenbloom's (1993) analysis of data from the *Nineteenth Annual Report of the Commissioner of Labor*.[12] This report actually contains annual data for the period from 1890 through 1903, but there were only

[11] This interpretation is also supported by the evidence presented later that factory earnings in the South Central region fell progressively farther behind northern levels after 1890.

[12] Rosenbloom and Sundstrom used Haines' (1989) city- and state-level cost-of-living indices for 1890 to adjust for spatial variations in prices.

minor changes in relative wages across cities during this period. The regional pattern of variation closely parallels that shown in Table 5.1. Wage levels in the North Central region were within 5 to 10 percent of those in the Northeast, while wages in the West remained 15 to 25 percent above the Northeast. Wages in the Southeast were again consistently lower than in the North, with the differential greatest for unskilled labor, while wages in the South Central region were relatively high for skilled workers but below northern levels for unskilled labor.

Geographic Variation in Factory Earnings

Average factory earnings data that can be derived from the censuses of manufacturers provide a largely independent test of conjectures based on the occupational wage data. Covering many more places and a much broader segment of the labor force, they reinforce conclusions based on the wage data, while making it possible to extend comparisons to many more cities and over a much longer time period. Beginning with the 1880 census, the collection of industrial statistics in major cities was turned over to special agents knowledgeable about manufacturing conditions in their districts. The resulting returns are generally regarded as being of substantially higher quality than the manufacturing returns collected for other areas by regular census enumerators. As the appendix to this chapter describes, it is possible to calculate from the published census volumes the average earnings of adult male wage earners in a consistent sample of 100 cities for each census year from 1879 through 1914.[13]

The census earnings figures are nominal. To obtain real earnings, I deflated them by state cost of living indices based on Michael Haines's (1989) analysis of retail price data from the Aldrich Report.[14] There are no data to construct location-specific cost-of-living estimates between 1870 and 1890, so I used Haines's

---

[13] Actually, the manufacturing data are available through at least 1939, but the analysis in this chapter is confined to the period before 1915.

[14] Haines's index included commodities representing approximately 86 percent of consumer expenditures for this period. Although Haines also reported indices for 70 individual cities, I used the state-level index because there are a large number of cities for which there are earnings data but no cost-of-living index.

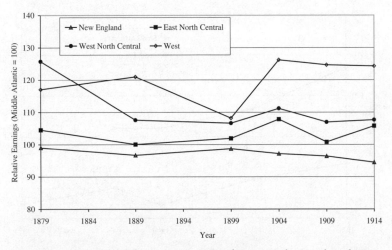

Figure 5.3   Relative Real Earnings in Manufacturing, the North and West, 1879–1914. *Note:* Observations for each region are unweighted averages of earnings in major cities adjusted for intercity differences in the cost of living. Real earnings in the Middle Atlantic are set equal to 100 in each year. *Source:* Rosenbloom (1996, p. 635).

index for 1890 to deflate earnings in both 1879 and 1889. For subsequent years, I adjusted his indices for differences in regional price trends on the basis of data reported by the U.S. Department of Labor (1912, 1915). Figures 5.3 and 5.4 summarize regional variations in real average earnings from 1879 through 1914. Figure 5.3, which traces earnings in the northern and western parts of the country relative to the Middle Atlantic, shows that as early as 1879 real average earnings were nearly equalized across New England, the Middle Atlantic and East North Central regions. Earnings in the West North Central were substantially higher than in the East in 1879, but they converged rapidly (though not completely) toward equality. In the West – comprising cities in the Pacific and Mountain states – factory earnings were approximately 20 percent higher than in the Middle Atlantic in both 1879 and 1889. Earnings converged temporarily in 1899, but then diverged again after the turn of the century.

Figure 5.4 compares earnings in the South Atlantic and South Central regions with those in the Middle Atlantic. In the South Atlantic, earnings, which were 16 percent below the Middle

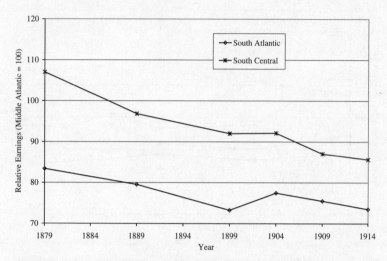

Figure 5.4 Relative Real Earnings in Manufacturing, the South Atlantic and South Central, 1879–1914. *Notes:* Observations for each region are unweighted averages of earnings in major cities adjusted for intercity differences in the cost of living. Real earnings in the Middle Atlantic are set equal to 100 in each year. *Source:* Rosenbloom (1996, p. 635).

Atlantic in 1879, diverged steadily. By 1914, the wage gap had grown to 26 percent. In the South Central region, relative earnings followed a similar declining trend. In 1879, they were slightly above the Middle Atlantic, but by the next census in 1889, they had slipped below northern levels. By 1914, the decline of earnings in the West South Central region had reduced earnings there to 86 percent of the average level in the Middle Atlantic.

Because census earnings data are an average over possibly heterogeneous groups of workers, differences in labor force composition across cities could, in principal, affect interregional comparisons. In practice, the extent of any such effect seems limited. During the late-nineteenth century, technological changes in manufacturing were promoting the increasing homogenization of the factory work force (Gordon, Edwards, and Reich 1982, pp. 79–100). Moreover, Rosenbloom (1996) showed that controlling for differences across cities in occupational composition as well as the age structure and literacy of the labor force actually tends to reinforce the pattern of interregional differentials; within the North,

Table 5.3. *Within-Region Coefficient of Variation of Real Average Earnings of Male Manufacturing Wage Earners, 1879–1914*

Region	1879	1889	1899	1904	1909	1914
MA	0.124	0.133	0.086	0.081	0.077	0.073
NE	0.149	0.117	0.104	0.116	0.114	0.112
ENC	0.068	0.094	0.064	0.089	0.079	0.104
WNC	0.118	0.117	0.100	0.086	0.085	0.101
SA	0.304	0.204	0.236	0.196	0.197	0.125
SC	0.325	0.173	0.147	0.158	0.108	0.097
West	0.058	0.072	0.092	0.047	0.078	0.054

Note: The coefficient of variation is calculated as the ratio of the standard deviation of earnings to the real average level of earnings across all cities for which data are available in each region at each date. Regional abbreviations: MA – Middle Atlantic; NE – New England; ENC – East North Central; WNC – West North Central; SA – South Atlantic; SC – South Central; West – West.
Source: Rosenbloom (1996, table 3).

interregional variation is reduced, and the North-South earnings gap is increased slightly.[15]

Because the census earnings data contain information on a large number of cities within each region, they can also be used to examine the extent of wage equalization within regions. Table 5.3 reports one widely used measure of within-region dispersion, the coefficient of variation of earnings.[16] In 1879, the greatest dispersion of earnings occurred within the two southern regions, where the coefficient of variation was greater than 0.3, roughly two to three times as large as for any of the other regions. In both the South Atlantic and South Central regions, however, dispersion fell sharply, indicating that substantial within-region equalization coincided with the increasing wage equalization between these two southern regions. In the North, where within-region dispersion was already relatively low, there was nonetheless a downward tendency in the coefficient of variation in three of the

[15] Rosenbloom (1996) used a regression framework to control for variations not only in labor force composition, but also in locational amenities and temporary disequilibrating shocks.
[16] The coefficient of variation normalizes the standard deviation of wages across cities within each region by expressing it as a fraction of the average wage within the region.

four regions considered. Only in the East North Central region, where dispersion was initially quite low, did dispersion tend to increase.

Market Integration

The wage and earnings data both suggest that a well-integrated northern labor market capable of achieving a substantial redistribution of population without producing large or lasting wage differentials existed in the decades immediately following the Civil War. This market did not, however, extend to the far West or the South. Despite relatively large population movement into the West, wages and earnings in this region remained above eastern levels (Eldridge and Thomas 1964, pp. 117–20). The combination of high rates of migration and continued wage differentials suggests that the rapid pace of labor demand growth in this region simply outstripped the ability of the labor market to respond.

In the South, despite the substantial population movements from the low-wage South Atlantic region toward higher-wage areas in the South Central region that were noted in Chapter 2 and an impressive within region convergence, wages and earnings fell further behind northern levels, especially for less-skilled labor, without inducing any significant migration northward. By 1890, wages of unskilled laborers in the South Atlantic and East South Central regions were 20 to 30 percent lower than were wages in the Northeast, while wages in the West South Central had reached equality with northern levels. Thereafter, the census earnings data imply a continuing decline in relative real wages until at least 1914. Compared to wage gaps within the North or South, these differentials are quite substantial.

Wages for skilled workers throughout the South were close to northern levels in 1890, but without data for subsequent years it is unclear whether this reflects a greater degree of North-South integration in markets for more skilled labor, or simply a difference in the relative regional supply and demand of skilled versus unskilled workers. Compared both to the degree of equalization achieved within the North and to the magnitude of trans-Atlantic wage differentials considered later, the North-South wage gap that had emerged by the turn of the century appears relatively large.

WAGE DIFFERENTIALS IN THE LONG RUN

Recent work by Robert Margo (2000) makes it possible to place the pattern of late-nineteenth century interregional wage differentials described earlier in a longer run historical context. Drawing on newly collected archival evidence on wages paid to civilian employees at military forts, Margo constructed measures of relative wages adjusted for regional differences in living costs for four different regions in each decade between 1820 and 1860. Based on these data, it is apparent that the tendency toward East-West convergence within the North had its roots in the antebellum period. So, too, did the divergence of wages between the North and South. On the other hand, it appears that the wage gap between the South Central and South Atlantic regions was much smaller prior to the Civil War than it was to become afterward.

Table 5.4 reports the log differences in regional real wages from the national average in each decade for two groups of workers – common labor and skilled artisans.[17] Within the North, the Midwest-Northeast wage gap was substantially larger for skilled than unskilled workers in each decade, though both differences displayed a marked tendency toward convergence between the 1820s and 1850s. For common laborers, the differential fell from 32.5 percent in the 1820s to around 15 percent after 1840; for artisans, the differential dropped from over 75 percent in the 1820s to about 30 percent after 1840. These differentials within the North contrast strikingly with the small size of interregional differentials within the South, around 13 percent in most decades for unskilled workers and between 9 and 17 percent among skilled workers.

Considering North-South differences, wages for common labor in the South Atlantic were initially above those of common labor in the Northeast in the 1820s, but this differential was reversed by the 1830s. In the 1840s the northern advantage widened to around 20 percent, but in the 1850s the differential had dropped

---

[17] For relatively small magnitudes, these log differences are approximately equal to the percentage difference in wage levels, but this approximation becomes worse as the magnitude of the differences increases. The percentage differences can be obtained by exponentiating the log differences reported in the table and multiplying by 100 – that is, the percentage difference $= 100 * e^{(\log \text{ difference})}$.

Table 5.4. *Regional Log Real-Wage Differences from the National Average, Civilian Employees at Military Forts, by Occupational Category, 1820–1860*

Region	1821–30	1831–40	1841–50	1851–60
Common labor				
Northeast	−0.084	−0.078	−0.009	−0.052
Midwest	0.197	0.230	0.131	0.101
South Atlantic	−0.038	−0.160	−0.192	−0.118
South Central	0.082	0.028	−0.062	−0.005
Interregional differences				
Midwest-Northeast	0.281	0.308	0.140	0.153
South Central-South				
Atlantic	0.120	0.189	0.130	0.113
Northeast-South				
Atlantic	−0.046	0.082	0.183	0.066
Artisans				
Northeast	−0.189	−0.189	−0.136	−0.121
Midwest	0.378	0.272	0.093	0.142
South Atlantic	0.177	0.164	0.142	0.035
South Central	0.260	0.246	0.250	0.197
Interregional differences				
Midwest-Northeast	0.567	0.461	0.229	0.263
South Central-South				
Atlantic	0.083	0.082	0.108	0.162
Northeast-South				
Atlantic	−0.366	−0.353	−0.278	−0.156

Note: The national average wage is constructed as a weighted average of regional wages, where each region is weighted by its share of national employment in the appropriate occupational classes. Wages are deflated by regional cost-of-living indices. *Source:* Margo (2000, pp. 104–5).

back to around 7 percent. In contrast, wages for skilled artisans throughout the South were comparable to those in the Midwest, and consequently well above levels in the Northeast.

Figure 5.5 combines data from Margo's antebellum wage series with interregional comparisons drawn from a variety of the sources discussed earlier to depict long-run trends in interregional wage and earnings differences from 1820 through 1914. The upper (solid) line shows real wages and earnings in the North Central region relative to wages or earnings in the Northeast, and the lower (dashed) line shows real wages and earnings in the South Atlantic relative to the Northeast. The various sources used to construct this graph drew their data from different locations and cover a

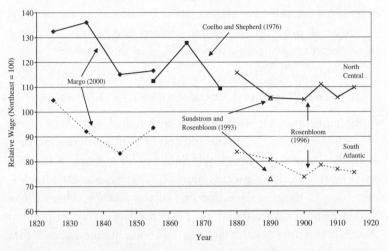

Figure 5.5   Real Wages and Earnings Relative to the Northeast, 1820–1914. *Notes:* Real manufacturing earnings in the Northeast calculated as an unweighted average of real earnings in the Middle Atlantic and New England regions. Real manufacturing earnings in the North Central region calculated as an unweighted average of real earnings in the East and West North Central regions. *Source:* Margo (2000, pp. 104–5; Coelho and Shepherd (1976, p. 218); Sundstrom and Rosenbloom (1993, p. 386); Rosenbloom (1996, p. 635).

changing selection of occupations; nonetheless, the picture that emerges is suggestive of the long-run trends in market integration. Combining Margo's antebellum data with our earlier examination of postbellum wage trends reinforces the earlier conclusion that northern and southern labor markets developed in isolation from one another throughout the nineteenth century. Wage differentials between these regions had begun to emerge prior to the Civil War and were further exacerbated by the shock of emancipation and reconstruction. On the other hand, it appears that, within the South, labor markets were working very well prior to the Civil War. Apparently the Civil War and the changes in labor market institutions that followed the abolition of slavery in the region created a great deal of labor market turmoil, which took a long time to repair. Within the North, it is apparent that labor market institutions were already in place to facilitate interregional supply responses prior to the Civil War. Wage equalization continued to progress after the Civil War, however, and was especially dramatic in markets for skilled labor. By the end of the century, interregional differentials in these markets had been reduced to 5 to 10 percent, comparable to those for unskilled workers.

INTERNATIONAL LABOR MARKET INTEGRATION

At the same time that labor markets within the United States were becoming increasingly closely integrated with one another, they were also becoming more closely linked to labor markets in other parts of the world, especially Europe. The large volume of immigration in these years is one sign of this linkage. There is less evidence about international wage differentials in this period than there is about intercity and interregional ones, but the evidence that is available indicates that, over the course of the late-nineteenth century, the northern United States was increasingly becoming part of a larger, trans-Atlantic labor market.

Undoubtedly the more than 50 million people who emigrated from Europe to labor-scarce regions in the Americas and Australasia between 1860 and 1914 were responding to a wide variety of different influences. But it is also apparent that economic forces were a central factor in directing these unprecedented population movements.[18] One indication of this is the close correlation between the volume of immigration and fluctuations in economic activity within the United States (Jerome 1926). As Figure 5.6 shows, between 1890 and 1914, the volume of immigration tended to move inversely with fluctuations in the unemployment rate. Additional evidence of the economic motivations behind international migration comes from data on the intended destinations of arriving immigrants. Studies analyzing this information have shown that the rate of immigration to different states within the United States was positively correlated with differences in state per capita income (Dunlevy and Gemery 1978; Dunlevy 1980; Dunlevy and Saba 1992).

Within Europe, rates of emigration varied widely across countries and over time (see Table 5.5). The reasons for this variation have

---

[18] Prior to the second half of the nineteenth century, the only comparable intercontinental migration was the forced movement of black slaves from Africa to the Americas and the Caribbean (Hatton and Williamson 1994a, p. 4).

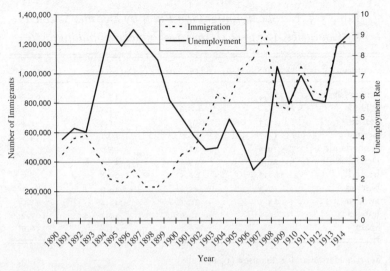

Figure 5.6 Immigration and Unemployment, 1890–1914. *Source:* Weir (1992, p. 341); U.S. Bureau of the Census (1975, Series C-89).

been the subject of considerable study.[19] Hatton and Williamson's (1994b) regression analysis of decadal average emigration rates from 11 European countries showed that close to three-quarters of the variation in emigration rates could be explained by a small number of economic and demographic factors. In particular, they found a strong positive relationship between emigration rates and the wage gap between sending and receiving regions. In addition, they found that emigration rates were positively related to the rate of population growth 20 years earlier, negatively related to the share of the labor force employed in agriculture, and positively related to the stock of previous migrants in the destination country. The positive effects of the growth rate of population 20 years earlier may be interpreted as the consequence of a supply shock that both raised the proportion of the population in the prime emigration age group and increased competition at home for scarce resources such as land. The share of the labor force in agriculture can be seen as a proxy for the disruptive effects of industrialization on domestic agricultural labor markets. As this share dropped, signaling the onset of industrialization, the disruptive effects of this

[19] Hatton and Williamson (1994a, pp. 8–15) reviewed the literature on this subject in greater depth.

Table 5.5. *European Emigration Rates by Decade, Selected Countries, 1871–1910 (per 1,000 mean population)*

Country	1871–1880	1881–1890	1891–1900	1901–1910
British Isles	50.4	70.2	43.8	65.3
Belgium		8.6	3.5	6.1
France	1.5	3.1	1.3	1.4
Germany	14.7	28.7	10.1	4.5
Netherlands	4.6	12.3	5.0	5.1
Denmark	20.6	39.4	22.3	28.2
Ireland	141.7	88.5	69.8	
Norway	47.3	95.2	44.9	83.3
Sweden	23.5	70.1	41.2	42.0
Italy	10.5	33.6	50.2	107.7
Spain		36.2	43.8	56.6

Source: Hatton and Williamson (1994a, p. 7).

change were likely to increase the pool of potential emigrants. The relationship between emigration rates and the stock of previous migrants in the destination can be explained by the role of earlier emigrants in lowering the costs of job search and helping to finance the transactions costs of migration. The greater the number of prior immigrants, the more likely that potential emigrants would know someone at their destination who could provide them with information and financing.

To gauge the impact of European immigration to the United States on trans-Atlantic labor market integration, it is necessary to look at the magnitude and evolution of international real-wage differentials. Fortunately, several recent studies have attempted to make such comparisons for the late-nineteenth and early-twentieth centuries. The most extensive comparison is offered by Jeffrey Williamson (1995), who constructed a data set of internationally comparable real wages from 1830 to the present for 11 European and 4 New World countries. Williamson intended his data to reflect national averages, but judging from his sources for the United States, it would be most appropriate to view his wage series as a measure of labor market conditions in the Northeast and North Central regions of the country. Wage rates in each country refer to unskilled labor. To make comparisons across countries, Williamson first deflated the wage series for each country by a national cost-of-living series. He then converted the resulting real-wage series to internationally comparable levels using purchasing-power-parity price indices calculated at benchmark dates.

Williamson (1995) was interested in measuring international wage convergence, but his focus was on relatively aggregated measures, such as the coefficient of variation across various groups of countries. As his analysis demonstrated, there was a pronounced international wage rate convergence between 1870 and 1913, explained in large part by reductions in the wage gap between the New World and the Old.[20] To understand what this convergence meant for American labor markets, it is useful, however, to look more closely at the gap between wages in the United States and each of the European countries in Williamson's data. Figures 5.7 and 5.8 plot Williamson's relative real-wage data for two groups of countries. For the major economies of Northwest Europe (Great Britain, Germany, France, Belgium, and the Netherlands), which are depicted in Figure 5.7, despite substantial short-run fluctuations, the wage gap with the United States remained relatively stable. Among these countries, wage levels were highest in Great Britain, fluctuating between 60 and 70 percent of American levels, and lowest in France, where wages were between 40 and 50 percent of those in the United States. The persistence of these gaps suggests that they reflect a relatively stable equilibrium situation. Indeed, as Table 5.5 shows, emigration rates from most of the countries shown in Figure 5.7 were quite low after 1870, implying that the remaining wage gaps created little incentive for trans-Atlantic immigration. Only British emigration rates remained relatively high, suggesting that the wage gap may overstate the transactions costs in this case.

Figure 5.8 traces relative wage movements in Scandinavia, Southern Europe, and Ireland. In most of these countries, wage levels in 1870 were much lower than in the countries depicted in

---

[20] Taylor and Williamson (1994) and O'Rourke, Williamson, and Hatton (1994) argued that this convergence would have been even more pronounced had international capital markets been less integrated. The parallel flow of capital from Europe to the New World helped to offset the effects of migration on the capital-labor ratio in both the Old and New World and thus reduced the effects of labor movements on the wage gap.

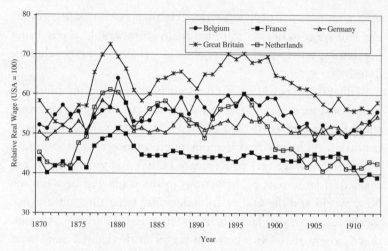

Figure 5.7   Relative European Wages, 1870–1913. *Source:* Williamson (1995, pp. 178–80).

Figure 5.7. They were, however, converging toward those in the United States (and their European neighbors) quite rapidly. In Ireland, Sweden, and Denmark, by the 1890s, wage ratios had reached levels only slightly below those in Great Britain. Convergence in Norway and Italy was slower and less complete but is nonetheless quite apparent. Only Spain – where wage levels were falling farther behind the United States and Europe – is an exception to this pattern. Overall, we seem to be observing a process of gradual adjustment toward international labor market equilibrium. Consistent with this view, Table 5.5 shows that the emigration rates from these countries were higher than for the countries with stable wage gaps.

In another recent study of international labor market integration, Robert Allen (1994) compared real-wage levels in the English-speaking world from 1880 to 1913. Allen compiled wages for unskilled laborers and bricklayers, as well as average factory earnings for six cities in England, Canada, the United States, and Australia. Allen found that consistent with evidence of a persistent outflow of labor from England, wages there were below those in all three New World countries. The magnitude of these differentials varied substantially, however, and was not closely correlated with the volume of migration going to different destinations, indicating

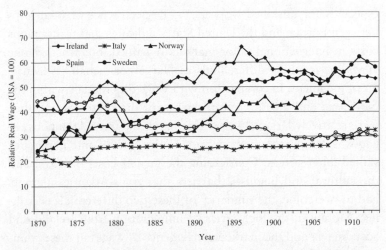

Figure 5.8   Relative European Wages, 1870–1913. *Source:* Williamson (1995, pp. 178–80).

that migration streams were not very responsive to differences in economic incentives across destinations.

Consistent with the evidence on international differences in skill premia discussed in Chapter 4, Allen found that differentials varied substantially by skill level. Comparing British and American real wages, he concluded that real wages of unskilled labor were essentially equalized across the two countries, but that the wages of bricklayers and average factory earnings in the United States were roughly twice what comparable workers in Britain earned. The discrepancy between Allen's finding of equalization between British and American unskilled wages and Williamson's data, which suggest that American unskilled wages were perhaps 50 percent higher than comparable British wages, is presumably a result of differences in the methods of currency conversion used in the two studies and suggests that some caution must be used in assessing the absolute magnitude of international wage gaps. What we can say is that over the 1870–1913 period, long-run trends in wages were quite similar in the United States and the countries of northwest Europe.

Together international wage and migration data point to the emergence and extension of an increasingly well-integrated trans-Atlantic labor market in the decades after the U.S. Civil War, especially for unskilled workers.[21] The persistence of wage gaps between Europe and the United States indicates that transactions costs in international labor markets remained, but whether one views the resulting differentials as "large" or "small" is a matter of judgment. In comparison with wage differentials within the Northeast and North Central regions of the United States, they were relatively large. On the other hand, the trans-Atlantic wage gap was comparable in magnitude to the North-South gap in unskilled labor wages. Considering the greater costs of travel and the cultural and linguistic barriers that trans-Atlantic migrants had to overcome, the similarity of these two differentials is striking. Moreover, the high levels of immigration from Ireland and Scandinavia and the marked convergence of wages in these countries toward U.S. levels point to an impressive expansion of the scope of trans-Atlantic labor markets at this time. Meanwhile, the stability of long-run wage differentials between the United States and other countries of Northwest Europe despite short-run fluctuations suggests that American employers faced a relatively elastic international supply of labor.

LABOR MARKET INSTITUTIONS AND LABOR MARKET INTEGRATION

The wage and earnings data considered in this chapter demonstrate the broad geographic scope of American labor markets in the late-nineteenth and early-twentieth centuries. However, the pattern of geographic integration that they reveal was uneven and selective. In the decades after the Civil War, labor markets across the Northeast and North Central regions of the United States were part of an effectively unified labor market and, in turn, were increasingly integrated with labor markets throughout Europe. At the same time, labor markets across the South were becoming increasingly integrated with each other. On the

---

[21] In principal, international wage convergence could have been achieved without labor market integration through the effects of factor price equalization. The large magnitude of population flows at this time suggests, however, that factor price equalization cannot be the whole story. General equilibrium analysis also suggests that factor price equalization was not a major factor in wage equalization at this time (Williamson 1996, pp. 285–8).

other hand, rising North-South wage gaps and the small volume of migration between North and South imply that southern labor markets remained largely isolated from northern and international markets.

Falling transportation and communication costs after the Civil War provided a powerful impetus for the expansion of markets, but they cannot explain the uneven character of market integration documented in this chapter. Rather, the interaction between falling transportation and communication costs and labor market institutions shaped patterns of geographic integration. The labor market institutions that facilitated long-distance movements of labor during the nineteenth century emerged as the result of the interaction between employers and workers. Because of the interdependent nature of actions by these two groups, once particular channels of labor recruitment were developed, the costs of using these channels fell, helping to perpetuate their use, even after the conditions that had originally led to their development had vanished.

As Chapters 2 and 3 showed, the networks of communication and assistance that were instrumental in mobilizing labor in this period developed along lines that were established in the first half of the nineteenth century, at a time when slavery created a sharp North-South division in labor market institutions. By the end of the Civil War, northern employers had access to well-developed mechanisms of recruiting arriving European immigrants, and the elaboration of this system, in turn, encouraged the continued migration of European job seekers. Within the South, a parallel set of institutions developed to facilitate the flow of information and population between the South Atlantic and South Central regions. In contrast, there were few connections between northern and southern labor markets and little incentive to establish them as long as European immigration continued. Northern employers could meet most of their labor needs from the stream of European immigrants, while opportunities in the South Central region offered southerners seeking to improve their lot through geographic mobility an opportunity to move toward a region of relatively higher wages.[22]

---

[22] Fishback (1998), in particular, emphasized the importance of the attractions of employment in the South Central region as a factor explaining the lack of migration from the South Atlantic to the North.

Not until World War I brought large-scale European immigration to an end did northern employers begin to invest in the mechanisms needed to recruit southern workers.

The history of labor market integration is interesting as an illustration of the role of history in shaping economic institutions. But the evidence about labor market integration examined here also has broader implications for our understanding of late-nineteenth century labor and social history. Most importantly, the integration of labor markets implies that we cannot hope to comprehend developments in this period by focusing on particular communities or even the nation as a whole without reference to the larger context in which they existed. Labor market integration was not perfect, of course, and in the short run local conditions probably did matter; however, in the longer run, communities were integrated into much broader markets, and this connection profoundly influenced the determination of wages and working conditions. Thus, the relatively slow growth of real wages in the United States as compared to labor productivity in this period appears to be explained by the depressing effects of immigration on domestic wage levels. It also appears from the widening of skill premia in this period that the effects of this competition were greatest among unskilled workers. The competitive pressures created by the extension of labor markets also offers some insights into the history of organized labor in this period. As Chapter 6 elaborates, high rates of mobility encouraged the widespread use of strikebreakers, which in turn served to undermine the efforts of workers to gain recognition of their right to organize and bargain collectively with employers.

How the course of American economic development would have differed in the absence of European immigration must remain speculative. Any such judgment rests on specification of a counterfactual model of the economy that can be used to evaluate outcomes in the absences of immigration. But specification of such a model is not straightforward because it depends on assumptions about the relative substitutability of immigrant and native-born workers, differences in savings rates, how immigration affected international capital flows, and a host of other factors, about which we lack strong priors.[23] Nonetheless, the findings of this chapter suggest that, in the absence of a pool of European job seekers, northern employers would likely have been much quicker to seek out low-wage southern workers and to establish channels of labor market recruitment similar to those that directed trans-Atlantic migration before World War I. For northern workers, it would probably have mattered little whether they faced competition from migrants from the low-wage South or from Europe. For the southern economy, however, integration into a broader national labor market would have had profound consequences. Instead of pursuing a distinctive low-wage path of development, as it actually did, the South would most likely have followed the same high-wage development path taken by the rest of the country.[24]

APPENDIX 5A: CENSUS EARNINGS DATA

Although the census of manufacturers did not report the earnings of manufacturing employees, average earnings can be calculated from the census as the ratio of total wage payments to the average number of wage earners employed during the calendar year preceding the census.[25] For 1889, 1899, and 1904, average employment and total wages were reported separately for men over 15 years of age, women over 15 years, and children, making it possible to calculate separate earnings figures for each of these groups. Although the published returns for other years reported average employment separately for these three age-sex categories, they provided only a

---

[23] See Carter and Sutch (1999) for a recent survey of efforts to evaluate the impact of immigration on the economy and labor market that emphasizes the linkage between assumptions (both implicit and explicit) about the appropriate counterfactual model of the economy and the resulting conclusions.

[24] Wright (1986) documented the impacts of the low-wage development path on the Southern economy that was actually followed in the postbellum era.

[25] Until 1905, the Census Bureau defined the census year for manufacturing data to be the 12 months ending on May 31 of the census year, but firms were allowed to submit reports for the business year coinciding most closely with the census year. In most cases, the reported data seem to pertain to the preceding calendar year. Beginning with the 1905 census, the census year was shifted to coincide with the previous calendar year to reflect this practice, and greater efforts were made to ensure that all firms reported statistics for this period (Easterlin 1957, pp. 679–80).

single aggregate wage figure.[26] For these years, it is necessary to impute the earnings of male manufacturing workers on the basis of the age and sex composition of the manufacturing labor force and the earnings of women and children relative to adult males in the years that these data are available.

By definition, total earnings for all workers in a given city can be written as

$$E = WM^* L^m + WF^* L^f + WC^* L^c \qquad (5A.1)$$

where WM, WF, and WC are average earnings of men, women, and children, respectively, and L^m, L^f, and L^c are the average employment of these three groups. Defining $F = WF/WM$ as the ratio of wages of adult females to those of adult males and $C = WC/WM$ as the ratio of wages of children to those of adult males and solving for WM yields:

$$WM = E/\{L^m + F^* L^f + C^* L^c\} \qquad (5A.2)$$

F, C, and WM can be calculated directly in 1889, 1899, and 1904, but for the other years it is necessary to substitute estimates of F and C to obtain an estimate of WM. Goldin (1990, pp. 63–6) offered evidence in support of the long-run stability of the ratio of female-to-male manufacturing earnings. Because of changes in census industry coverage, I used the average earnings ratios for 1889 and 1899 to impute male earnings in 1879, and used the average earnings ratios for 1904 to impute male earnings in 1909 and 1914.

Between 1879 and 1914, two important changes took place in census methods and coverage, but their impact on average earnings figures appears to be quite limited. The first change involved a shift in the methods used to measure average employment. For 1879 and 1889, instructions to enumerators indicate that employers were asked to report a single number reflecting average employment during that part of the year when the plant was in operation. Beginning with the 1899 census, separate employment figures were

---

[26] In 1914, employment was reported separately by age and sex only for December. I have assumed that the proportions of men, women, and children in the labor force remained constant throughout the year to obtain average employment figures by age and sex for this census.

requested for each month, and the census bureau computed average employment by summing these figures and dividing by 12. The procedure used in 1879 and 1889 may have produced some downward bias in average earnings. If workers seasonally unemployed at one establishment were successful in finding alternative employment during times of slack demand, census procedures would have counted them more than once, thus biasing upward average employment and biasing downward the resulting earnings estimate.[27]

In contrast, the procedure used in 1899 appears likely to understate employment and hence overstate earnings. In effect, the measure of employment adopted in 1899 reflects the number of full-time workers that would have been needed were production spread evenly throughout the year. To the extent that employment was seasonal or plants shut down for one or more months due to slack demand, this figure will be biased downward relative to actual employment during those periods when the plant was in operation. Consequently, earnings estimates for these years would be biased upward. For 1899 and later, average earnings are best interpreted as the amount that a full-time worker would earn if employed year-round. That is, they are an estimate of the daily (hourly) wage rate multiplied by the number of days (hours) worked per year by a year-round employee. As such, what they measure is conceptually quite similar to what occupational wage data measure.

In practice, the consequences of this shift in census employment concepts were small. Seasonal fluctuations were highly correlated across industries, and agricultural cycles did not mesh well with fluctuations in industrial demand, so opportunities for reemployment were limited (see Engerman and Goldin 1994, pp. 111–16). A more direct test of the effects of this shift is provided by comparisons of the employment to population ratio in each city before and after the shift in employment concepts. Rosenbloom (1996, p. 633) showed that there was little change, and, to the extent that there was any shift in this ratio, it was consistent across cities and

[27] In addition, since the earnings data are confined to manufacturing, if some seasonally unemployed workers found jobs in other sectors, the average earnings figures would understate their true annual income.

regions so that it is unlikely to have affected the size of regional differentials.

The second discontinuity in the census data is the result of a shift in the scope of census coverage. There were minor changes in coverage at each census, and a major redefinition in 1904 (Easterlin 1957, pp. 641–52). In 1904, handicraft and neighborhood industries were excluded from the enumeration, removing most of the building trades and a number of branches of clothing manufacture. These changes reduced overall employment and payrolls by about 20 percent and the number of establishments by nearly 50 percent. These changes in coverage make it more difficult to use the census to identify long-run trends in the levels of earnings and other variables, but they affect intercity and interregional differentials at a point in time only to the extent that changes in coverage varied across locations. The extent of this effect can be assessed directly, since the Census Bureau recalculated returns from 1899 to make the coverage comparable with that adopted in 1904. Comparing the two sets of 1899 data, average annual earnings fell by just 2 percent as a result of the exclusion of hand and neighborhood trades. Moreover, the effect on earnings was quite uniform across cities and regions (Rosenbloom 1996, p. 634).

6

LABOR MARKET INTEGRATION AND THE USE OF STRIKEBREAKERS

The integration of local labor markets into broader regional and national labor markets during the nineteenth century increased competitive pressures on wages and working conditions (Commons et al. 1918, pp. 43–4; Lebergott 1964, pp. 132–6). As the tendency for wage equalization documented in Chapter 5 illustrates, the scope for local variations in the terms of employment declined. In many industries, the competitive pressures caused by increased market integration were further compounded by technological changes that encouraged the increasingly fine division of labor and enabled employers to replace skilled craft workers with semiskilled operatives or unskilled laborers. The impact of these developments on American workers was profound. Broader labor markets and technological changes expanded employment opportunities for some workers, but for others they undermined efforts to increase wages and improve working conditions.[1]

The increasing elasticity of labor supply resulting from the geographic integration of labor markets severely constrained unions' efforts to improve wages and working conditions. Having won higher wages and more control over piece rates in 1881, for example, carpenters in St. Louis found that "our advances in wages would soon be lost through the influx of men from cities where

---

[1] Whatley (1993) argued, for example, that strikebreaking provided an important source of opportunities for African Americans. Based on accounts of 141 incidents of African American strikebreaking between the Civil War and the 1930s, he found that strikebreaking helped to encourage migration out of the South and opened doors to industries and occupations from which African Americans had previously been barred by racial discrimination.

wages were lower. Day after day men came from other states where wages were $1.75 to $2" (quoted in Tygiel 1981, p. 366). A skilled butcher in Chicago put the matter more bluntly, observing simply that the threat of being replaced by less-skilled workers was "the club held above our heads at all times" (quoted in Tuttle 1969, p. 412). The effects of increasing competition went beyond the purely economic, however, as a letter to a local newspaper from a coal miner in Ohio's Hocking Valley made clear. When new arrivals displaced long-time employees in the 1870s, he wrote that the displaced workers experienced "about the same emotions that an ordinary person would if robbed of his home" (quoted in Gutman 1962, p. 247).

One of the most visible and contentious manifestations of the increasing competitive pressures in American labor markets in the late-nineteenth century was the widespread use of strikebreakers.[2] The aggregate statistics reproduced in Table 6.1 show that between 1881 and 1900 employers hired over half a million replacement workers. This amounts to close to 10.8 percent of the 4.7 million workers who went on strike in this period. Of these replacements, over 40 percent were brought to the location of the strike from somewhere else, suggesting the important role that the recruitment of labor by employers played in expanding local labor supply. Employers' ability to replace striking workers has long been regarded by labor historians as one of the most potent weapons available to them in their efforts to defeat labor's demands for improvements in employment conditions. Philip Foner (1975, p. 17) argued, for example, that "the failure of a great number of strikes in the cotton textile, mining, iron and steel, cigar, railroad, and other industries must be attributed in no small measure to the ability of employers to make use of unskilled labor obtained from the labor exchanges and steamship companies as strikebreakers."

[2] Although the widespread use of strikebreakers in this period has sometimes been attributed to the large volume of immigration in the late-nineteenth century, Ehrlich (1974) argued that recent immigrants were no more likely to serve as strikebreakers than were the native born or members of older immigrant groups. Based on articles and letters published in the *National Labor Tribune*, a major labor weekly in the late-nineteenth century, he attributed the frequency of strikebreaking in the late-nineteenth century to the abundant labor supply in this period rather than to the volume of immigration.

Table 6.1. *Aggregate Strike Statistics, 1881–1900*

Year	Number of strikes	Number on strike	New employees		New employees brought from other places	
			Number	Percent of strikers	Number	Percent of new employees
1881	471	101,070	10,957	10.8	3,949	36.0
1882	454	120,857	11,353	9.4	5,356	47.2
1883	478	122,198	11,434	9.3	4,450	38.9
1884	443	117,313	11,833	10.1	4,324	36.5
1885	645	158,584	19,077	12.0	7,224	37.9
1886	1,432	407,152	39,854	9.8	12,932	32.4
1887	1,436	272,776	39,549	14.5	18,173	46.0
1888	906	103,218	16,700	16.2	5,237	31.4
1889	1,075	205,068	16,725	8.2	6,802	40.7
1890	1,833	285,900	31,034	10.9	12,393	39.9
1891	1,717	245,042	34,115	13.9	17,378	50.9
1892	1,298	163,499	25,847	15.8	13,492	52.2
1893	1,305	195,008	21,907	11.2	11,017	50.3
1894	1,349	505,049	75,092	14.9	35,198	46.9
1895	1,215	285,742	24,726	8.7	9,221	37.3
1896	1,026	183,813	13,289	7.2	5,128	38.6
1897	1,078	332,570	16,108	4.8	7,344	45.6
1898	1,056	182,067	19,064	10.5	7,335	38.5
1899	1,797	308,267	36,303	11.8	16,171	44.5
1900	1,779	399,656	31,590	7.9	11,331	35.9
Total	22,793	4,694,849	506,557	10.8	214,445	42.3

Source: U.S. Bureau of Labor (1901, pp. 340–3).

This chapter uses data from a random sample of over 2,000 individual strikes between 1881 and 1894 to examine systematically the impact of labor market integration on the use of strikebreakers.[3]

---

[3] The data come from reports compiled by the U.S. Commissioner of Labor and are discussed at length later. Several other recent studies have also explored the relationship between strikebreaking and other strike characteristics using disaggregated strike data. Mullin (1993) conducted a similar study on a smaller scale, examining the propensity to use replacement workers in a sample of 395 strikes in Illinois between 1881 and 1886. Currie and Ferrie (2000) found that the legal environment had a strong but "sometimes surprising" effect on the use of strikebreakers. Analyzing data on over 12,000 strikes in 13 states in the Northeast and North Central regions, they found that laws legalizing unions and banning blacklists – both apparently prolabor in their intentions – had the perverse effect of increasing the probability that strikebreakers would be used, but that the use of strikebreakers was less likely in states that had passed laws establishing maximum hours for any group of male workers.

In addition to providing the opportunity to explore systematically variation in the use of strikebreakers, the disaggregated data collected by the Bureau of Labor underscore the impact that strikebreaking had on late-nineteenth century labor conflicts. The data show that the use of strikebreakers was remarkably widespread, occurring in more than 40 percent of the strikes in the sample, and that the use of replacement workers had a powerful effect on the likelihood of strike success.[4] Of those strikes in which replacements were hired, just 21 percent ended successfully, and only 6.3 percent were partially successful. In contrast, when replacements were not hired, 63 percent of strikes were successful, and another 9.8 percent were partially successful.[5]

The data reveal several interesting regularities in the use and recruitment of strikebreakers. First, consistent with evidence presented in Chapter 5 indicating the increasing geographic integration of labor markets in this period, the propensity to use strikebreakers did not vary systematically by either city size or region. This finding contradicts Herbert Gutman's (1970) hypothesis that, in smaller communities, the greater solidarity between the community at large and striking workers made it more difficult for employers to use strikebreakers.[6] Second, consistent with

---

[4] In comparison, Cramton and Tracy (1995) reported that between 1985 and 1989 replacement workers were employed in just 11 percent of strikes involving 1,000 or more workers and 17 percent of smaller strikes.

[5] The classification of strikes as successful, partially successful, or failed was performed by the Bureau of Labor investigators who gathered the strike data. They based their judgments on a comparison of the objectives of the strike and its outcome. The impact of strikebreaking on strike success is equally pronounced after conditioning on a wide range of other factors likely to affect the probability of strike success, including industry, location, establishment size, union authorization, and the number of strikers.

[6] One way in which community support for workers' demands could manifest itself was in community resistance to the importation of replacement workers. "Although the mill owners in large cities such as St. Louis, Indianapolis, and Cincinnati found it easy to bring in new workers from outside," according to Gutman (1970, p. 41), "it was another story in small towns. They could easily hire new hands in Pittsburgh, Philadelphia, and other eastern cities, but the social environment...made it difficult to keep these men." Because workers often sought to dissuade strikebreakers verbally or to block their way into factories or mines, there was always the potential for violence, and the leanings of local law enforcement and militia forces could tip the balance in such confrontations either way. Brecher (1972, pp. 6–7) argued that it was precisely this sort of difference in community attitudes that explained why, during the Great Railroad strike of

the argument that employer recruitment of labor was an important factor in initiating new streams of migration, employers in
smaller communities and in locations outside the Northeast were
much more likely to use replacements brought from other places.
Third, differences in the skill level of striking workers had little impact on employers' use of strikebreakers, but there was substantial
variation in the use of replacements across industries. Employers
were most likely to use strikebreakers in transportation, printing
and publishing, and food processing and meatpacking, and least
likely to hire replacements in construction and mining. Fourth,
although there is no indication of any relationship between aggregate economic fluctuations and the use of strikebreakers, it does
appear that employers were more likely to turn to replacements in
the years immediately following the massive upheavals of 1886.
Finally, the data indicate that strikebreaking was less likely to occur
in union-authorized strikes after 1886, suggesting that organized
labor was becoming either more effective in controlling geographic
mobility or more adept at picking those fights that they had a high
probability of winning.

THE EVOLUTION OF STRIKE BEHAVIOR IN THE
NINETEENTH CENTURY

To contemporaries, the 1880s and early 1890s appeared to be
an era of unprecedented turbulence in the history of labor relations. Labor journalist John Swinton described the mid-1880s
as "revolutionary." In an 1887 report, the New York Bureau of
Labor Statistics noted that "the year 1886 has witnessed a more
profound and far more extended agitation among the members
of organized labor than in any previous year in the history of
our country" (quoted in Foner 1975, p. 11). There is no comprehensive quantitative evidence on strike activity before 1881,
but based on a mixture of qualitative and quantitative indicators,

1877, employers were able to replace striking workers in Baltimore, but failed
to do so in Martinsburg, West Virginia. Bennett and Earle (1982) interpreted an
inverse relationship between strike rates and population for communities with
populations of less than 85,000 as partially confirming Gutman's hypothesis, but
examination of strikebreaking would appear to be a more direct way of testing
his conjecture.

David Montgomery (1980) identified the 1870s as a crucial turning point in the nature of labor conflict. Prior to the mid-1840s, according to Montgomery, strikes were rare, and riots were the primary vehicle for the expression of working-class discontent. In the three decades after 1845, strikes spread out geographically and industrially, but for the most part they remained spontaneous and primarily defensive actions prompted by employer-initiated wage cuts or the effects of rapid inflation on real-wage levels. Beginning sometime in the 1870s, however, the extent and nature of strike activity shifted perceptibly. Increasingly, strike objectives shifted from defensive responses to employer actions toward the achievement of recognition of labor's right to bargain collectively over wages and work rules.

The causes of this transition were undoubtedly complex, but there is little question that the rapid pace of economic change in the decades after the Civil War was an important factor contributing to the growth of union membership. The trade-union movement in the United States can be traced back to at least the 1830s; however, until the post–Civil War period, most labor unions remained transitory organizations, forming during prosperous periods and collapsing during hard times. Not until the 1860s were the first successful national unions formed (Ulman 1955, pp. 3–7; Commons et al. 1918, pp. 43–4). Beginning in the late-1870s with several highly publicized successes won by the Knights of Labor, union membership climbed rapidly. Although the Knights of Labor proved unable to sustain this enthusiasm after the mid-1880s, membership in craft unions affiliated with the American Federation of Labor (AFL) continued to grow throughout the late-nineteenth century.

One reason for the growing popularity of organized labor was the increased importance of "workplace public good" – aspects of the employment relationship that were common to all workers at an establishment, such as safety conditions, hours of work, and seniority rules – caused by the growing size of manufacturing establishments at this time. When decisions about these aspects of the employment relationship are market determined, they will reflect the preferences of the marginal worker, that individual just on the verge of coming or going. The presence of a union provides a mechanism for collective choice that gives more weight to the preferences of less mobile, intramarginal workers.[7]

Because strikes are ex post inefficient, most economic models assume that they occur because workers and employers do not have access to the same information about firm profitability or the costs that a strike will impose on employers.[8] Increasing geographic integration, together with shocks to supply and demand caused by the emergence of big business and the spread of organized labor, disrupted existing employment relationships and must have created considerable uncertainty about the relative bargaining power of workers and employers. The effects of changes in technology and business organization were not, however, confined to employees in rapidly expanding firms. As large manufacturers consolidated national markets, smaller, more traditional firms faced increasingly intense competition in product markets. Responding to these changes, they sought to increase the intensity of work effort or cut wages to remain competitive with larger, more efficient producers.[9]

Although employers and workers were generally aware of the changes in market integration, business structure, and labor organization taking place around them, it was difficult for them to assess how these changes might affect their bargaining power. In the late 1860s, for example, officials at the McCormick reaper works in Chicago were aware of the rising volume of European immigration but uncertain about the relative costs and benefits of replacing their existing labor force. In an 1867 letter, Leander McCormick wrote: "I have thought . . . whether it would not be well to employ an agent to send us [immigrants] as I have seen that [there] are large numbers arriving" (quoted in Ozanne 1967, p. 7). But there is no evidence that this effort was pursued, suggesting that the cost of recruiting immigrants proved greater than initially anticipated. Later, in the 1880s, the McCormicks did attempt to replace striking iron molders, using their dealers to recruit potential

---

[7] Freeman and Medoff (1984) argued that providing a vehicle for negotiating over workplace public goods is one of the important functions of unions. See also Wright (1987a, p. 334).

[8] Strikes are inefficient because, whatever the final outcome, both sides could have been better off if they had reached this solution without the costs of foregone production and earnings caused by a strike. See Kennan (1986).

[9] This point was made by Currie and Ferrie (1995, p. 3).

strikebreakers. Although a number of men accepted train tickets to Chicago, the firm had great difficulty retaining any of them. "Out of the lot of men you sent us yesterday," they wrote to one dealer in Des Moines, Iowa, "but two of them showed up in Chicago . . . the balance having deserted along the way." To another dealer they complained: "the gentleman you sent us as a molder . . . did not remain over an hour or two until he packed his valise and skipped" (quoted in Ozanne 1967, p. 15).

A gap between workers' and employers' perception of their respective bargaining power is also evident in the 1890 strike of leather workers in Lynn, Massachusetts. According to John Cumbler's (1974, pp. 403–4) account of this conflict, the workers believed that because of the general prosperity of the industry and the value of their skills, employers would quickly concede to their demands. The employers, on the other hand, were determined not to give up any of their control over the workplace and believed that the cost of breaking the union would be smaller than the cost of accepting their employees' demands.

THE STRIKE DATA

Prompted by the rapidly increasing level of labor conflict during the first half of the 1880s, the U.S. Commissioner of Labor in 1886 initiated an effort to compile a comprehensive listing of all strikes that had occurred since 1881. Agents of the Bureau of Labor combed newspapers and other publications to compile a list of strikes and lockouts for these years. Then field agents were dispatched to investigate each conflict. Whenever possible, these agents interviewed representatives of both sides in the conflict so as to corroborate the facts they had gleaned from published accounts. A subsequent report extended the collection of data from 1886 through the middle of 1894. Together these two reports include data on more than 12,000 strikes.[10] Previous analysts have regarded the Bureau of Labor's strike data as both "comprehensive

[10] U.S. Bureau of Labor (1888, 1896). Although the bureau continued to collect data on strikes after 1894, subsequent publications provided only aggregate figures by state, industry, and year, rather than listing individual strikes, making it impossible to extend the analysis to later years.

and reliable" (Montgomery 1980, p. 86).[11] Recently, however, Gary Bailey (1991) raised questions about the completeness of their coverage. Based on a comparison between local newspapers in Terre Haute, Indiana, and the strike statistics for 1881 to 1894, he found that of 34 strikes mentioned in the local press, only about half were included in the Bureau of Labor's tabulation. Although this finding does raise some concern about the comprehensiveness of the data, it poses less of a problem for studies, such as this one, that explore the relationship between various aspects of individual strikes.

For each strike in its tabulation, the bureau reported, among other facts, the industry and occupation of the workers on strike; whether the strike was authorized by a union; the number of workers on strike; employment, wages, and hours before the strike; the duration of the conflict; its cause(s) and outcome(s), including the number (if any) of replacement workers hired; and the number of such workers brought from other locations. The data do not, however, provide any additional information about the sources from which outside strikebreakers were recruited or when during the strike they were hired.

This chapter employs a random sample of 2,070 strikes drawn from the strike data.[12] The strike statistics are augmented with population data drawn from the censuses of 1880, 1890, and 1900 and a measure of the skill level of the workers involved based on the occupational titles reported by the Bureau of Labor.[13] Table 6.2 summarizes selected characteristics of the strikes for the sample, as well as for those strikes in which strikebreakers were hired, and those in which strikebreakers were brought from other places. The table clearly documents the quantitative significance

[11] The data collection effort is described in U.S. Bureau of Labor (1888, 1896, 1901). For additional discussion of the data, see Edwards (1981), Friedman (1988), Card and Olson (1995), and Currie and Ferrie (2000).

[12] The data consist of a 1-in-5 random sample of strikes between 1881 and 1886, and a 1-in-10 random sample of strikes between 1887 and 1894. These data were originally collected in machine-readable form by Gerald Friedman who has generously made them available to me.

[13] Population data were available for cities with populations in excess of 25,000 in 1900. I estimated the population between census years by assuming a constant rate of population increase. I determined skill levels based on a comparison of occupational titles with the classification scheme elaborated in Edwards (1933).

Table 6.2. *Selected Strike Characteristics, 1881–1894*

	All strikes	Strikes with replacements	Strikes with replacements brought from elsewhere
Number of observations	2,070	851	269
Average employment before strike	408.42	579.75	1060.33
Average number on strike	202.91	282.81	633.79
Average duration in days	21.50	28.27	39.45
Average number of replacements hired	25.77	62.68	129.85
Average number of replacements brought from elsewhere	12.33	29.13	94.81
Fraction authorized by union	0.657	0.632	0.695
Fraction fully successful	0.460	0.217	0.178
Fraction partially successful	0.088	0.074	0.093
Fraction in cities with 250,000 or more population	0.356	0.326	0.175
Fraction in cities with less than 25,000 population	0.453	0.424	0.542
Fraction in Northeast region	0.639	0.636	0.501
Fraction in North Central region	0.290	0.287	0.394
Fraction for increase in wages	0.373	0.368	0.323
Fraction for reduction in hours	0.076	0.082	0.082
Fraction involving skilled workers	0.368	0.374	0.415
Fraction in which replacement workers hired	0.411	1.00	1.00
Fraction in which replacement workers brought from elsewhere	0.130	0.316	1.00

Source: Strike sample data described in text.

of strikebreaking during the late-nineteenth century. Replacement workers were hired in 851 strikes (41 percent of the total), and in these instances employers hired an average of nearly 63 replacement workers. If anything, these figures are likely to understate employers' efforts to replace striking workers. Striking workers and their supporters often attempted to prevent strikebreakers from taking up their jobs through persuasion and the threat or use of force. Only when employers were, in fact, successful in putting replacements to work would they appear in the strike statistics. The use of outside strikebreakers was also quite common, occurring in nearly one-third of the strikes in which any replacement workers were hired.

It is also apparent that strikes in which replacements were hired differed in a number of ways from those in which they were not. The use of replacements appears to have been associated with larger strikes and larger establishments. There is also a positive correlation between the use of strikebreakers, especially from outside the community, and strike duration, but without knowing when during the strike replacements were hired, it is impossible to determine whether longer duration was a cause or a consequence of the use of replacements. These differences are all even more pronounced for the sample of strikes in which replacements were brought from other places.

DETERMINANTS OF THE USE OF STRIKEBREAKERS

As Table 6.2 makes clear, the characteristics of strikes in which employers used strikebreakers differed systematically from those in which they did not use strikebreakers, and strikes in which strikebreakers were brought from other places differed from those in which strikebreakers were obtained locally. Disentangling the effects of location and other strike characteristics on decisions about whether to use strikebreakers and where to obtain them requires a multivariate statistical analysis. This section begins by specifying a model of employers' decisions about whether to use strikebreakers and then discusses econometric estimates of this model. In the next section, I employ this same framework to consider the decision about whether to recruit strikebreakers locally or to bring them from other places.

Once a strike began an employer faced a choice between recruiting replacement workers or waiting for a settlement to be negotiated without hiring replacements.[14] Hiring replacements presumably increased the likelihood that the conflict would end on terms that the employer viewed favorably. But it also obliged the employer to incur direct and indirect costs associated with recruiting new workers. Presumably, an employer's decisions about whether to recruit replacements reflected the employer's evaluation of the relative magnitudes of these costs and benefits. In other words,

---

[14] See Cramton and Tracy (1995) for a more extensive discussion of the inclusion of the use of strikebreaking within standard bargaining models of strikes.

we would expect that an employer would hire replacements when the expected benefits of doing so exceeded the costs, and that the number of replacements hired would be chosen to maximize the expected benefit net of costs.

We can express employers' expected net benefit from hiring strikebreakers mathematically as

$$B = P(S, X) * V(Y) - C(S, Z) \qquad (6.1)$$

where $P(S, X)$ is the probability that the strike ends successfully for the employer, $V(Y)$ is the value to the employer of a successful outcome, and $C(S, Z)$ is the cost of recruiting replacement workers. In these equations, S denotes the number of replacement workers hired, and X, Y, and Z are vectors of other exogenous variables that affect, respectively, the probability of a successful outcome, the value to the employer of a successful outcome, and the cost of recruiting replacements. Presumably increasing the number of replacements, S, would raise the probability of a successful outcome. In the extreme, if the employer replaced all the striking workers, the strike would, by definition, have ended successfully for the employer. On the other hand, it seems likely that the costs of recruiting replacements would increase with the number of replacements hired.

Within this framework, the employer's decision can be viewed as choosing the value of S that maximizes his net benefit, B. Solving the employer's maximization problem, the number of replacements that is optimal will be a function of all the exogenous variables in equation (6.1). Denoting this number by S^*, we can write

$$S^* = G(X, Y, Z) \qquad (6.2)$$

subject to the constraint that S^* must be nonnegative.[15] After the exogenous variables to be included have been identified, it is possible to estimate their effects on the optimal number of strikebreakers using data drawn from the Bureau of Labor's strike reports.

---

[15] The constraint that S^* must be nonnegative arises because employers cannot hire a negative number of replacement workers. It should be apparent that equation (6.2) is a "reduced form" expression in which the coefficients do not have any structural interpretation.

A wide variety of factors may have influenced the costs of re-cruiting replacement workers. Despite increasing geographic inte-gration in this period, it seems possible that location continued to affect the costs of hiring replacements. The bulk of European immigration passed through port cities in the Northeast, and this situation may have lowered the cost of recruiting replacements in this region. On the other hand, the use of convict leasing in the South may have lowered the cost of obtaining strikebreakers in this region. In an imperfectly integrated labor market, employers in smaller places would also face a smaller supply of potential strike-breakers, and hence a higher cost of recruiting replacements. If the residents of smaller communities were more likely to feel a sense of solidarity with striking workers, as Herbert Gutman (1970) and others have speculated, this effect would be reinforced by the greater community opposition to strikebreaking in smaller places. It also seems possible that the supply of potential strikebreakers would vary with aggregate economic fluctuations, increasing as the unemployment rate rose.

The issue of controlling migratory labor was central to the emergence in this period of national trade unions (Ulman 1955, chs. 2–3; Commons et al. 1918, pp. 307–12). To the extent that unions were effective in achieving this goal, the supply of strike-breakers would be smaller in union-authorized strikes; hence, the cost of hiring replacements would be higher. The effect of union authorization seems likely to have increased after the mid-1880s as national unions affiliated with the American Federation of Labor became more adept at using strike funds to discipline local unions and maintain solidarity among striking workers. Gerald Friedman (1988) found that after 1886 the shift in union strategy did indeed increase the likelihood of success for union-authorized strikes.

The cost of recruiting strikebreakers also depended on the ex-tent of training that they required and the amount of hostility that introducing new workers might induce among current employees. To some extent, these factors are likely to be a function of the skill level of the striking workers, but they may also have been at least partly functions of industry characteristics.

Turning to factors affecting the benefits of a successful outcome, employers in this period evidenced a great deal of hostility toward

unions, a fact that seems likely to have figured in their calculation of the benefits of recruiting strikebreakers. The bitter Homestead conflict of 1892, for example, was motivated by Andrew
Carnegie's desire to break the union (Foner 1975, pp. 208–9). Similarly, when leather workers in Lynn, Massachusetts, went on strike
in 1890, the manufacturers agreed to fight the union and bring the
open shop to the city (Cumbler 1974, pp. 403–4). These observations suggest that the perceived benefits of winning a strike may
have been greater when it was authorized by a union than when
it was a spontaneous protest. Employers may also have viewed
the benefits of winning as greater when the strike was offensive
in nature (over issues such as wage increases, hours reductions, or
work rules), than when it was a spontaneous, defensive response
to employer-initiated wage cuts. Because the costs of foregone production imposed by a strike were likely to be an increasing function
of establishment size, the benefits of ending a strike should be an
increasing function of prestrike employment. The costs imposed
by a work stoppage (and hence the benefits of ending it) would
also vary across industries depending on the ability of employers
to build up inventories in anticipation of a strike and the potential
loss of customers that would follow from a temporary interruption in supplies. As a result, employers in service industries and
industries with highly perishable products or highly competitive
markets would have perceived the benefits of using replacements
to be greater.

Finally, the expected benefit that employers perceived from recruiting replacements depended not only on the cost saving they
anticipated from a successful conclusion of the strike, but also on
the probability that this event would occur. Other things being
equal, it seems likely that the probability of winning would be a
decreasing function of the number of workers on strike.

Table 6.3 reports the results of econometric estimates of the impact of strike characteristics on the use of replacement workers.
Many of the explanatory variables are categorical. To capture
locational differences in the supply of strikebreakers, I included
zero-one indicator variables for three regions and four city-size
classes. I controlled for the effects of skill and industry on the

Table 6.3. *Determinants of the Use of Replacements and the Log of the Number of Replacements Hired*

Variable	Mean	S.D.	Probit regression for use of replacements[a]		OLS regression for log(number of replacements)	
			Coefficient	t-statistic	Coefficient	t-statistic
City-size effects[b]						
25,000–49,999	0.060	0.237	−0.0042	−0.087	0.3013	2.064**
50,000–99,999	0.073	0.259	−0.0077	−0.169	0.4213	3.549***
100,000–249,999	0.085	0.278	0.0712	1.615*	0.3191	1.816**
250,000 or more	0.356	0.479	−0.0666	−2.365**	−0.1743	−1.234
Regional effects[c]						
North Central	0.289	0.454	−0.0234	−0.891	0.0107	0.120
South	0.061	0.240	0.0004	0.009	0.0429	0.326
West	0.010	0.098	−0.0180	−0.160	−1.0183	−1.814*
Industry and occupation effects[d]						
Transportation	0.054	0.226	0.1036	1.890*	0.6605	2.877***
Construction	0.167	0.373	−0.1191	−2.756***	−0.2336	−1.009
Mining	0.087	0.281	−0.1784	−3.827***	−0.1353	−0.360
Stone quarrying and cutting	0.043	0.203	−0.0442	−0.710	0.1588	0.891
Metals and metallic goods	0.094	0.292	−0.0613	−1.367	−0.0736	−0.407
Machinery	0.022	0.146	−0.0652	−0.817	0.2847	1.091
Printing and publishing	0.032	0.176	0.1836	2.523**	0.7609	2.352**
Furniture	0.033	0.178	0.0286	0.415	0.1537	0.696
Wooden goods	0.024	0.152	−0.0091	−0.117	0.1067	0.459
Boots and shoes	0.046	0.210	−0.0383	−0.656	−0.2095	−1.051
Clothing	0.074	0.262	0.0449	0.889	−0.0179	−0.098
Tobacco and cigars	0.079	0.269	0.0198	0.395	0.0547	0.324
Glass	0.021	0.143	−0.1088	−1.357	−0.3658	−1.070
Food preparation, canning, butchering	0.022	0.147	0.1311	1.605*	0.1535	0.419
Skilled occupation	0.368	0.482	0.0413	1.354	0.1058	0.863
Strike cause effects[e]						
Wage increase	0.373	0.484	−0.0417	−1.574		
Hours reduction	0.076	0.265	0.0180	0.383		
Defensive	0.147	0.355	−0.0434	−1.219		
Strike characteristic effects						
Log(No. of employees)	4.539	1.580	0.0435	3.597***	0.2424	3.070***
Log(No. of strikers)	3.691	1.538	−0.0299	−2.412**	0.4181	6.531***
Authorized by union	0.657	0.475	0.0176	0.468	0.1594	1.249
Authorized by Union, 1887–94	0.396	0.489	−0.0872	−1.826*	−0.0961	−0.490

Table 6.3. (*cont.*)

Variable	Mean	S.D.	Probit regression for use of replacements[a]		OLS regression for log(number of replacements)	
			Coefficient	t-statistic	Coefficient	t-statistic
Year Effects[f]						
1882	0.043	0.202	0.0917	1.209	0.0362	0.135
1883	0.048	0.213	0.1769	2.430**	0.5321	1.500
1884	0.065	0.207	0.0484	0.649	0.1919	0.768
1885	0.065	0.246	0.0124	0.182	0.1742	0.719
1886	0.173	0.378	0.0688	1.160	−0.0101	−0.043
1887	0.081	0.237	0.1001	1.392	0.2943	0.973
1888	0.050	0.219	0.1435	1.807*	0.3787	1.147
1889	0.060	0.238	0.0723	0.953	0.2366	0.842
1890	0.098	0.297	0.0381	0.540	−0.1025	−0.393
1891	0.098	0.297	0.0572	0.804	0.0399	0.155
1892	0.074	0.263	0.0725	0.994	−0.1451	−0.536
1893	0.072	0.259	0.0712	0.970	−0.1057	−0.389
1894	0.048	0.215	0.0926	1.170	0.3058	1.088
Constant					−1.4010	−1.277
Inverse Mill's ratio					1.2110	1.293
N			2,045		838	
Chi-squared			117.29			
R-squared					0.507	

Note: The t-statistics are computed using heteroscedasticity-corrected standard errors. The observed probability of strikebreaking is 0.4098, and the predicted probability is 0.4058.
*Statistically significantly different from zero at the 10 percent level.
**Statistically significantly different from zero at the 5 percent level.
***Statistically significantly different from zero at the 1 percent level.
[a]Coefficients are reported as the partial derivatives of the probability with respect to each variable, evaluated at the sample mean values of the other independent variables. For zero-one categorical variables, the coefficient shows the change in probability for a discrete change in that variable from zero to one. The t-statistics reported are calculated using the original probit parameters and their corresponding standard errors.
[b]Omitted category is cities with population under 25,000.
[c]Omitted category is Northeast region.
[d]Omitted category is all other industries.
[e]Omitted category is strikes over work rules.
[f]Omitted category is 1881.
Source: Strike sample data described in the text.

costs and benefits of employing strikebreakers using an indicator variable for highly skilled workers and a set of indicators for 14 of the most common industries in the data. I also included indicator variables for each year to control for macroeconomic fluctuations that might have affected the supply of potential strikebreakers.

To measure the effects of strike causes, I used indicator variables for defensive strikes and for strikes initiated by labor demands for higher wages or shorter hours. The excluded category is strikes over work rules. I also used indicator variables to measure the effects of union authorization and possible changes in this effect after 1886. Finally, to control for scale effects, I included two continuous variables – the number of workers employed before the strike and the number of workers on strike.

The first two columns of the table report the mean and standard deviations of each of the explanatory variables. The remainder of the table reports the results of the analysis in two stages. Columns 3 and 4 show the results of the first stage, in which I examine the decision whether to use replacements at all. Columns 5 and 6 report the results of analyzing the determinants of the number of replacements hired (in logarithms) in those strikes in which any replacements were used.[16] The variables used to estimate both equations are similar, but because the reasons for a strike's occurrence are likely to affect an employer's willingness to use strikebreakers, but not the number of replacements needed to defeat the strike, I exclude strike cause effects from the second-stage estimation of the determinants of the number of replacements hired. To control for possible sample selection bias in the second-stage equations, I include the inverse Mill's ratio.[17]

---

[16] Because of the large number of strikes in which no strikebreakers were used, Ordinary Least Squares (OLS) is not an appropriate method of estimating equation (6.2). It would be possible to employ a Tobit model to estimate equation (6.2), but the two-stage procedure employed here allows for the possibility that the function G is discontinuous at zero. On this choice, see Maddala (1983, ch. 6). In terms of signs and relative magnitudes, Tobit estimates (not reported here) closely resemble the results obtained from the first-stage probit estimation. As will be seen later, however, the impact of several variables on the number of replacements hired appears to be quite different from that on employers' propensity to use replacements. The first-stage estimates are obtained using a probit model in which the dependent variable takes the value one if any strikebreakers were used and zero otherwise. The second-stage estimates are obtained by Ordinary Least Squares applied to those strikes in which a positive number of replacement workers were hired.

[17] The need to correct for sample selection arises because the OLS regression is restricted to only those observations for which S is nonzero. The problem can be seen most clearly by considering an empirical analog of equation (6.2), which adds an error term u to reflect the impact of unobserved characteristics. Letting i index individual observations and assuming that the function $G(X, Y,$

In column 3, the estimated parameters show the effect of each variable on the probability that replacement workers will be used. For the zero-one indicator variables, this is the implied effect on the predicted probability of using replacement workers that would result from changing the variable's value from zero to one when all the other independent variables are set at their sample means. For the continuous variables, the table reports the implied partial derivative of the probability of using replacement workers with respect to that variable, where the derivative is evaluated at the sample means of the independent variables.

The first-stage estimates indicate that locational effects on the probability of using replacement workers were quite limited. None of the regional effects is large in magnitude or statistically significant. Several of the city-size variables are statistically significant, but the direction of these effects is inconsistent, and not especially large. Employers in cities with populations of 250,000 or more appear to have been somewhat less likely to use replacements, whereas those in the next largest size class – those with populations between 100,000 and 250,000 – were somewhat more likely to use replacements. On the basis of these estimates, there is no indication that employers in smaller places faced higher costs of recruiting replacements.

In contrast to the limited impact of location, industry effects were much more pronounced. Employers in transportation, printing, and food preparation were 10 to 20 percentage points more likely to use replacement workers than were employers in the excluded category of miscellaneous industries. Evaluated at the predicted

Z, u) can be approximated as linear in its arguments, the model then becomes $S_i = aX_i + bY_i + cZ_i + u_i$, where a, b, and c are vectors of coefficients. Rearranging terms, it is apparent that the condition $S_i > 0$ is equivalent to the condition that $u_i > -aX_i - bY_i - cZ_i$. Thus, even if it is assumed that the expected value of u_i is uncorrelated with the explanatory variables across the entire sample, this will not be true for the set of strikes for which S_i is nonzero, violating one of the underlying assumptions of the OLS model. Heckman (1979) showed, however, that this problem can be resolved by adding an estimate of the expected value of u_i to the regression. This additional regressor, often referred to as the inverse Mills' ratio, is equal to $\phi(Z_i)/\Phi(-Z_i)$, where ϕ and Φ are, respectively, the density and distribution functions of the standard normal variable, and Z_i is an estimate of u_i divided by its standard error derived from the probit estimates over the full sample. See Maddala (1983, pp. 158–9), for additional discussion and references.

probability of using replacements of 40 percent, this implies that the use of replacements was one-quarter to one-half more likely in these industries. In view of the relative successes of organized labor in the building trades, it is perhaps not surprising that the use of replacements was 12 percentage points less likely in construction than in miscellaneous industries. Of greater note, however, the data indicate that despite numerous accounts of strikebreaking and violence aimed at strikebreakers in mining, employers in this industry were nearly 18 percentage points less likely to use replacements than in the excluded category. If there is a pattern here, it appears to be that employers in industries with perishable products were more likely to use replacements, other things being equal, than those in industries where the durability of products reduced the short-run costs of strike-caused interruptions in production. After controlling for industry, there does not appear to be any significant effect of skill levels on the probability of strikebreaking. This result may reflect the fact that it was no more difficult to recruit skilled strikebreakers than it was to recruit unskilled ones, or it may be that this variable is poorly constructed, and industry effects are already capturing the important variations in skill levels.

None of the strike cause effects is large or statistically significant, but the variable for union authorization after 1886 enters with a negative and statistically significant effect. This suggests that either unions were becoming better at choosing which struggles they were likely to win or union control of mobility was becoming more effective in limiting strikebreaking during the late 1880s and early 1890s, and that these effects outweighed any impact of employer antipathy toward unions in this period.

Both of the scale variables enter the regression significantly and with the expected signs.[18] Employers were more likely to turn to replacements the larger the establishment or the smaller the number of workers on strike. The magnitudes of the two coefficients suggest that effects of establishment size were somewhat stronger

---

[18] The coefficients imply that a one-standard-deviation increase in the number of employees before the strike would raise the probability of using replacement workers by 7 percentage points, whereas a one-standard-deviation increase in the number of workers on strike would lower the probability of using replacements by 4.6 percentage points.

than those of the number of strikers, so that, holding constant the fraction of workers on strike, the use of replacements was more common in large establishments than in small ones.

Only a few of the year effects are statistically significant, and their pattern does not suggest any consistent cyclical effects on employers' propensity to use strikebreakers. On the other hand, the large positive effects in 1886, 1887, and 1888 suggest that employers may have increased their use of replacement workers in the wake of the pronounced unrest that culminated in the strike wave of 1886.

The estimates of the determinants of the number of replacements hired reported in column 5 indicate that the strongest explanatory factors are scale effects. The log of the number of strikers is highly significant (both statistically and quantitatively) and suggests that employers attempted to replace a little over 40 percent of their striking workers. Holding the number of workers on strike constant, the number of replacements hired was also increasing with establishment size. The coefficient on this variable implies that every 10 percent increase in establishment size increased the number of replacements by 2.4 percent.

Several other interesting patterns also emerge after controlling for these scale factors. First, the city-size effects suggest that, when employers in mid-sized cities turned to replacements, they hired larger numbers of them than was true of employers in cities with populations either under 25,000 or above 249,999. Only two of the industry effects enter the regression significantly, but both are in industries in which the propensity to hire replacements was higher than usual. In both transportation and printing and publishing, not only were employers more likely to use replacement workers, but, when they used replacements, they also tended to hire more of them. Finally, the insignificant coefficient on the inverse Mill's ratio indicates that the hypothesis of no sample selection bias cannot be rejected at standard confidence levels.

THE RECRUITMENT OF STRIKEBREAKERS

That location had little impact on employers' decisions about whether to employ replacement workers is consistent with the emergence of an increasingly integrated national labor market after the Civil War and suggests that employers in smaller communities were able to tap into broader labor markets with relative ease. Using information on sources of strikebreakers sheds further light on the impact that high rates of labor mobility had on labor conflict in this period and confirms the important role that employer recruitment played in mobilizing labor.

Anecdotal evidence makes it clear that strikebreakers were sometimes recruited over long distances. Cumbler (1974, pp. 407, 409), for example, reported that leather manufacturers in Lynn, Massachusetts, advertised in Montreal for replacements, and many of the strikebreakers whom they hired appear to have come from Newark. According to Tuttle (1966), during the Chicago meatpacking strike of 1904, replacements came from as far away as Baltimore. Foner (1975, pp. 208–9, 233) reported that in Coeur D'Alene, Idaho, mine operators recruited replacements from Duluth, Minnesota; and during the Homestead strike, Andrew Carnegie advertised for replacements in newspapers in Boston, St. Louis, and Philadelphia. Although it is possible to analyze the use of outside strikebreakers, the strike data do not provide information about the sources from which outside replacements were recruited, so I am unable to draw firm conclusions about the distances over which most recruitment occurred.

To analyze the determinants of employers' decisions about whether to recruit replacement workers locally or from other locations, I employed essentially the same framework developed in the previous section to analyze the choice of whether to use replacement workers. Restricting the scope of analysis to those strikes in which replacement workers were used, I assumed that employers weighed the expected benefits of using outside strikebreakers against the costs and chose the number of outside strikebreakers that maximized the difference between expected costs and benefits. Again, I used a two-stage estimation procedure in which the first stage examines the decision whether to use outside strikebreakers and the second stage considers the choice of how many outside strikebreakers to employ. The independent variables used in the two equations are identical to those used earlier, and the results of estimating these two equations are reported in Table 6.4.

Table 6.4. *Determinants of the Use of Replacements Brought from Other Places and the Log of the Number of Replacements Brought from Other Places*

Variable	Probit regression for use of outside replacements[a]		OLS regression for log(number of outside replacements)	
	Coefficient	t-statistic	Coefficient	t-statistic
City-size effects[b]				
25,000–49,999	0.0509	0.689	−0.0423	−0.211
50,000–99,999	−0.0865	−1.521	0.2283	0.833
100,000–249,999	−0.1345	−2.637***	−0.4381	−1.339
250,000 or more	−0.2619	−6.734***	−0.6523	−1.603
Regional effects[c]				
North Central	0.2094	5.156***	0.4177	1.513
South	0.1011	1.346	0.3081	1.446
West	0.1197	0.650	0.2856	0.888
Industry and occupation effects[d]				
Transportation	0.0735	0.999	0.3184	1.185
Construction	0.0364	0.507	−0.1691	−0.668
Mining	−0.0649	−0.851	0.0822	0.256
Stone quarrying and-cutting	0.1973	1.919*	0.0559	0.151
Metals and metallic goods	0.0446	0.645	−0.2622	−0.907
Machinery	0.0881	0.812	0.5567	1.317
Printing and publishing	0.3736	3.701***	0.1538	−0.313
Furniture	−0.0714	−0.630	−0.8814	−1.852*
Wooden goods	−0.2251	−2.537***	−0.5916	−0.866
Boots and shoes	0.1304	1.454	−0.5039	−1.330
Clothing	0.0411	0.541	−0.6254	−2.023**
Tobacco and cigars	−0.0767	−1.028	−0.8274	−2.844***
Glass	0.0456	0.349	0.0831	0.165
Food preparation, canning, butchering	0.1228	1.082	0.5533	0.690
Skilled occupation	−0.0103	−0.226	−0.2074	−1.070
Strike cause effects[e]				
Wage Increase	−0.0037	−0.090		
Hours Reduction	0.0782	1.065		
Defensive	0.0914	1.676*		
Strike characteristic effects				
Log(No. of employees)	−0.0236	−1.321	0.0632	0.803
Log(No. of strikers)	0.0881	4.658***	0.6600	5.071***
Authorized by union	0.1312	2.401**	0.4581	1.567
Authorized by union, 1887–94	0.0007	0.011	0.0427	0.161
Year effects[f]				
1882	−0.0303	−0.288	−0.3361	−0.998
1883	−0.0515	−0.536	−0.2599	−0.739

Table 6.4. (*cont.*)

Variable	Probit regression for use of outside replacements[a]		OLS regression for log(number of outside replacements)	
	Coefficient	t-statistic	Coefficient	t-statistic
1884	−0.0030	−0.030	0.2164	0.677
1885	−0.0853	−0.890	−0.5509	−1.353
1886	−0.0811	−0.972	−0.3593	−1.060
1887	0.0558	0.508	−0.0953	−0.221
1888	−0.0241	−0.207	−0.2576	−0.671
1889	0.1534	1.253	−0.2097	−0.487
1890	−0.0471	−0.441	−0.8098	−1.986**
1891	0.0741	0.659	−0.0926	−0.245
1892	−0.0602	−0.574	−0.6641	−1.601
1893	0.0727	0.631	−0.2173	−0.519
1894	0.1020	0.809	−0.2386	−0.549
Constant			−0.6807	−0.547
Inverse Mill's ratio			0.7727	1.109
N	838		263	
Chi-squared	183.33			
R-squared			0.615	

Note: The t-statistics are computed using heteroscedasticity-corrected standard errors. The probability of bringing replacement workers from elsewhere is estimated using the sample of strikes in which some replacement workers were hired. The observed probability of bringing replacements from elsewhere in this sample is 0.3127, and the predicted probability is 0.2742.
*Statistically significantly different from zero at the 10 percent level.
**Statistically significantly different from zero at the 5 percent level.
***Statistically significantly different from zero at the 1 percent level.
[a] Coefficients are reported as the partial derivatives of the probability with respect to each variable, evaluated at the sample mean values of the other independent variables. For zero-one categorical variables, the coefficient shows the change in probability for a discrete change in that variable from zero to one. The t-statistics reported are calculated using the originally estimated probit parameters and their corresponding standard errors.
[b] Omitted category is cities with population under 25,000.
[c] Omitted category is Northeast region.
[d] Omitted category is all other industries.
[e] Omitted category is strikes over work rules.
[f] Omitted category is 1881.
Source: Strike sample data described in the text.

In contrast to the limited effect of location on employers' use of strikebreakers, Table 6.4 reveals strong and systematic locational effects on the use of outside replacements. Beginning with cities of 50,000 or more population, city-size effects are negative and grow increasingly large in magnitude as city size increases. Overall, outside replacements were used in about 30 percent of strikes in which any replacements were hired. The estimated city-size effects imply that the probability of using outside replacements was reduced to just 17 percent in cities between 100,000 and 250,000 population and was less than 5 percent in cities with populations of 250,000 or more. Even after controlling for city size, employers outside the Northeast were substantially more likely to use outside replacements than employers in the Northeast. Because of small sample sizes in the South and West, however, only the coefficient estimate for the North Central region is statistically significant.

The industry effects do not suggest any very clear pattern. Printing and publishing, in which both the likelihood of using replacement workers and the number of replacements hired were higher than average, was also characterized by a higher probability of using outside replacements. Employers in stone quarrying and-cutting were also more likely to use outside replacements, whereas employers in wooden goods were less likely to use outside replacements.

Among the strike characteristics variables, it appears that employers were considerably more likely to recruit replacements from other places in the face of union-authorized strikes than in the case of those without union authorization. This tendency suggests that unions were able to enforce a degree of solidarity locally but that, as Lloyd Ulman (1955, chs. 2–3) argued, high rates of geographic mobility in this period posed a significant challenge for local unions' efforts to gain employer recognition and served as an important impetus in the movement toward the formation of national unions. The likelihood of recruiting strikebreakers from other places was also increasing with the number of workers on strike. This variable was also associated with increases in the use of replacement workers, suggesting that increases in the number of replacements that employers wished to hire may have caused them to have to look farther afield to find sufficient supplies of replacements.

The regression for the number of replacements recruited from outside reinforces the impression that, other things being equal, the number of replacements required was an important determinant of employers' need to recruit replacements at a distance. The log of the number of strikers enters with a large and statistically significant effect in this regression. This coefficient implies that a 10 percent increase in the number of workers on strike would increase the number of outside replacements hired by 6.6 percent.

Although none of the city-size or regional effects is statistically significant, their signs and relative magnitudes reinforce the impression gleaned from the first-stage estimation that employers in smaller cities and outside the Northeast tended to rely more heavily on outside replacements. In those rare instances when employers in cities with populations of 100,000 or more turned to outside replacements, the estimated coefficients imply that they used fewer of them than did their counterparts in smaller places. Similarly, when employers outside the Northeast recruited outside strikebreakers, they tended to recruit more of them than was true of employers within the Northeast. Finally, the coefficient on the inverse Mill's ratio implies that the hypothesis of no sample selection bias cannot be rejected at standard confidence levels.

STRIKEBREAKING AND LABOR MARKET INTEGRATION

During the late-nineteenth century, increasing labor market integration and technological change made it easier for employers to replace striking workers. Although labor historians have long believed that employers' use of strikebreakers was an important factor undermining organized labor in this period, discussion of strikebreaking has been based largely on evidence drawn from a few highly visible incidents. The individual strike data analyzed in this chapter confirm earlier impressions of both the ubiquity and significance of strikebreaking for labor relations in the 1880s and early 1890s. Strikebreaking was indeed quite common, occurring in over 40 percent of all strikes, and exerted a powerful influence on the chances of strike success.

Beyond this, however, the strike data also offer a number of important insights about variations in the effects of labor market integration on workers in different industries and locations. First, evidence of systematic variation across locations in the recruitment of outside replacements and the limited locational effects on employers' propensity to use strikebreakers suggest that neither geographic isolation nor community solidarity provided strikers with much protection against the threat of replacement. The greater propensity of employers to recruit outside strikebreakers in union-authorized strikes further underscores the impact that high rates of geographic mobility in this period had in undermining organized labor's efforts to win recognition in this period. Second, the risk of replacement varied substantially across industries. Industry is a proxy for a wide range of possible influences, but it appears that employers were most likely to replace striking workers in industries where the perishability of products made strikes most costly. Third, it appears that after 1886 either the efforts of national trade unions to use strike funds to control mobility among their members were successful in reducing the supply of strikebreakers in union-authorized strikes or the national unions were becoming more adept at selecting those conflicts in which they had the greatest chance of success.

7

LABOR MARKET INSTITUTIONS AND AMERICAN ECONOMIC GROWTH

Lessons from the Nineteenth Century

Efficient markets are an essential factor in a nation's economic success. In the United States, as elsewhere, during the nineteenth century, rapid technological advances in transportation and communication reduced the costs of migration and created the potential for broader, and hence more efficient, markets. Realizing this potential, however, required the creation of institutions capable of channeling information between buyers and sellers and providing the means for market participants to act on that information. As the preceding narrative shows, employers and workers responded to the opportunities that falling transportation and communication costs created, constructing labor market institutions that helped to facilitate the massive redistribution of labor that American industrialization required. The increased geographic integration of labor markets in the nineteenth century contributed to the efficient allocation of labor, but it also produced a number of other unanticipated results with significant consequences for the course of American economic development.

Three important themes characterize the development of American labor markets in this period. First, despite the widely noted importance of friends and family in conveying labor market information, the extension of labor markets was accomplished largely through the active involvement of employers in recruiting labor. Second, although the channels of recruitment created by employers and workers facilitated the increasing geographic integration of labor markets over the course of the nineteenth century, market integration did not advance uniformly. After connections between particular sources and destinations of labor were established, the actions of both employers and job seekers tended to reinforce these links at the expense of potential alternatives. As a result, the expansion of labor market boundaries tended to proceed in a path-dependent manner. In other words, history mattered. Third, the development of market institutions that promoted geographic mobility affected other dimensions of labor market performance in important ways. Especially important was the interaction between external recruitment and the internal allocation of labor within the firm. Differences in the development of market institutions for skilled and unskilled labor encouraged a growing reliance on on-the-job training as a source of skilled labor. High rates of mobility, however, discouraged the formation of long-term employment relationships that would have justified investments in this training, and contributed to a growing tension between the goals of efficient spatial labor allocation and the training of an adequate supply of skilled workers.

LABOR MARKET INSTITUTIONS AND GEOGRAPHIC INTEGRATION

Throughout the nineteenth and early-twentieth centuries the development of new, scale-intensive manufacturing technologies encouraged the growth of factory methods of production. In the United States, manufacturers who wished to take advantage of the opportunities created by these technologies repeatedly found themselves pressing up against the limits of locally available supplies of labor or, as economists would say, they found that the supply of labor was highly inelastic. Rather than accept the market-determined outcome of rising wages as they moved out along the existing labor supply curve, many employers chose to adjust along a different margin – investing in the development of channels of labor recruitment that expanded the boundaries of their labor markets. Improvements in transportation and communications technologies – the application of steam power to rail and water transportation, the introduction of the telegraph and telephone, and the falling costs of newspapers – all facilitated their efforts. But these advances would not have expanded the geographic scope of labor markets without the parallel development of mechanisms to channel information to prospective job seekers and to provide them with the assistance necessary to act on this information.

The declining costs of transportation and communication might have been expected to produce a more or less uniform broadening of market boundaries. The development of labor market institutions, however, reflected the influence of historical forces that produced a more uneven pattern of integration. Beginning in the 1840s, manufacturers in the northern United States turned increasingly to European immigrants as a source of labor. In the South, on the other hand, slave owners opposed economic development efforts that would have encouraged an influx of immigrant workers and reduced the value of one of their most important assets, slave labor. As a result, antebellum immigration was almost exclusively a northern phenomenon. While the development of institutions capable of attracting and distributing European immigrant labor was central to the mobilization of labor within the North, in the South slave traders organized a profitable and active market in slaves that facilitated substantial movements of labor into highly productive agricultural lands in the South Central region of the country.

The divergent institutional paths followed by northern and southern labor markets were reinforced in the aftermath of the Civil War despite the abolition of slavery. The foundations of the northern immigrant-based labor market expanded and deepened. Employers actively encouraged chain migration patterns that perpetuated existing links between sources of labor supply in Europe and specific destinations in the United States. At the same time, a system of commercial services – employment agencies, labor bosses, immigrant banks, boardinghouses, saloons, and the like – that provided both information and assistance sprang up in major northern cities. Although these services could not compete directly with kin- and friendship-based channels of recruitment, they provided comparable services to immigrants who lacked access to such channels. The availability of these services both helped to stimulate an increased volume of European immigration and encouraged employers in need of labor to turn to employment agencies in northern cities as a source of mobile labor. The interdependence between the actions of employers and job seekers was mutually reinforcing, thus encouraging the centralization of institutions promoting the distribution of labor in a few major northern cities, such as New York and Chicago.

In the aftermath of the Civil War, southern employers in need of labor turned briefly to northern cities to hire temporary gang labor. Although the costs of recruiting labor in this way at first appeared lower than those of developing the institutional framework needed to recruit nearby workers, southern employers soon learned that, because of low southern wages, it was extremely difficult to retain immigrant workers. Rather than raise wages to compete with northern employers, southerners instead began to develop better channels of recruitment within the South. The result was the creation of a distinct set of southern labor market channels operating largely in isolation from those in the North.

In both regions of the country, market forces worked effectively to reallocate labor as is evidenced by the declining level of wage differentials within each region. In contrast, however, wage differentials between the two regions were growing larger, and the volume of migration from the low-wage South to the high-wage North remained quite small until World War I. That southerners did not move to the North is hardly surprising. Opportunities in the South Central region provided an attractive alternative for potential migrants in the southeast. Wages in the South Central region lagged only slightly behind northern levels for much of the postbellum period, and there must have been additional nonpecuniary benefits to remaining within the South, where agricultural conditions and more intangible cultural features were familiar. These attractions were reinforced by the presence of channels of information and assistance available to promote this movement. Employer recruitment and the activities of labor agents helped to facilitate East-West movements within the South, and these initial movements established the foundations for subsequent chain migrations. In contrast, few northern employers sought to recruit labor in the South, preferring instead to rely on European immigrants to meet their labor needs. As a result, most potential migrants in the South lacked access to networks that could provide them with labor market information from the North or assist them in migrating in response to the information that was available. Despite the individual rationality of the majority of southerners' decisions to remain within the South, their choices helped to perpetuate the separateness of the region and fostered the conditions for southern poverty in much of the twentieth century (Wright 1986).

Implicit in the preceding narrative is the view that had the development of labor market institutions followed a different path, the course of American economic history would have looked substantially different. We cannot go back and rerun the course of history to test this conjecture, but it is possible to gain some perspective from the "natural experiment" that is offered by the closing off of mass immigration during and after World War I. Confronted with strong wartime demand and labor shortages, northern employers began much more actively to recruit workers in the South. The impact of these changes is clearly evident in the shift in migration patterns out of the South after 1910. Migration rates from the South increased dramatically, rising by a factor of nearly 10 for whites, and by about 2.5 for blacks. For the first time, the West South Central region became a region of net emigration. With the establishment of substantial communities of southern migrants in northern cities, the basis for subsequent chain migration flows was established. If European immigration had been cut off earlier, or if the antebellum southern economy's reliance on slave labor had not contributed to the development of a distinct southern labor market, it seems plausible that these shifts in internal migration patterns would have emerged earlier.

LABOR MARKET INSTITUTIONS, MARKET EFFICIENCY, AND ECONOMIC DEVELOPMENT

The first instinct of an economist is to assess market performance in terms of the efficiency with which the market allocates scarce resources.[1] At first glance, it appears that American labor markets

---

[1] Robert Margo (2000, p. 153), for example, observed in a recent book about antebellum labor markets that "real world economies are characterized by a never-ending stream of decisions about how to allocate labor in response to economic

performed well by this criterion. Employer recruitment and hiring practices helped to encourage and perpetuate networks of information and assistance that effectively mobilized labor over increasingly large distances. The convergence of real wages and earnings within the North and South and the narrowing of trans-Atlantic wage differences is testimony to the growing geographic integration and efficiency of labor markets. Yet, this is only part of the story. For as we have seen, wage equalization operated only within market boundaries that were historically determined. Information and assistance flowed through channels that were shaped by past events. Establishing new networks was neither a continuous nor an automatic process. Not until the existing system of labor allocation was disrupted by the cessation of international migration during World War I did employers invest in the creation of labor market channels that would effectively link labor supply in the South to employers in the North.

Moreover, focusing exclusively on the efficiency of labor allocation at a point in time obscures the inherently multidimensional nature of market outcomes. As the preceding account has shown, the ways in which employers and workers responded to geographic imbalances in labor supply interacted in important and unpredictable ways with the incentives for skill creation and, through these, the organization of work within firms. More broadly, the high mobility regime that emerged in the course of the nineteenth century affected almost every dimension of employment relationships.

Initially employers sought to fill both skilled and unskilled positions through external recruitment, relying on craft apprenticeship to produce skilled artisans. However, the development of labor market institutions facilitating geographic mobility was more effective at meeting employers' demands for unskilled than skilled workers. Employers continued to recruit skilled craft workers on

opportunities created by initial conditions. . . . Broadly speaking, labor markets can be judged effective when they permit these opportunities to be realized relatively quickly, in the manner suggested by standard economic models of supply and demand." In a similar vein, Stanley Lebergott (1964, p. 131) concluded that "the course of American history suggests that the advance from imperfect labor markets to more perfect labor markets is one of the significant external economies that pace economic growth."

external markets, but they found that the relative cost of these workers was rising over the course of the century. By the end of the century, skill premia had reached historically high levels and were well above those found in most European countries. Because the institutions to train skilled workers in America were relatively underdeveloped, and skilled workers were less responsive to international wage differentials than unskilled workers, many employers attempted to address the relative scarcity of skilled labor by reorganizing the production process. Increasing the division of labor and substituting special-purpose capital equipment for skilled workers contributed to the emergence of a distinctive American manufacturing technology and reduced the need for traditional categories of skilled labor. But this approach did not eliminate the need for skilled labor; rather, it altered the types of skills required. The growing class of operatives needed to implement the new factory methods of production required new, employer-specific skills that evolved rapidly and were most easily learned through on-the-job training and experience. These skills could often be acquired more quickly than traditional craft skills, but the investments required to produce them could still be substantial.

For workers and employers to be willing to make the needed investments in on-the-job training, both parties had to be reasonably confident that the employment relationship would last long enough for them to recoup their up-front costs. Job tenure data indicate that the potential returns from additional training provided enough incentive for a significant minority of workers to enter into relatively lengthy employment relationships. Nineteenth-century labor market institutions that focused on promoting geographic mobility, however, did not foster long-term employment relationships but created instead an industrial labor force characterized by only limited attachment to industrial work. As a result, a much larger fraction of employment relationships remained short-term than is true today. It seems likely that the high rate of turnover among manufacturing workers at the end of the nineteenth century deterred additional investments in training. We cannot directly test this conjecture, but the dramatic shift in employment policies during and after World War I once again provides a useful quasi-experiment. Once immigration restrictions had created a more stable and experienced labor force, employers moved quickly to establish centralized personnel departments and introduced policies such as formal job ladders, pension plans, subsidized housing, and insurance schemes designed to encourage long-term job attachment (Slichter 1929; Wright 1987a, pp. 332–5).

The tension between promoting geographic mobility and encouraging investments in training that emerged in the late-nineteenth century is representative of other trade-offs between the various dimensions of labor market performance that are implicit in any set of market institutions. The expanding agenda of labor reform issues around the turn of the century – such as shorter hours, restrictions on the use of women and child workers, workers' compensation insurance, and unemployment insurance – suggests that workers were becoming increasingly dissatisfied with the outcomes produced by the relatively unfettered and externally competitive labor market institutions that had emerged during the course of the nineteenth century. In the case of workers' compensation, the existing system, which relied on the courts to adjudicate liability for workplace injuries and deaths, was clearly an inferior outcome for employers as well as workers, but moving to a solution that all sides regarded as superior was a lengthy process that ultimately required legislative intervention (Fishback and Kantor 2000).

During the nineteenth century, the dynamic nature of American economic growth caused imbalances between the supply of and demand for labor in particular locations. These imbalances, in turn, created opportunities for mutually beneficial exchange between employers in labor-scarce regions and job seekers in labor-abundant ones. Employers' responses to recurrent labor scarcity encouraged the emergence of labor market institutions that were well suited to promoting the geographic mobility of labor. In this sense, market institutions responded as economic theory predicts: working to promote the efficient allocation of labor by eliminating imbalances in supply and demand. But these market institutions had other important and largely unpredictable consequences. On the one hand, they reinforced the regional division of the country created by slavery for decades after the end of the Civil War. On the other hand, the high rates of labor mobility encouraged by these market institutions discouraged long-term employment relationships and inhibited investments in training that restricted the supply of skilled workers. By the early-twentieth century, the tension between the objectives of efficient spatial labor allocation and other dimensions of the market performance was growing more and more prominent. Not until World War I brought an end to the era of mass migration, however, was it possible to move toward a new labor market regime that addressed employers' and workers' dissatisfaction by placing a greater weight on promoting long-term jobs and building worker skills within internal labor markets.

REFERENCES

Abbot, Grace. 1908. "The Chicago Employment Agency and the Immigrant Worker." *American Journal of Sociology* 14: 289–305.

Allen, Robert C. 1994. "Real Incomes in the English-Speaking World, 1879–1913." In George Grantham and Mary MacKinnon, eds. *Labour Market Evolution: The Economic History of Market Integration, Wage Flexibility and the Employment Relation*. London and New York: Routledge, pp. 107–39.

Atack, Jeremy, and Peter Passell. 1994. *A New Economic View of American History from Colonial Times to the Present*, 2nd ed. New York and London: W. W. Norton.

Bailey, Gary L. 1991. "The Commissioner of Labor's 'Strikes and Lockouts': A Cautionary Note." *Labor History* 32: 432–40.

Baron, James N., Frank R. Dobbin, and P. Devereaux Jennings. 1986. "War and Peace: The Evolution of Modern Personnel Administration in U.S. Industry." *American Journal of Sociology* 92: 350–83.

Barton, Josef J. 1975. *Peasants and Strangers: Italians, Rumanians, and Slovaks in an American City, 1890–1950*. Cambridge, MA: Harvard University Press.

Bemis, Edward W. 1891. "Relation of Trades-Unions to Apprentices." *Quarterly Journal of Economics* 6: 76–93.

Bennett, Sari, and Carville Earle. 1982. "The Geography of Strikes in the United States, 1881–1894." *Journal of Interdisciplinary History* 13: 63–84.

Ben-Porath, Yoram. 1980. "The F-connection: Families, Friends, and Firms in the Organization of Exchange." *Population and Development Review* 6: 1–30.

Bernstein, David E. 1995. "The Law and Economics of Post-Civil War Restrictions on Interstate Migration by African Americans." George Mason University, School of Law. Law and Economics Working Paper Series, no. 96–103.

Berridge, William A. 1929. "Labor Turnover in American Factories." *Monthly Labor Review* 29: 62–5.

Bessen, James. 2000. "The Skills of the Unskilled in the American Industrial Revolution." Research on Innovation, Working Paper, www.researchoninnovation.org/skills.pdf.

Bodnar, John. 1974. "The Procurement of Immigrant Labor: Selected Documents." *Pennsylvania History* 41: 189–206.

1985. *The Transplanted: A History of Immigrants in Urban America.* Bloomington, IN: University of Indiana Press.

Bodnar, John, Roger Simon, and Michael P. Weber. 1982. *Lives of Their Own: Blacks, Italians and Poles in Pittsburgh, 1900–1960.* Urbana, IL: University of Illinois Press.

Bogart, E. L. 1900. "Public Employment Offices in the United States and Germany." *Quarterly Journal of Economics* 14: 341–77.

Boyer, George R., and Timothy J. Hatton. 1994. "Regional Labor Market Integration in England and Wales, 1850–1913." In George Grantham and Mary MacKinnon, eds. *Labour Market Evolution: The Economic History of Market Integration, Wage Flexibility and the Employment Relation.* London and New York: Routledge, pp. 84–106.

Brecher, Jeremy. 1972. *Strike!* Boston: South End Press.

Breen, William J. 1987. "Sectional Influences on National Policy: The South, the Labor Department, and the Wartime Mobilization, 1917–1918." In Bruce Clayton and John A. Salmond, eds., *The South is Another Land: Essays on the Twentieth-Century South.* New York; Westport, CT; and London: Greenwood Press, pp. 69–84.

Brissenden, Paul F., and Emil Frankel. 1920. "Mobility of Labor in American Industry." *Monthly Labor Review* 10: 1342–62.

Broadberry, S. N. 1997. *The Productivity Race: British Manufacturing in International Perspective, 1850–1990.* Cambridge and New York: Cambridge University Press.

Brody, David. 1960. *Steelworkers in America.* Cambridge, MA: Harvard University Press.

Brown, John K. 1995. *The Baldwin Locomotive Works, 1831–1915: A Study in American Industrial Practice.* Studies in Industry and Society, no. 8. Baltimore and London: Johns Hopkins University Press.

Brown, Martin, and Peter Philips. 1985. "The Evolution of Labor Market Structure: The California Canning Industry." *Industrial and Labor Relations Review* 38: 392–407.

1986a. "The Historical Origin of Job Ladders in the U.S. Canning Industry and Their Effects on the Gender Division of Labour." *Cambridge Journal of Economics* 10: 129–45.

1986b. "Craft Labor and Mechanization in Nineteenth-Century American Canning." *Journal of Economic History* 46: 743–56.

Card, David, and Craig A. Olson. 1995. "Bargaining Power, Strike Durations, and Wage Outcomes: An Analysis of Strikes in the 1880s." *Journal of Labor Economics* 13: 32–61.

Carosso, Vincent J. 1970. *Investment Banking in America.* Cambridge, MA: Harvard University Press.

Carter, Michael J., and Susan B. Carter. 1985. "Internal Labor Markets in Retailing: The Early Years." *Industrial and Labor Relations Review* 38: 586–98.

Carter, Susan B., and Elizabeth Savoca. 1990. "Labor Mobility and Lengthy Jobs in Nineteenth-Century America." *Journal of Economic History* 50: 1–16.

Carter, Susan B., and Richard Sutch. 1999. "Historical Perspectives on the Economic Consequences of Immigration into the United States." In Charles Hirschman, Philip Kasinitz, and Josh DeWind, eds. *The Handbook of International Migration: The American Experience.* New York: Russell Sage Foundation, pp. 319–41.

Carter, Susan B., Roger L. Ransom, and Richard Sutch. 1991. "The Historical Labor Statistics Project at the University of California." *Historical Methods* 24: 52–65.

Chandler, Alfred D., Jr. 1977. *The Visible Hand: The Managerial Revolution in American Business.* Cambridge, MA: Harvard University Press.

Chicago. 1914. *Report of the Mayor's Commission on Unemployment.* Chicago: n.p.

Coelho, Philip R. P., and James F. Shepherd. 1974. "Differences in Regional Prices: The United States, 1851–1880." *Journal of Economic History* 34: 551–91.

1976. "Regional Differences in Real Wages: The United States, 1851–1880." *Explorations in Economic History* 13: 203–30.

1979. "The Impact of Regional Differences in Prices and Wages on Economic Growth: The United States in 1890." *Journal of Economic History* 39: 69–85.

Cohen, William. 1991. *At Freedom's Edge: Black Mobility and the Southern White Quest for Racial Control, 1861–1915.* Batton Rouge, LA, and London: Louisiana State University Press.

Collins, William J. 1997. "When the Tide Turned: Immigration and the Delay of the Great Migration." *Journal of Economic History* 57: 607–32.

Commons, John R. 1904. "Labor Conditions in Meat Packing and the Recent Strike." *Quarterly Journal of Economics* 9: 1–32.

Commons, John R., and associates. 1918. *History of Labour in the United States,* Vol II. New York: Macmillan.

Conner, J. E. 1907. "Free Public Employment Offices in the United States." *Bulletin of the Bureau of Labor* no. 68: 1–115.

Corcoran, Mary, Linda Datcher, and Greg J. Duncan. 1980. "Information and Influence Networks in Labor Markets." *Five Thousand American Families – Patterns of Economic Progress: Vol. 8, Analyses of the First Eleven Years of the Panel Study of Income Dynamics.* Ann Arbor, MI: Institute for Social Research, pp. 1–38.

Cowgill, Theodore Thomas. 1928. "The Employment Agencies of Chicago." M.A. thesis, University of Chicago.

Cramton, Peter C., and Joseph S. Tracy. 1995. "The Use of Replacement Workers in Union Contract Negotiations: The U.S. Experience, 1980–1989." NBER Working Paper, no. 5106.

Creamer, Daniel. 1941. "Recruiting Contract Laborers for the Amoskeag Mills." *Journal of Economic History* 1: 42–56.

Cumbler, John T. 1974. "Labor, Capital, and Community: The Struggle for Power." *Labor History* 15: 395–415.

Currie, Janet, and Joseph Ferrie. 1995. "Strikes and the Law in the U.S., 1881–1894: New Evidence on the Origins of American Exceptionalism." NBER Working Paper, no. 5368.

2000. "The Law and Labor Strife in the United States, 1881–1894." *Journal of Economic History* 60: 42–66.

David, Paul A. 1987. "Industrial Labor Market Adjustment in a Region of Recent Settlement: Chicago, 1848–1868." In Peter Kilby, ed. *Quantity and Quiddity: Essays in U.S. Economic History.* Middletown, CT: Wesleyan University Press, pp. 47–97.

Davis, Lance E. 1963. "Capital Immobilities and Finance Capitalism: A Study of Economic Evolution in the United States, 1820–1920." *Explorations in Entrepreneurial History* 1: 88–105.

1965. "The Investment Market, 1870–1914: The Evolution of a National Market." *Journal of Economic History* 25: 355–99.

Dawson, Andrew. 1979. "The Paradox of Dynamic Technological Change and the Labor Aristocracy in the United States, 1880–1914." *Labor History* 20: 325–351.

De Schweinitz, Dorothea. 1932. *How Workers Find Jobs: A Study of Four Thousand Hosiery Workers in Philadelphia.* Philadelphia: University of Pennsylvania Press.

Devine, Edward T. 1909. "Employment Bureau for the People of New York City." *Annals of the American Academy of Political and Social Science* 33: 225–38.

Doeringer, Peter B., and Michael J. Piore. 1985. *Internal Labor Markets and Manpower Analysis.* Armonk, NY: M. E. Sharpe.

Douglas, Paul H. 1921. *American Apprenticeship and Industrial Education.* New York: Columbia University.

Dublin, Thomas. 1979. *Women at Work: The Transformation of Work and Community in Lowell, Massachusetts, 1826–1860.* New York: Columbia University.

DuBoff, Richard B. 1982. "The Telegraph and the Structure of Markets in the United States, 1845–1890." *Research in Economic History,* vol. 8. Greenwich, CT: JAI Press, pp. 253–78.

Dunlevy, James A. 1980. "Nineteenth-Century European Immigration to the United States: Intended Versus Lifetime Settlement Patterns." *Economic Development and Cultural Change* 29: 77–90.

Dunlevy, James A., and Henry A. Gemery. 1977. "The Role of Migrant Stock and Lagged Migration in the Settlement Patterns of Nineteenth Century Immigrants." *Review of Economics and Statistics* 59: 137–44.

1978. "Economic Opportunity and the Response of 'Old' and 'New' Migrants to the United States." *Journal of Economic History* 38: 901–18.

Dunlevy, James A., and Richard P. Saba. 1992. "The Role of Nationality-Specific Characteristics on the Settlement Patterns of Late Nineteenth-Century Immigrants." *Explorations in Economic History* 29: 228–49.

Easterlin, Richard A. 1957. "Estimates of Manufacturing Activity." In Everett S. Lee, Ann Ratner Miller, Carol P. Brainerd, and Richard Easterlin, *Population Redistribution and Economic Growth, United States, 1870–1950: Vol. 1, Methodological Considerations and Reference Tables.* Philadelphia: American Philosophical Society, pp. 635–702.

Edwards, Alba M. 1933. "A Social-Economic Grouping of the Gainful Workers in the United States." *Journal of the American Statistical Association* 28: 377–87.

Edwards, P. K. 1981. *Strikes in the United States, 1881–1974.* Oxford: Basil Blackwell.

Ehrlich, Richard L. 1974. "Immigrant Strikebreaking Activity: A Sampling of Opinion Expressed in the 'National Labor Tribune.'" *Labor History* 15: 529–42.

Elbaum, Bernard. 1984. "Making and Shaping of Job and Pay Structures in the Iron and Steel Industry." In Paul Osterman, ed. *Internal Labor Markets.* Cambridge, MA: MIT Press, pp. 71–107.

1989. "Why Apprenticeship Persisted in Britain but Not in the United States." *Journal of Economic History* 49: 337–349.

Eldridge, Hope T., and Dorothy Swaine Thomas. 1964. *Population Redistribution and Economic Growth, United States, 1870–1950: Vol. 3, Demographic Analyses and Interrelations.* Philadelphia: American Philosophical Society.

Engerman, Stanley, and Claudia Goldin. 1994. "Seasonality in Nineteenth-Century Labor Markets." In Thomas Weiss and Donald Schaefer, eds. *American Economic Development in Historical Perspective.* Stanford, CA: Stanford University Press, pp. 99–127.

Erickson, Charlotte. 1957. *American Industry and the European Immigrant, 1860–1885.* Cambridge, MA: Harvard University Press.

  1972. *Invisible Immigrants: The Adaptation of English and Scottish Immigrants in Nineteenth Century America.* Coral Gables, FL: University of Miami Press.

  1984. "Why Did Contract Labor Not Work in the Nineteenth Century United States." In Shula Marks and Peter Richardson, eds. *International Migration: Historical Perspectives.* London: Temple Smith for the Institute of Commonwealth Studies, pp. 34–56.

Ernst, Robert. 1949. *Immigrant Life in New York City, 1825–1863.* New York: King's Crown Press.

Field, Alexander James. 1978. "Sectoral Shifts in Antebellum Massachusetts: A Reconsideration." *Explorations in Economic History* 15: 146–71.

  1992. "The Magnetic Telegraph, Price and Quantity Data, and the New Management of Capital." *Journal of Economic History* 52: 401–14.

Fishback, Price V. 1992. *Soft Coal, Hard Choices: The Economic Welfare of Bituminous Coal Miners, 1890–1930.* New York: Oxford University Press.

  1998. "Operation of 'Unfettered' Labor Markets: Exit and Voice in American Labor Markets at the Turn of the Century." *Journal of Economic Literature* 36: 722–65.

Fishback, Price V., and Shawn Everett Kantor. 2000. *A Prelude to the Welfare State: The Origins of Workers' Compensation.* Chicago and London: University of Chicago Press.

Foner, Philip S. 1975. *History of the Labor Movement in the United States: Vol. II, From the Founding of the American Federation of Labor to the Emergence of American Imperialism,* 2nd ed. New York: International Publishers.

Freeman, Richard. 1998. "Spurts in Union Growth: Defining Moments and Social Processes." In Michael D. Bordo, Claudia Goldin, and Eugene White, eds., *The Defining Moment: The Great Depression and the American Economy in the Twentieth Century.* Chicago and London: University of Chicago Press, pp. 265–96.

Freeman, Richard, and James L. Medoff. 1984. *What Do Unions Do?* New York: Basic Books.

Friedman, Gerald. 1988. "Strike Success and Union Ideology: The United States and France, 1880–1914." *Journal of Economic History* 48: 1–26.

  1992. "Dividing Labor: Urban Politics and Big-City Construction in Late-Nineteenth Century America." In Claudia Goldin and Hugh Rockoff, eds. *Strategic Factors in Nineteenth Century American Economic History: A Volume to Honor Robert W. Fogel.* Chicago and London: University of Chicago Press, pp. 447–64.

REFERENCES

Gallaway, Lowell E., Richard K. Vedder, and Vishwa Shukla. 1974. "The Distribution of the Immigrant Population in the United States: An Econometric Analysis." *Explorations in Economic History* 11: 213–26.

Garraty, John. 1978. *Unemployment in History: Economic Thought and Public Policy*. New York: Harper & Row.

Gates, Paul Wallace. 1957. *The Illinois Central Railroad and Its Colonization Work*, Harvard Economic Studies, Vol. 42. Cambridge, MA: Harvard University Press.

Gjerde, John. 1985. *From Peasants to Farmers: Migration from Balestrand, Norway to the Upper Middle West*. Cambridge and New York: Cambridge University Press.

Goldin, Claudia. 1990. *Understanding the Gender Gap: An Economic History of American Women*. New York and Oxford: Oxford University Press.

Goldin, Claudia, and Lawrence F. Katz. 1999. "The Returns to Skill in the United States Across the Twentieth Century." NBER Working Paper, no. 7126.

Gordon, David M., Richard Edwards, and Michael Reich. 1982. *Segmented Work, Divided Workers: The Historical Transformation of Labor in the United States*. Cambridge and New York: Cambridge University Press.

Gospel, Howard F. 1992. *Markets, Firms, and the Management of Labour in Modern Britain*. Cambridge and New York: Cambridge University Press.

Granovetter, Mark S. 1974. *Getting a Job: A Study of Contracts and Careers*. Cambridge and New York: Cambridge University Press.

Great Britain, Board of Trade. 1911. *Cost of Living in American Towns*. Reprinted by U.S. Senate, 62nd Congress, 1st sess., Sen. Doc. 22, vol. 4. Washington, DC: GPO.

Gutman, Herbert G. 1962. "Reconstruction in Ohio: Negroes in the Hocking Valley Coal Mines in 1873 and 1874." *Labor History* 3: 243–64.

   1970. "The Worker's Search for Power: Labor in the Gilded Age." In H. Wayne Morgan, ed. *The Gilded Age: A Reappraisal*. Syracuse, NY: Syracuse University Press, pp. 31–54.

Haines, Michael R. 1989. "A State and Local Consumer Price Index for the United States in 1890." *Historical Methods* 22: 97–105.

Hamilton, Gillian. 2000. "The Decline of Apprenticeship in North America: Evidence from Montreal." *Journal of Economic History* 60: 627–64.

Hanagan, Michael. 1997. "Markets, Industrial Relations, and the Law: Britain and France: 1867–1906." In Louise A. Tilly and Jytte Klausen, eds. *States, Citizenship Rights and European Integration*. London: Rowman and Littlefield, pp. 127–46.

Harney, Robert F. 1974. "The Padrone and the Immigrant." *Canadian Review of American Studies* 5: 101–18.

   1979. "Montreal's King of Italian Labor: A Case Study of Padronism." *Labour/Le Travailleur* 4: 57–84.

Harris, Howell John. 1991. "Getting It Together: The Metal Manufacturers Association of Philadelphia, c. 1900–1930." In Sanford M. Jacoby, ed. *Masters to Managers: Historical and Comparative Perspectives on American Employers*. New York: Columbia University Press, pp. 111–31.

REFERENCES

Harrison, Shelby M., Bradley Buell, Mary La Dame, Leslie E. Woodcock, and Frederick Alonzo King. 1924. *Public Employment Offices: Their Purpose, Structure, and Methods.* New York: Russell Sage Foundation.

Hatton, Timothy J., and Jeffrey G. Williamson. 1994a. "International Migration 1850–1939: An Economic Survey." In Timothy Hatton and Jeffrey G. Williamson, eds. *Migration and the International Labor Market, 1850–1939.* New York and London: Routledge, pp. 3–32.

1994b. "What Drove the Mass Migrations from Europe in the Late Nineteenth Century." *Population and Development Review* 20: 533–59.

Heckman, James J. 1979. "Sample Selection Bias as a Specification Error." *Econometrica* 47: 153–61.

Holmes, William F. 1980. "Labour Agents and the Georgia Exodus, 1899–1900." *South Atlantic Quarterly* 79: 436–48.

Hounshell, David A. 1984. *From the American System to Mass Production, 1800–1932: The Development of Manufacturing Technology in the United States.* Baltimore and London: Johns Hopkins University Press.

Jackson, Robert Max. 1984. *The Formation of Craft Labor Markets.* Orlando, FL: Academic Press.

Jacoby, Daniel. 1991a. "Legal Foundations of Human Capital Markets." *Industrial Relations* 30: 229–50.

1991b. "The Transformation of Industrial Apprenticeship in the United States." *Journal of Economic History* 51: 887–910.

Jacoby, Sanford M. 1985. *Employing Bureaucracy: Managers, Unions, and the Transformation of Work in American Industry, 1900–1945.* New York: Columbia University.

Jacoby, Sanford M., and Sunil Sharma. 1992. "Employment Duration and Industrial Labor Mobility in the United States, 1880–1980." *Journal of Economic History* 52: 161–79.

James, John A. 1978. *Money and Capital Markets in Postbellum America.* Princeton, NJ: Princeton University Press.

1994. "Job Tenure in the Gilded Age." In George Grantham and Mary MacKinnon, eds. *Labour Market Evolution: The Economic History of Market Integration, Wage Flexibility and the Employment Relation.* London and New York: Routledge, pp. 185–204.

Jaynes, Gerald David. 1986. *Branches without Roots: Genesis of the Black Working Class in the American South, 1862–1882.* New York and Oxford: Oxford University Press.

Jerome, Harry. 1926. *Migration and Business Cycles.* New York: National Bureau of Economic Research.

Jones, Maldwyn A. 1980. "Immigration." In Glen Porter, ed., *Encyclopedia of American Economic History: Studies of the Principal Movements and Ideas,* vol. 3. New York: Charles Scribner's Sons, pp. 1068–86.

Kamphoefner, Walter D. 1987. *The Westfalians: From Germany to Missouri.* Princeton, NJ: Princeton University Press.

Kapp, Friedrich. 1870. *Immigration and the Commissioners of Emigration.* New York: The Nation Press; reprinted New York: Arno Press and the New York Times, 1969.

Kellor, Frances. 1915. *Out of Work: A Study of Unemployment.* New York and London: G. P. Putnam's Sons.

Kennan, John. 1986. "The Economics of Strikes." In Orley Ashenfelter and Richard Layard, eds. *Handbook of Labor Economics,* 2 vols., Amsterdam: North-Holland, pp. 1091–1138.

REFERENCES

Keyssar, Alexander. 1986. *Out of Work: The First Century of Unemployment in Massachusetts*. Interdisciplinary Perspectives in Modern History. Cambridge and New York: Cambridge University Press.

Klug, Thomas. 1989. "Employers' Strategies in the Detroit Labor Market, 1900–1929." In Nelson Lichtenstein and Stephen Meyer, eds. *On the Line: Essays in the History of Auto Work*. Urbana and Chicago: University of Illinois Press, pp. 42–72.

Koren, John. 1897. "The Padrone System and Padrone Banks." *Bulletin of the Department of Labor* no. 9: 113–29.

Lebergott, Stanley. 1964. *Manpower in Economic Growth: The American Record Since 1800*. New York: McGraw-Hill.

1984. *The Americans: An Economic Record*. New York and London: W. W. Norton.

Leiserson, William M. 1914. "The Theory of Public Employment Offices and the Principles of their Practical Administration." *Political Science Quarterly* 29: 28–46.

Licht, Walter. 1983. *Working for the Railroad: The Organization of Work in the Nineteenth Century*. Princeton, NJ: Princeton University.

1992. *Getting Work: Philadelphia, 1840–1950*. Cambridge, MA: Harvard University Press.

Long, Clarence D. 1960. "Wages and Earnings in the United States, 1860–1890." *National Bureau of Economic Research, General Series*, no. 67. Princeton, NJ: Princeton University Press.

MacDonald, John S., and Leatrice D. MacDonald. 1974. "Chain Migration, Ethnic Neighborhood Formation and Social Networks." In Charles Tilly, ed. *An Urban World*. Boston: Little Brown, pp. 226–36.

Maddala, G. S. 1983. "Limited-Dependent and Qualitative Variables in Econometrics." *Econometric Society Monographs*, no. 3. Cambridge and New York: Cambridge University Press.

Mandle, Jay. 1978. *The Roots of Black Poverty*. Durham, NC: Duke University Press.

Mankiw, N. Gregory. 1998. *Principles of Economics*. Fort Worth, TX: Dryden Press.

Margo, Robert A. 2000. *Wages and Labor Markets in the United States, 1820–1860*. Chicago and London: University of Chicago Press.

Marshall, Alfred. 1961. *Principles of Economics*, 9th (variorium) ed. annotated by C. W. Guillebaud. London: Macmillan.

Massachusetts Bureau of Statistics of Labor. 1894. *Twenty-Fourth Annual Report*. Boston: Wright and Potter.

Mater, Dan H. 1940. "The Development and Operation of the Railroad Seniority System." *Journal of Business* 13: 384–419.

McHugh, Cathy L. 1988. *Mill Family: the Labor System in the Southern Cotton Textile Industry, 1880–1915*. New York and Oxford: Oxford University Press.

Meade, Emily Fogg. 1907. "The Italian on the Land: A Study of Immigration." *Bulletin of the Bureau of Labor* no. 70: 473–533.

Minnesota Bureau of Labor. 1895. *4th Biennial Report (1893–1894)*. St. Paul: Pioneer Press.

Missouri Bureau of Labor Statistics. 1891. *Thirteenth Annual Report, 1891*. Jefferson City, MO: Tribune Printing Company.

Moch, Leslie Page. 1989. "Europeans Leave Home: Internal, International, and Transatlantic Migrations in the Nineteenth and Early Twentieth Centuries." Photocopy, University of Michigan–Flint.

Montgomery, David. 1980. "Strikes in Nineteenth-Century America." *Social Science History* 4: 81–104.

Morawska, Ewa. 1990. "The Sociology and Historiography of Immigration." In Virginia Yans-McLaughlin, ed. *Immigration Reconsidered: History, Sociology, and Politics*. New York and Oxford: Oxford University Press.

Mullin, Debbie. 1993. "The Porous Umbrella of the AFL: Evidence from Nineteenth-Century State Labor Bureau Reports on the Establishment of American Unions." Ph.D. Diss., University of Virginia.

Murayama, Yuzu. 1991. "Information and Emigrants: Interprefectural Differences of Japanese Emigration to the Pacific Northwest, 1880–1915." *Journal of Economic History* 52: 125–47.

Myers, Charles A., and Rupert Maclaurin. 1943. *The Movement of Factory Workers: A Study of a New England Industrial Community, 1937–1939 and 1942*. New York: John Wiley & Sons.

Myers, Charles A., and George P. Shultz. 1951. *The Dynamics of a Labor Market*. New York: Prentice Hall.

Nelli, Humbert S. 1970. *Italians in Chicago, 1880–1930: A Study in Ethnic Mobility*. New York and Oxford: Oxford University Press.

Nelson, Daniel. 1975. *Managers and Workers: Origins of the New Factory System in the United States, 1880–1920*. Madison, WI: University of Wisconsin Press.

Nelson, Philip. 1959. "Migration, Real Income and Information." *Journal of Regional Sciences* 1: 43–73.

New York. 1909. *Report of the Commision on Immigration of the State of New York*. Albany, NY: J. B. Lyon.

New York, Bureau of Labor Statistics. 1886. *Third Annual Report*. Albany, NY: Argus.

   1909. "Industrial Training." *26th Annual Report*, Part I. Albany, NY: State Dept. of Labor.

New York, Commissioners of Emigration. 1869–1874; 1880–1886. *Annual Reports*. New York: n.p.

New York Times. 1868a. "Emigration and the Labor Market." 2 February, p. 4.

   1868b. "Unemployed Emigrants." 3 February, p. 8.

   1868c. "Emigrant Labor." 23 July, p. 1.

Odell, Kerry A. 1989. "The Integration of Regional and Interregional Capital Markets: Evidence from the Pacific Coast, 1883–1913." *Journal of Economic History* 49: 297–310.

Ohio, Bureau of the Statistics of Labor. 1889. *Twelfth Annual Report, 1888*. Columbus, OH: n.p.

O'Hanlon, John. 1976. *Reverend John O'Hanlon's "The Irish Emigrant's Guide for the United States,"* A Critical Edition with Introduction and Commentary by Edward J. Maguire. New York: Arno Press.

O'Rourke, Kevin, Jeffrey G. Williamson, and Timothy J. Hatton. 1994. "Mass Migration, Commodity Market Integration and Real Wage Convergence: The Late-Nineteenth-Century Atlantic Economy." In Timothy J. Hatton and Jeffrey G. Williamson, eds. *Migration and the International Labor Market, 1850–1939.* New York and London: Routledge, pp. 203–20.

Ozanne, Robert. 1967. *A Century of Labor Management Relations.* Madison, WI: University of Wisconsin Press.

Peck, Gunther William. 1994. "Reinventing Free Labor: Immigrant Padrones and Contract Laborers in North America, 1880–1920." Ph.D. Diss., Yale University.

Perloff, Harvey S., E. S. Dunn, E. E. Lampard, and R. F. Muth. 1965. *Regions, Resources, and Economic Growth.* Lincoln, NB: University of Nebraska Press.

Piore, Michael J. 1979. *Birds of Passage: Migrant Labor in Industrial Societies.* Cambridge and New York: Cambridge University Press.

Rees, Albert, and George P. Shultz. 1970. *Workers and Wages in an Urban Labor Market.* Chicago and London: University of Chicago Press.

Reynolds, Lloyd G. 1951. *The Structure of Labor Markets: Wages and Labor Mobility in Theory and* Practice. New York: Harper & Brothers.

Richardson, Reed C. 1963. *The Locomotive Engineer, 1863–1963: A Century of Railway Labor Relations and Work Rules.* Ann Arbor, MI: University of Michigan.

Rosenberg, Nathan. 1976. *Perspectives on Technology.* Cambridge and New York: Cambridge University Press.

Rosenbloom, Joshua L. 1988. "Labor Market Institutions and the Geographic Integration of Labor Markets in the Late Nineteenth Century United States." Ph.D. Diss., Stanford University.

1990. "One Market or Many? Labor Market Integration in the Late Nineteenth-Century United States." *Journal of Economic History* 50: 85–107.

1996. "Was There a National Labor Market at the End of the Nineteenth Century? New Evidence on Earnings in Manufacturing." *Journal of Economic History* 56: 626–56.

Rothenberg, Winifred B. 1988. "The Emergence of Farm Labor Markets and the Transformation of the Rural Economy: Massachusetts, 1750–1855." *Journal of Economic History* 48: 537–66.

Sargent, Frank B. 1911. "Statistics of Unemployment and the Work of Employment Offices." *Bulletin of the United States Bureau of Labor*, Misc. Ser. No. 109.

Sautter, Udo. 1983. "North American Government Labor Agencies Before World War One: A Cure for Unemployment?" *Labor History* 24: 366–93.

1991. *Three Cheers for the Unemployed: Government and Unemployment Before the New Deal.* Cambridge and New York: Cambridge University Press.

Saxonhouse, Gary, and Gavin Wright. 1984. "Two Forms of Cheap Labor in Textile History." In Gary Saxonhouse and Gavin Wright, eds. *Technique, Spirit and Form in the Making of Modern Economies: Essays in Honor of William N. Parker*, Research in Economic History, Supplement 3. Greenwich, CT, and London: JAI Press, pp. 3–32.

Shergold, Peter R. 1983. "'Reefs of Roast Beef': the American Worker's Standard of Living in Comparative Perspective." In Dirk Hoerder, ed. *American Labor and Immigration History, 1877–1920s: Recent European Research.* Urbana, IL: University of Illinois Press, pp. 78–106.

Sheridan, Frank J. 1907. "Italian, Slavic, and Hungarian Unskilled Immigrant Laborers in the United States." *Bulletin of the Bureau of Labor* no. 15: 403–86.

Slichter, Sumner. 1929. "The Current Labor Policies of American Industries." *Quarterly Journal of Economics* 43: 393–435.

Smelser, D. P. 1919. *Unemployment and American Trade Unions.* Baltimore: The Johns Hopkins Press.

Smiley, Gene. 1975. "Interest Rate Movements in the United States, 1888–1913." *Journal of Economic History* 35: 591–620.

Snowden, Kenneth. 1987a. "Mortgage Rates and American Capital Market Development in the Late Nineteenth Century." *Journal of Economic History* 47: 671–92.

——— 1987b. "American Stock Market Development and Performance, 1871–1929." *Explorations in Economic History* 24: 381–420.

Sobek, Matthew 1995. "Occupation and Income Scores." *Historical Methods* 28: 47–51.

Sobek, Matthew, and Lisa Dillon. 1995. "Interpreting Work: Classifying Occupations in the Public Use Microdata Samples." *Historical Methods* 28: 70–3.

Spiller, Pablo T., and Cliff J. Huang. 1986. "On the Extent of the Market: Wholesale Gasoline in the Northeastern United States." *Journal of Industrial Economics* 35: 131–45.

Stark, Oded. 1984. "Bargaining, Altruism, and Demographic Phenomena." *Population and Development Review* 10: 679–92.

Stephens, George Asbury. 1911. "Influence of Trade Education upon Wages." *Journal of Political Economy* 19: 17–35.

Stigler, George J., and Robert A. Sherwin. 1985. "The Extent of the Market." *Journal of Law and Economics* 28: 555–85.

Stone, Katherine. 1974. "The Origins of Job Structures in the Steel Industry." *Review of Radical Political Economics* 6: 113–73.

Stover, John F. 1961. *American Railroads.* Chicago: University of Chicago Press.

Stromquist, Shelton. 1983. "Enginemen and Shopmen: Technological Change and the Organization of Labor in an Era of Railroad Expansion." *Labor History* 24: 485–99.

——— 1987. *A Generation of Boomers: The Pattern of Railroad Labor Conflict in Nineteenth-Century America.* Urbana, IL: University of Illinois.

Sundstrom, William A. 1986. "Studies in the Evolution of the Employment Relationship in American Manufacturing, 1880–1930." Ph.D. diss., Stanford University.

——— 1988. "Internal Labor Markets before World War I: On-the-Job Training and Employee Promotion." *Explorations in Economic History* 25: 424–45.

Sundstrom, William A., and Joshua L. Rosenbloom. 1993. "Occupational Differences in the Dispersion of Wages and Working Hours: Labor Market Integration in the United States, 1890–1903." *Explorations in Economic History* 30: 379–408.

Sylla, Richard. 1969. "Federal Policy, Banking Market Structure and Capital Mobilization in the United States, 1863–1913." *Journal of Economic History* 29: 657–86.

Tadman, Michael, 1989. *Speculators and Slaves: Masters, Traders, and slaves in The Old South.* Madison, WI: University of Wisconsin Press.

Taylor, Alan M., and Jeffrey G. Williamson. 1994. "Convergence in the Age of Mass Migration." NBER Working Paper, no. 4711.

Taylor, George Rogers, and Irene D. Neu. 1956. *The American Railroad Network, 1861–1890.* Cambridge, MA: Harvard University Press.

Thompson, Carl William. 1907. "Labor in the Packing Industry." *Journal of Political Economy* 15: 88–108.

Tilly, Charles. 1990. "Transplanted Networks." In Virginia Yans-McLaughlin, ed. *Immigration Reconsidered: History, Sociology, and Politics.* New York and Oxford: Oxford University Press, pp. 79–95.

Tuttle, William M., Jr. 1966. "Some Strikebreakers' Observations of Industrial Warfare." *Labor History* 7: 193–96.

    1969. "Labor Conflict and Racial Violence: The Black Worker in Chicago, 1894–1919." *Labor History* 10: 408–32.

Tygiel, Jules. 1981. "Tramping Artisans: The Case of the Carpenters in Industrial America." *Labor History* 22: 348–76.

Ulman, Lloyd. 1955. *The Rise of the National Trade Union.* Cambridge, MA: Harvard University Press.

U.S. Bureau of Labor. 1888. *Third Annual Report of the Commissioner of Labor.* Washington, DC: GPO.

    1896. *Tenth Annual Report of the Commissioner of Labor.* Washington, DC: GPO.

    1901. *Sixteenth Annual Report of the Commissioner of Labor.* Washington, DC: GPO.

U.S. Bureau of the Census. 1975. *Historical Statistics of the United States, Colonial Times to 1970,* Bicentennial Edition. Washington, DC: GPO.

U.S. Congress, House of Representatives. 1886. *Report on the Statistics of Wages in Manufacturing with Supplementary Reports.* Joseph D. Weeks. House Misc. Doc. 42, vol. 13, part 20, 47th Cong., 2nd Sess. Washington, DC: GPO.

    1889. *Select Committee to Inquire into the Alleged Violations of the Laws Prohibiting the Importation of Contract Laborers, Paupers, Convicts and Other Classes.* 50th Cong. 2nd sess. Washington, DC: GPO.

U.S. Congress, House of Representatives, Industrial Commission. 1901. *Relations and Conditions of Capital and Labor.* 57th Cong., 2nd sess. Washington, DC: GPO

U.S. Congress, Senate. 1892. *Retail Prices and Wages.* Senate Report no. 986, 52nd Cong., 1st sess., 3 parts. Washington, DC: GPO.

    1911. Reports on the Immigration Commission. "Immigrants in Industries." 61st Cong., 2nd sess., Senate doc. 633. Washington, DC: GPO.

U.S. Department of Commerce and Labor. 1905. *Nineteenth Annual Report of the Commissioner of Labor.* "Wages and Hours of Labor." Washington, DC: GPO.

U.S. Department of Interior, Census Office. 1897. *Eleventh Census, 1890.* Washington, DC: GPO.

U.S. Department of Labor. 1898. "Wages in the United States and Europe, 1870–1898." *Bulletin* no. 18: 665–93.

    1904. *Regulation and Restriction of Output.* Eleventh Special Report of the Commissioner of Labor. Washington, DC: GPO.

    1908. "Cost of Living of the Working Class in the Principal Industrial Towns of Germany." *Bulletin* no. 78: 523–48.

    1909. "Cost of Living of the Working Class in the Principal Industrial Towns of France." *Bulletin* no. 83: 66–87.

1910. "Cost of Living of the Working Class in the Principal Industrial Towns of Belgium." *Bulletin* no. 87: 608–25.

1912. "Retail Prices 1890 to June 1912." *Bulletin* no. 106: 1–205.

1915. "Retail Prices, 1907 to December 1914." *Bulletin* no. 156: 1–397.

Bureau of Labor Statistics (BLS). 1985. "How Workers Get Their Training." *Bulletin* no. 2226: 1–59.

Ward, David. 1971. *Cities and Immigrants: A Geography of Change in Nineteenth-Century America*. New York: Oxford University Press.

Ware, Caroline F. 1931. *The Early New England Cotton Manufacture: A Study in Industrial Beginnings*. Boston and New York: Houghton Mifflin.

Way, Peter. 1993. *Common Labour: Workers and the Digging of North American Canals, 1780–1860*. New York and Cambridge: Cambridge University Press.

Weir, David R. 1992. "A Century of U.S. Unemployment, 1890–1990." In Roger L. Ransom, Richard Sutch, and Susan B. Carter, eds. *Research in Economic History*, vol. 14. Greenwich, CT, and London: JAI Press, pp. 301–46.

Weyl, Walter E., and A. M. Sakolski. 1906. "Conditions of Entrance to the Principal Trades." *Bulletin of the Department of Labor* no. 67: 681–780.

Whatley, Warren C. 1990. "Getting a Foot in the Door: 'Learning,' State Dependence, and the Racial Integration of Firms." *Journal of Economic History* 50: 43–60.

1993. "African-American Strikebreaking from the Civil War to the New Deal." *Social Science History* 17: 555–8.

Wiener, Jonathan. 1978. *Social Origins of the New South*. Baton Rouge, LA: Lousiana State University Press.

Williamson, Jeffrey G. 1995. "The Evolution of Global Labor Markets Since 1830: Background Evidence and Hypotheses." *Explorations in Economic History* 32: 141–96.

1996. "Globalization, Convergence, and History." *Journal of Economic History* 56: 277–306.

Williamson, Jeffrey G., and Peter H. Lindert. 1980. *American Inequality: A Macroeconomic History*. New York: Academic Press.

Wright, Gavin. 1979. "Cheap Labor and Southern Textiles before 1880." *Journal of Economic History* 39: 655–80.

1986. *Old South, New South: Revolutions in the Southern Economy Since the Civil War*. New York: Basic Books.

1987a. "Labor History and Labor Economics." In Alexander J. Field, ed. *The Future of Economic History*. Boston: Kluwer-Nijhoff, pp. 313–48.

1987b. "Postbellum Southern Labor Markets." In Peter Kilby, ed. *Quantity and Quiddity*. Middletown, CT: Wesleyan University Press, pp. 98–134.

Yellowitz, Irwin. 1968. "The Origins of Unemployment Reform in the United States." *Labor History* 9: 338–60.

INDEX

3 5282 00527 4157